RICHARD DEMARCO has personally experienced e' inception in 1947, as well as contributing to its histor of the visual and performing arts, plus conference: underline the importance of introducing an academic and Fringe programmes so that they integrate completely and significant, in the '40s, '50s, '60s and into the '70s.

The Eighties began with an inevitable confrontation between the ethos of The Demarco Gallery and the ethos of the Scottish Arts Council. Joseph Beuys believed that 'everyone is an artist'. Did that include those criminals serving life imprisonment? The Scottish Arts Council believed that art was firmly controlled by the concept of an art industry, that, indeed, art was part of a leisure industry and that the Minister of Culture was also the Minister for Tourism.

Richard Demarco has always believed that art and education are two sides of the same coin and that is why the Arts Council of Scotland came to the conclusion, in 1980, that Richard Demarco had 'brought dishonour to the meaning of art, brought dishonour to the meaning of art in Scotland, and brought dishonour to The Demarco Gallery' and, for that reason, he did not deserve to be supported by annual central government funding.

Richard Demarco has also always believed, from his ten years of experience as a primary and secondary school teacher (1957–1967), that the use of the language of all the arts expresses the incontrovertible fact that, as Joseph Beuys maintained, every human being possesses a birthright to be creative.

All expressions of art, particularly on the highest level, are a gift and, indeed, ascend to the condition of prayer, in gratitude for the gift of Life. As a gift, it cannot be attached to a price tag. He acknowledges the fact that his experience of the Edinburgh Festival, from his boyhood to this troubled computerised world of the Third Millennium, is a blessing upon his life and, indeed, a blessing upon Edinburgh as the city of his birth.

The Edinburgh Festival came into being against all the odds when the pain endured by humanity in the aftermath of World War II seemed insufferable. A small group of friends were eager to support Rudolf Bing's belief that Edinburgh could become an ideal British version of Austria's pre-war Salzburg Festival. They took the language of art most seriously as the one language given to human beings which could begin the process of healing the wounds of global conflict. Ironically, therefore, without the suffering caused by the Second World War, the Edinburgh Festival could not have come into being. According to the Lord Provost, John Falconer, as the first Chairman in 1947, the Edinburgh Festival was an expression of 'the flowering of the human spirit' and therefore 'it was in no way a commercial venture'.

When Richard Demarco asked Joseph Beuys to explain the quintessential nature of his art, Joseph Beuys replied succinctly 'my art is my teaching'. In 1972, The Demarco Gallery's experiment in education through all the arts was entitled with the use of two words – EDINBURGH ARTS. It was inspired by Black Mountain College, the American equivalent of the Bauhaus, and by Edinburgh as the world capital of all the arts.

From 1957 to 1967, Richard Demarco was the Art Master of Edinburgh's Scotus Academy and worked closely with his colleague, Arthur Oldham, who was the Academy's Music Master. Together, they firmly believed that every Scotus Academy boy was born to be creative. Richard Demarco extended his Scotus Academy art room to be identified with the Paperback Bookshop created by Jim Haynes in the late 1950s and early 1960s. From the year 1963 to 1967, Richard Demarco became the Vice-Chairman of what was in fact a slight enlargement of the Paperback Bookshop.

This came to be known as the Traverse Theatre Club and was housed in an 18th-century eight-storey tenement in Edinburgh's Lawnmarket in close proximity to Edinburgh Castle on the historic Royal Mile. It was also, under Richard Demarco's directorship, Scotland's first art gallery focused completely on the international art world and the need for a powerful dialogue between Scotland and the European art world on both sides of the Iron Curtain.

As such, the Traverse Theatre Club established an international reputation for both the visual and performing arts. However, when Jim Haynes moved his concept of the Traverse to London, the Traverse spirit of internationalism continued to shine bright within the Edinburgh New Town house of what was to be known as The Richard Demarco Gallery. It was actually the Edinburgh version of Roland Penrose's London-based Institute of Contemporary Art. It seemed inevitable that, in 1972, The Demarco Gallery should become a 'university of all the arts' in collaboration with Edinburgh University's Schools of Scottish Studies and Extra-Mural Studies.

In 2013, Richard Demarco was invited to the European Parliament in Brussels. There, Martin Schulz, as President of the Parliament, awarded him a medal as a European Citizen of the Year. His European citizenship is well defined in the publication entitled Demarco 2020 as a celebration of his 90th birthday.

The Demarco Archive is a large-scale collaborative work of art – a unique Gesamtkunstwerk. It exists predominantly in nature. It could, therefore, be compared to Ian Hamilton Finlay's Gesamtkunstwerk of Little Sparta. It exists in a farmscape known as 'Stonypath' in the landscape of Lanarkshire.

EDINBURGH ARTS linked the Edinburgh cityscape with the farmscape of Kinross-shire. Meikle Seggie is a working farm. It is a point of departure which leads to a journey through time and space to the Apennine farmscapes of Richard Demarco's Roman ancestors around the town of Picinisco, near to the Abbey of Monte Cassino and the city of Cassino.

Picinisco existed in Roman times, close to the villa of Cicero. The citizens of this village are known as 'Ciceroni' – the children of Cicero. They have become famous as artists' models as a direct result of their lifestyle as farmers and shepherds. In this world, mankind has related to the extreme forces of nature from pre-historic times. As proof of this thought-provoking fact, there exists pre-historic rock carvings of shepherds and their sheep in the mountainous wilderness around Picinisco.

By focusing on The Road to Meikle Seggie, Richard Demarco is responding to a need to celebrate his Roman forebears who once regarded Scotland as the north-western frontier of the Roman Empire. Richard Demarco regards himself as a teacher, mainly on primary and secondary levels, using the language of all the arts. This provides proof positive that Scotland remains, from its earliest history, a unique and important manifestation of the cultural heritage of Europe.

RODDY MARTINE was born in South East Asia but brought home to Scotland by his parents to be educated at Edinburgh Academy. From launching an Edinburgh Festival magazine in his schooldays, he has followed the progress of the Edinburgh International Festival, Edinburgh Fringe Festival and Edinburgh Military Tattoo for over 60 years. For four years, he was co-opted as a judge for the Edinburgh Festivals' Cavalcade.

As a columnist with five major newspapers during the 1990s, and editor of a succession of Scottish lifestyle magazines, he has always regarded Edinburgh as his home and has published 30 books largely relating to Scottish lifestyle topics – history, biography, interiors, Scotch whisky, tartan and the supernatural. For his involvement in the Scotch Whisky Industry, he was made a Keeper of the Quaich in 1996, and a Master of the Quaich in 2006.

He was a Trustee of the Edinburgh International Festival during the 1970s, and served as a Trustee of The 369 Gallery of Contemporary Art throughout the 1980s. As a writer and photo journalist, he has attended The Grandfather Mountain Highland Games in North Carolina, and Tartan Week in New York and Washington, USA; the International Gathering of the Clans in Nova Scotia, and, in 2003, he was honoured as the Scottish Australian Heritage Council's Guest from Scotland for Sydney Scottish Week.

He was an early supporter of the Traverse Theatre in the Lawnmarket and subsequently in the Grassmarket where, although almost 20 years younger than its founder members, he knew them well. He was a cheerleader for The Demarco Gallery from the moment it first opened its doors in its original manifestation in Melville Crescent.

For Roddy Martine, with all the personalities he befriended, and all of the comings and goings he has witnessed over the years, the enduring and challenging world of Demarco's Edinburgh has always embodied the uplifting spirit of the Edinburgh Festivals.

DR CHARLIE ELLIS is a researcher and EFL teacher who writes on culture education and politics. He is a regular contributor to The Scottish Review and Modern English Teacher. He has authored several academic articles on politics and public intellectuals and is currently working on a book for Edinburgh University Press on British conservatism and culture.

TERRY ANN NEWMAN is an artist born in Wiltshire in 1944 and educated in Southampton, gaining a Diploma in Fine Art from the College of Art in 1987. Since meeting Richard Demarco in 1983, she has travelled extensively in Europe, particularly in Eastern Europe during the 1980s and 1990s with The Demarco Gallery's EDINBURGH ARTS; she has been a director of the Demarco European Art Foundation since 1992, and deputy to Richard Demarco since 2000. Her art works are in private and public collections, including the National Galleries of Lithuania and Hungary.

Demarco's Edinburgh

RICHARD DEMARCO and RODDY MARTINE

Luath Press Limited

EDINBURGH

www.luath.co.uk

First published 2023

ISBN: 978-1-80425-095-2

The paper used in this book is recyclable. It is made from totally
chlorine-free pulp produced in a low-energy, low-emission manner
from renewable forests.

Printed and bound b
Robertson Printers, Forfar

Typeset in 11.5 point Sabon LT
by Main Point Books, Edinburgh

In Memory of Hugo Burge
of Marchmont, Greenlaw, Berwickshire

Contents

Edinburgh is too large to know what it fundamentally thinks about anything; and the people who want something livelier of their Festival (are *The Fantastic Symphony* or *The Beggar's Opera* so deadly?) really mean different. Dankworth instead of Debussy, Acker Bilk rather than Bach, Brubeck and not Britten.

The 7th Earl of Harewood, Artistic Director of the Edinburgh Festival 1961–1964, *Lens Magazine*, 1963

Preface

AS AN IMPECUNIOUS teenager, suspiciously alien, albeit exotic from having been born on the island of Borneo, *Demarco's Edinburgh* was, and remains for me, MY Edinburgh. More importantly, *Demarco's Edinburgh* embodies the Edinburgh Festival that both Richard and I, 18 years apart in age, discovered for ourselves as schoolboys.

Gallery Director, Artist and Teacher Richard Demarco was aged 17 in August 1947, and he was in at the very start of it. How I envy him. Kathleen Ferrier, Bruno Walter, the Vienna Philharmonic, Edinburgh Castle floodlit for the first time since before World War II. I wish I had been there. Born at the very beginning of that same year, my involvement began as late as 1963 when, at the age of 16, I edited an Edinburgh Festival magazine called *Lens – A Youthful Focus on the Edinburgh Festival*.

During the 1960s, The Demarco Gallery in Edinburgh's Melville Crescent, and thereafter in its several re-locations – Blackfriars Street, the Forrest Hill Poorhouse, St Mary's School in Albany Street, Skateraw, Craigcrook Castle, Summerhall, and now Milkhall – was a beacon of excitement. It was where Edinburgh's permanent and perhaps scornful and alarmed residents were invited to embrace bohemia. It was where the Georgian grandeur of Edinburgh's New Town spilled effortlessly and mischievously into suburbia, and far beyond. The Demarco Gallery was the meeting place for all of the arts in Scotland, be they high or low in affectation, be they parochial or worldly wise or just simply inspirational. The Demarco Gallery was where the Enlightenment and those who aspired to a better world found enlightenment. And it was always international.

Despite a Haddington-shire ancestry stretching back into the somewhat dimmed mists of time, the reign of King David to be precise, I saw my first light of day in Sarawak. However, like the Edinburgh-born Italo-Scot Richard Demarco, I consider myself, first and foremost, a Scot. At the same time, we are both non-political Europeans or, rather more pretentiously, Citizens of the World. My parents were multilingual, my mother fluent in French; my father, in German, various Chinese dialects and Malay (not languages much called upon in Corstorphine where they latterly lived). Even so, it was through such versatility of mind that they sent me to summer schools in Switzerland and France.

For nine years, I commuted to work in Glasgow (as Editor of *Scottish Field*) and probably this is why I have never been susceptible to the propriety of Middle Class Edinburgh, so spectacularly out of kilter with its dazzling annual international festival of music, theatre and, until the 1990s, the visual arts.

Like Richard Demarco, I have embraced the concept of The Road to Meikle Seggie: that all roads throughout the world lead finally to the centre of Scotland, and that all roads from Meikle Seggie connect to Infinity. Both of us mourn the absence of global visual art, traditional and contemporary, in the official Festival programme, and the international vision that this embraced.

However, those who seek a definitive and forensic history of the Edinburgh International Festival must turn to David Pollock's masterly *Edinburgh's Festivals: A Biography*. In contrast, *Demarco's Edinburgh* is a deeply alternative personal read.

In *Demarco's Edinburgh*, Richard and I have set out, warts and all, to explain in two sections, his and mine, our individual observations on how Scotland's Capital City came to showcase its greatest 20th-century achievement and how this has impacted upon our lives. Not as a gateway for Scottish tourism. Not as a hub for financial expertise. Not for Scotland's devolved United Kingdom legislature, but for hosting 76 years of an extraordinary, fantastic and breathtakingly innovatory International Festival, unlike any other, anywhere else.

These are Richard Demarco's memories coupled with mine, his mainstream and mine slipstream, but held together by a cast of characters far beyond your wildest imagination, and who must never ever be forgotten. This is *Demarco's Edinburgh*.

Roddy Martine, July 2023

Introduction

Requiem for the Unknown Artist

THIS IS THE TITLE which Joseph Beuys gave to his significant art work in 1970 as part of the Edinburgh International Festival's programme of artists from Düsseldorf devised by Richard Demarco and presented by The Richard Demarco Gallery in the setting of Edinburgh College of Art and entitled *Strategy: Get Arts*. It could also be the title of the great art work that Richard has created over the decades in which he places the 'unknown artist' into the international public domain of the Edinburgh Festival. Richard is an artist, both as a painter and as an instigator and challenger, who causes new insights into the creativity of his friends.

As co-creator of the Traverse Theatre Club, The Richard Demarco Gallery and The Demarco European Art Foundation, Richard has brought thousands of artists together, through the years, in order to maintain the excitement of the early days of the Edinburgh International Festival. Together with his friends who were saddened when 'the circus left town', he presented Edinburgh with the possibility of enjoying exciting new experiences for 52 weeks of the year. Without this stimulation and challenge, Richard would not have remained in Edinburgh; it is entirely due to the founding principles of the 1947 Festival that Edinburgh has benefited from the years of his strenuous endeavours.

I came to Edinburgh in 1986 to The Demarco Gallery as it moved into the exciting location of Blackfriars Church and helped to prepare it for the great opening of Polish art. Having met Richard in 1983, I recognised the international understanding of art that Richard championed and which could be found on the Continent of Europe and in the world of Christendom. Richard Demarco epitomises this understanding. He takes risks for the best possible reasons with so very many actually succeeding due to his determination to enable artists to flourish.

Demarco's Edinburgh carefully expresses this sensibility.

The world of Richard Demarco was, and is, such a very exciting, constantly evolving, expression of a journey, a journey through landscape with friends and into the history of ideas. This is the journey that he has named The Road to Meikle Seggie.

It is this sense of a journey that runs throughout Richard's work for the Edinburgh Festival, from his first experience as a schoolboy in 1947, right up to this year, his 94th! There is no sense of his stopping, of resting on his laurels. This would be simply impossible.

Terry Ann Newman, July 2023

Taking the Long View:
What drives Richard Demarcos' relentless search for truth and beauty?

Dr Charlie Ellis

RICHARD DEMARCO'S RELENTLESS, unremitting energy and passion for new projects are frequently mentioned in profiles of him. Now aged 93, this proselytising passion for art still burns as he rages against the dying of the light. Every conversation sees his interlocutors probed and prodded and ambitious new collaborations mooted. Animated recollections and connections are stimulated by every piece of art or photo he encounters.

So, where does this energy come from? What is fuelling his impassioned pleas? Throughout Demarco's public pronouncements and cultural interventions, certain themes are returned to time and time again. They reveal the wellspring of his cultural vision and why he remains so zealous about it. This chapter identifies and contextualises the abiding themes of Demarco the public intellectual, sometimes masked by Demarco the hyperbolic showman. The discussion here draws on Demarco's recent public pronouncements, as well as private discussions.[1] In particular, those relating to the 75th anniversary of the Edinburgh Festival, marked and celebrated in 2022, and Marco Federici's film *Rico: The Richard Demarco Story*. Demarco used these events to outline his central mission and the values which inspire it.

As a totality, Demarco offers a unique perspective as a public intellectual. However, Demarco also echoes the thoughts of a number of leading figures in the sphere of cultural politics. A number of Demarco's abiding themes are also highly relevant to a series of still-smouldering debates in the sphere of culture and in relation to the Edinburgh Festival and Fringe. We can crystallise Demarco's singular vision by comparing and contrasting him with them. Doing so helps explain why Demarco, despite his huge influence, remains something of an outsider without a natural set of allies or supportive institutions. The temporary, uncertain status of his *Gesamtkunstwerk* manifests the imperilled character of the cultural vision expressed through it.

A Healing Balm

Demarco is rarely seen without a camera or sketchbook[2] in his hand. At any cultural event or conversation, he will be snapping away, keen to capture the moment. Disconcertingly, he even takes photos of his interviewers while he is being interviewed! As he relates, 'I've been taking photos since I was a child', and isn't likely to stop now. This 'genre' of art, which Demarco defines as 'Event Photography', seeks to use the camera to document and amplify the work of other artists. Telling cultural history through photography.[3] As a result, there are about two million photographs in his vast archive. Only a portion (around 15,000 images) have been digitised so far – by Dundee University.

From this vast number, Demarco highlights the significance of a photo of the German artist Joseph Beuys reverently surveying the names inscribed on the war memorial at Edinburgh University. Demarco collaborated with Beuys many times[4] and considers him to be 'the most important artist of the second half of the 20th century'. Demarco reflects that Beuys spent five years in a Nazi uniform, 'fighting people such as these'. Beuys himself, Demarco believes, died early due to his war wounds, suffered in a near-fatal plane crash in the Crimea in 1943. Trauma and repair would become key themes of Beuys' art.[5]

Beuys' eight visits to Edinburgh and participation in 'Strategy: Get Arts' were part of the healing process. That 1970 event, dominated by artists based in Düsseldorf, expressed that 'Germany was no longer our enemy'.

That these artists were so warmly received in a country where 'German' had been 'a swear word' only 25 years before was evidence of some degree of amelioration. The photo of Beuys at the war memorial manifests Demarco's faith in art as a unifying force, and as 'a healing balm for the pain the human race has suffered'.

The photo also demonstrates how deeply woven Demarco's cultural life is into much wider, geopolitical change. In short, the post-war reconstruction of Europe, the cultural revolution of the 1960s, the Cold War and, more recently, the apparent 'backslide' towards national populism.[6] Demarco has not been a passive observer of these shifts but intimately involved in them, promoting some and vigorously opposing others. He has done so using art as a language that forms bonds and connections across borders and social divides.

Demarco's numerous engagements with artists in Eastern Europe exemplify this in the fullest. Those behind the Iron Curtain had been in 'the largest prison in the world', with very few in the art world prepared to try and connect to it. He took around 60 trips to Eastern Europe in that period to help 'maintain a cultural lifeline'.[7] He brought many of them to Edinburgh, which he considered a form of 'universal space'. What seemed to propel him was Camus' view that 'tyrants know that the work of art is an emancipatory force'.[8]

For Demarco, the apparent shifts towards national populism that we see today[9] in Europe and further afield (Bolsonaro, Trump, Modi) is a great threat. It threatens to undo the partial reunification of Europe that occurred at the end of the Cold War 'emerging from the debris of the Berlin Wall'.[10]

For Demarco, this trend was typified by Brexit, something which 'appals' him ('what a madness!'). Demarco had hoped that we were finally 'putting the 20th century behind us', but this has not happened. History has bitten back. This all leaves Demarco fearing that we might be nearing a *third* world war. The brave Ukrainian soldiers are, Demarco believes, 'fighting for *our* freedom'. He holds that, 'if they lose, this will put European culture in serious jeopardy'. We are, Demarco believes, 'living not in interesting times but times of chaos, where everything's falling apart'.

The photo of Beuys highlights the centrality of World War II to Demarco's cultural perspective. The Festival was, in Demarco's view, 'born out of the horror of World War II'. The war is therefore 'embedded' in the history of the Festival. This drives Demarco's abiding internationalism and his faith in art. Art gave him a tool for promoting a very different perspective, focusing on the fundamental commonalities between people across borders. The Festival had revealed that 'that which contains darkness also contains the prospect of light'. Something wondrous was created in a time of general scarcity with many European cities flattened.

One of the worst affected cities in the UK was Coventry. Its post-war rebirth was led by Basil Spence who, like Demarco, studied at Edinburgh College of Art. Spence was inspired to design a cathedral by the destruction he witnessed in Normandy. In many ways, the cathedral he designed was primarily a work of art rather than a practical building. For Spence, art was an essential component of architecture.[11] Coventry Cathedral subsequently became home of The Centre for the Study of Forgiveness and Reconciliation and regularly hosts cultural events. Those involved in the design and building of the 'Phoenix at Coventry' were not defeated by the destruction but inspired towards rebirth.[12] Their faith was tested but not extinguished. Demarco has a similar belief in art's ability to reconcile. For both Demarco and Spence, it was World War II which inspired them to their greatest achievements.

What had caused the conflagration was nationalism. What lay behind this was an 'othering' and demonisation of certain groups. Demarco himself felt that from an early age, vilified as a 'wop',[13] and bullied and ostracised by classmates as 'an alien child'. As both Italian and Roman Catholic he was 'deeply questionable'. Demarco saw how quickly this xenophobia could quickly transmogrify into aggressive and violent nationalism. During the war he was evacuated to Largs, thought to be safer than Edinburgh. He arrived just in time to witness some of the heaviest bombardments of the conflict. From the tenement he was staying in he saw 'the sky light up' and heard the sounds of the destructive 'blitz' on Clydebank of March 1941. Through his first experience of the Festival (in 1947), he saw a way that such fissures could be overcome. This helps explain the zeal with which he promotes art and the Festival.

Elitist or Egalitarian?

Demarco's urgent energy came across in spades in his various public performances during the 2022 Festival. Though he can't stand the form, Demarco's 'performance' at the Quaker Meeting House owed something to stand-up comedy.[14] Prowling across the stage he delved into his memories, his sometimes halting voice suddenly sweeping into fervent crescendos. At times, he stepped into the audience, clasping the hands of some, grasping the shoulders of others, so keen was he to get across his message.

As part of a new collaboration with the Signet Library, Demarco and his team displayed a 'tiny smidgen' of his archive, chronicling the evolution of the Edinburgh Festival and his involvement with it. Again, Demarco implored visitors to take the original vision of the Edinburgh Festival seriously; 'I'm not messing around.' Those in Edinburgh during August should not act merely as 'cultural tourists', passively encountering the Festival. The challenge Demarco makes to those who attend the contemporary Festival is simply 'Are you serious?' Rather than cultural tourists, Demarco wishes to see committed 'artistic explorers'.

Demarco's forthright critique of the contemporary Edinburgh Fringe might invite charges of golden-ageism and cultural elitism. When sharing memories of past Festivals it's typical for him to utter 'there was a time when' before bemoaning an aspect of the Festival now absent. He also talks of 'the Festival that I knew' as something entirely different, and superior, to its current form. He sees the Festival as it is now as 'symbolic of a cultural decline'. Declinist narratives certainly populate much of our public discourse. They are very prominent in cultural debates and those concerning the built environment. Those areas of the internet devoted to Edinburgh's past are awash with them. A pervasive sense of a city in decline, 'not what it used to be'.

This charge of being a conservative figure, livid with nostalgia, has been levelled at the likes of Richard Hoggart. He was a central figure in the evolution of cultural studies as an academic discipline but is sometimes dismissed as a figure primarily of the past.[15] Between 1992 and 2000, Demarco held the position of Professor of European Cultural Studies at the University of Kingston. Some might see Demarco's disenchantment with the present state of the Festival in similar fashion. His public pronouncements, perhaps inevitably at 93, tend to be backward looking. This perhaps makes communicating the relevance of his archive difficult. Nostalgia is widely seen, as Samuel puts it, not primarily about the past 'but about felt absences or "lack" in the present'.[16] Certainly, Demarco sees much lacking in the contemporary Festival. When comparing it with the programme of The Demarco Gallery (when based in Blackfriars Street) in 1992, he finds it hard not to see it as unrivalled within the contemporary scene.

His narrative of dilution and decline might be dismissed as typical of the Jeremias expressed by cultural figures uneasy about contemporary trends.[17] From this perspective, the history of the Festival and Fringe, as charted by David Pollock, is one of evolution not decline.[18] The Fringe has certainly grown massively in recent decades and is considered a major success story by many. It could be seen as a story of cultural democratisation. That, what was performed and enjoyed by an incestuously small group in the early decades of the Festival and Fringe is now enjoyed by many multiples more. To paraphrase Kingsley Amis, more need not mean worse. Are Demarco's criticisms of the contemporary Fringe the product of cultural elitism?

How could Demarco counter such changes? Highly relevant to Demarco are the cultural writings of Russell Keat.[19] He drew a distinction between 'elitism of access' (which could be translated as, good culture 'is only for the likes of us') and 'elitism of judgement' (that good culture 'is what we few who can judge these matters say it is').[20] These are themes which David Hume wrestled with in his essay 'On the Standard of Taste'. Keat also echoes Richard Hoggart who believed that 'saying that some things are better than others' was something which should be encouraged if based on judgements which you are prepared to substantiate'.[21] In his Reith Lectures, Hoggart spoke of 'powerful resistance within British culture as a whole to making distinctions, recognising different standards'.[22]

Demarco has no such reticence to making distinctions when discussing culture. The Festival should be, in his view, about bringing the best art to

Edinburgh from around the world, as judged by 'the highest standards'. While showing people around his archive, judgements come thick and fast: 'Why am I the only person who can explain why this is a work of genius?!' These judgements are, however, borne of his long involvement in the artistic sphere. If he isn't qualified to make such judgements, then who is? Though Demarco might continually repeat Beuys' view that 'everyone is an artist', this is not the same as saying that 'everyone is a good artist'.

There are certainly a number of links between Demarco and 'left culturalist' thinkers such as Hoggart, a near contemporary of Demarco. According to this view, 'everyone should have the opportunity to share the good things that the upper classes had customarily enjoyed'. In short, 'serious' culture need not be the sole property of a 'leisured elite'.[23] Hoggart embodied a broadening of British cultural life in the 1950s and 1960s which drew in many from working-class backgrounds. Though he became an influential figure within British cultural institutions, Hoggart always felt like an outsider, caught 'between two worlds'.[24] This parallels Demarco's sense of never feeling fully at home in Scotland. As a natural outsider, he has held an inherent sympathy for the marginalised.

This egalitarian, democratic desire to see the world of art opened up is illustrated in Demarco's involvement with the Craigmillar Festival.[25] Here he collaborated with its founder Helen Crummy, whose son Andrew has subsequently made an impact through works such as the Great Tapestry of Scotland. From his years as a school teacher, Demarco became aware that artistic potential could be found in all corners of society. At the time Craigmillar was dismissed by many as a 'scheme' riven by irresolvable social problems. Craigmillar was peripheral geographically and also considered so culturally. The idea that artistic ability was in plentiful supply in Craigmillar went against the snobbery embedded in Edinburgh society.

Local engagement, led by members of the community, was far more likely to discover artistic potential than 'outreach' work by national cultural institutions. The Craigmillar Festival has inspired similar events in areas such as Easterhouse in Glasgow.

One of the major works produced for the Craigmillar Festival was *The Gentle Giant* (aka Gulliver) sculpture by Jimmy Boyle. This was the centrepiece of the 1976 event. Demarco was involved, alongside Joseph Beuys, with Jimmy Boyle and the Special Unit at 'Britain's worst prison', Barlinnie. The principle that 'everyone was an artist', included convicted criminals behind bars. This was Demarco's most high profile involvement with marginalised groups. It also caused a great deal of consternation and led to Demarco coming into conflict with the established arts institutions.

He was condemned for having, in a statement much quoted by Demarco, 'brought dishonour to the world of art'. His involvement with the Special Unit again emphasised Demarco's belief in the power of art as a healing balm. It sought to embrace those 'cut off' from society, to whom art was 'so alien'.[26] It was borne of a love of art which 'knew no bounds'.[27] Demarco's sense of being an outsider was accentuated by this controversy – but also the sense that he enjoys being on the edge and getting 'up the noses' of those in the 'cosy little world' of the arts institutions.

In No Way a Commercial Venture

In relation to the Edinburgh Festival, what drives him is a sense that something magnificent was achieved but that this legacy is being squandered. This helps explain the restless, discontented character of many of his public interventions. One aspect of this is his view that art 'should not be aligned with tourism and market forces'. Becoming profit driven has, in Demarco's eyes, eroded the true meaning of the Festival. Demarco often quotes John Falconer, the Festival's patron in 1947, who proclaimed the event to be about the 'flourishing of the human spirit' and 'in no way a commercial venture'. Demarco now sees the Fringe as a 'money-making machine', largely controlled by the major venues.

In seeing commercial forces as the chief source of decline, he again links to cultural critics such as Hoggart and Jim McGuigan. They see cultural populism as the inevitable result of a cultural sphere in which commercial values dominate.[28] Though this position is contested, such as in the work of the economist and long-time Edinburgh resident Alan Peacock[29], this 'market scepticism' is widely held. It connects to the idea that there exists a fundamental 'contradiction' between the values of the market and those of art.[30] In Demarco's case, it has been the idea of art as a commodity which has been so insidious. He believes that 'art has been commodified so that unless it is about profit it is not taken seriously by our local or national government masters'. In short, a commercial view of art has permeated many cultural institutions, who are increasingly 'controlled by the power of mammon'. In relation to the Fringe, this commercialisation is manifested in the move away from the visual arts towards comedy.

Demarco's vision of the Festival and Fringe unites the two aspects of Ancient Greek performance: Comedy and Tragedy. It should aim to strike 'the perfect balance between tragedy and laughter'. For Demarco, the wholesale embrace of comedy and entertainment has undermined the cultural significance of the Festival and Fringe. He pleads with those running the Fringe not to 'turn everything into a circus'. That Fringe performances are now usually one-hour long is seen by Demarco as symbolic of this cultural shallowing. He contends, 'How can you do anything serious in one hour?'

In 'Richard Demarco's Edinburgh' map (of 1994), he charts the places he took Joseph Beuys. It included the Pleasance as one of the key Fringe venues. The original Pleasance is now known as the Pleasance Courtyard, illustrating the way the Pleasance (and the other big venues, such as Underbelly) have spread their tentacles out across the city. Some have resisted this takeover by the 'Big Four'. The Free Fringe (in both the PBH and Laughing Horse variants) has, since 1996, helped many performers access the Fringe. They have also made the Fringe more accessible to those on a limited budget. There are some similarities between Demarco and the central figure of the Free Fringe, Peter Buckley Hill.[31] Seen as disputatious troublemakers, both have regularly clashed with the leadership of the official Festival and Fringe. Both have also attracted a loyal band of followers and collaborators, which have kept their projects alive during tough times.

The Free Fringe has constantly been looking to carve out new venues and performance spaces. Places such as the Banshee Labyrinth, Liquid Rooms and Cabaret Voltaire have quickly become acclaimed venues. This follows in the footsteps of Demarco, who created fascinating venues in unpromising places such as the Forrest Hill Poorhouse and Gladstone's Court. He preferred this to the 'safety of an art gallery with clean white walls'.

However, most of the new venues unearthed by the Free Fringe have been in the heart of the Old Town; in the Cowgate and its 'environs'. This has made the Cowgate area even more difficult to navigate during August. Free Fringe venues a bit further out (such as the Omni Centre) have not been particularly successful.

While the Free Fringe offers a range of shows (spoken word, theatre, magic, etc), comedy tends to dominate. This is where parallels between Buckley Hill and Demarco end. There is no comparison in terms of cultural ambition. Buckley Hill has laudably striven to open up the Fringe; Demarco has constantly sought to raise the sights of those involved. The Free Fringe has accentuated existing trends. For example, the rise of the Free Fringe has accelerated the long-term trend towards comedy. Increasingly the Fringe is seen as synonymous with comedy, especially stand-up comedy.[32]

That such a view is also held by some who organise the Fringe indicated to Demarco of 'a loss of memory'. In short, a total lack of awareness of the history of the Festival. Demarco sees evidence of this around the city. Jim

Haynes' path-breaking Paperback Bookshop was on Charles Street, next to Bristo Square.[33] Demarco sees the sweeping away of the original street as typifying a cultural negligence. That Edinburgh University's Informatics Building now occupies the site of the bookshop is, for Demarco, evidence of a general shift away from the arts. For him, a 'proper education takes into account every aspect of culture'. Demarco sees his archive as one antidote to this deficiency, so is saddened that the University has no interest in acquiring his archive.

The rise of stand-up comedy has inevitably shifted the focus of the Fringe to the 'anglosphere', away from Europe. Christian Schulte-Loh (Germany) and Sofie Hagen (Denmark) are very rare instances of European stand-ups and they have to use English when in Edinburgh. Because of the 'infestation' of stand-up comedians the Fringe is now, Demarco suggests, 'fully rooted in English'. In contrast, a musician, visual artist, dancer can use 'the language of the arts' to communicate. For Demarco, 'no language is more important than the language of art'.

Demarco's very first experience at the Festival (in 1947) was watching the theatre of Molière – in French. For Demarco, the Festival and Fringe's loss of its international, multilingual aspect and its ability to truly 'challenge the audience'; have been key elements of its decline since the 1980s. The rise and rise of comedy has, in Demarco's eyes gone hand in hand with a commercialisation. Commercialisation has, Demarco believes, led to a cultural narrowing. The Festival and culture more generally 'have been absorbed into the world of entertainment'.

Demarco's concerns about commercialisation raises the interesting question of where he believes the funding of arts should come from. Again, a comparison with Richard Hoggart is illustrative. Hoggart in ways embodied the 'cultural consensus'[34] of the post-war era. This was a general political agreement that the public funding of the arts was efficacious.

There was 'general agreement among politicians of all parties that public subsidy should be continued', on the 'guiding principle of "the Best for Most"'.[35] In short, that high culture 'could be taken to deprived areas to widen horizons and cultivate souls'.[36] This consensus was manifested in CEMA (Council for the Encouragement of Music and the Art), established in 1940, and later the Arts Council.

For Hoggart and his ilk, public funding increased access to culture and led to cultural democratisation. Similarly, the BBC's protected position (through the Licence Fee) was seen as a way to ensure that it could look beyond. For Hoggart and others, the 1960s (under the Director-Generalship of Hugh Carleton Greene) saw the BBC make a significant contribution to British cultural life, through high profile documentary series by David Attenborough, Kenneth Clark, John Berger, and television dramas by the likes of Dennis Potter. For many, it is considered a neo-Reithian golden age.[37] For others, it is a golden age that never was.[38]

This parallels Demarco's sense that the 1960s and 1970s were something of a golden era for the Festival and Fringe. In visual arts, it was a period when Edinburgh had 'real significance', exemplified by Strategy: Get Arts. For him, what was put on in that era set a benchmark that has rarely, if ever, been met since. However, Demarco is keen to emphasise that memories of Strategy: Get Arts not be 'possessed of any trace of nostalgia'. Instead, though more than 50-years-old, it was 'more relevant, more alive', than most of the contemporary art world.

Demarco has continually crossed swords with the public funding bodies and now seems entirely alienated from them. His public talks are peppered with derogatory remarks about bodies such as Creative Scotland and the National Galleries. A severing of ties has forced him to depend on private patronage as a source of funding for his archive and other projects. 'I'm not able to get funding from the normal sources'. It's not always clear in Demarco's case whether this embrace of private patronage is one of necessity and principle. Certainly, there are many who are sceptical about public patronage. They fear that public bodies are often conditioned by 'groupthink', which can lead to a narrowing of vision in terms of what cultural activities are worthy of support. From Demarco's perspective, the advantage of private patronage is a degree of freedom, of not being beholden to institutional edict.

The downside of private patronage is a constant sense of uncertainty. This is evident in the peripatetic character of Demarco's cultural life and the sense of never having a secure base ('I've never owned a gallery'). The Traverse and The Demarco Gallery both had many locations. The archive has also lacked secure anchorage, being stored in a variety of places over the years. The 'biggest problem' with archives being simply 'where to put them'.[39] That it currently has some degree of security (if not true accessibility) is due to the support he gets from a key patron, Robert McDowell at Summerhall.

Demarco knows this cannot continue indefinitely, but he remains unsure as to the degree he wants the National Galleries of Scotland to be involved with his archive in the long term. 'I'm not sure if I should end up in the arms of the National Galleries'. This sense of alienation has become a dominant theme of Demarco's pronouncements. He has had a profound loss of faith in cultural institutions and now believes that 'the art world is not the right place for art'.

A Bloody Archive

This sense of alienation bleeds into his fluctuating feelings about his archive. Demarco switches between proclaiming the deep historical and artistic significance of his archive and threatening to burn it down due to the indifference it is shown.[40] For Demarco, this indifference reflects a failure to understand the true cultural enormity of the Edinburgh Festival and Fringe. Plans for the archive to have a long-term home in Granton (as part of 'The Art Works at Granton Waterfront') have taken many years to finalise.[41]

As of spring 2023, 'the ground has yet to be broken'. Demarco has accepted that he is unlikely to see this come to fruition in his lifetime ('at my age, you can't have a five-year plan'). What fuels his current efforts is a deep desire to ensure that the archive remains intact, and that a team is created to administer and care for it in perpetuity. But why does he care so much?

Demarco rejects many of the labels ascribed to him and his contribution. He 'hates' to be described, as he often is, as an arts impresario ('impresarios make money!'). Though the material he has collated is defined as the Demarco Archive, he abhors the idea of it as an inaccessible collection gathering dust and mould. 'I've not spent the whole of my life creating a bloody archive – my collection of boxes.' Indeed, he even rejects the very idea of an archive: 'My archive is not an archive but a homage to the Edinburgh Festival and the tribute to those I have worked with – many no longer with us.' He wanted to 'question to its very depth the idea of an archive'. In short, he does not want it to be a dormant collection of documents and pieces of art.

He much prefers to use the German word *Gesamtkunstwerk*, to express the collaborative, universal character of the project. A true *Gesamtkunstwerk* should, according to Hans Ulrich Obrist, not demonstrate its curator's 'own theory' but should be formed from conversations and collaborations.[42] Though certainly imprinted with his own vision, Demarco's Archive does seem to fit this definition, through the numerous collaborations and cross-pollinations it manifests.

Embodied in this is the idea of an archive that is living and breathing. They are not merely anthologies of the past but continue to evolve and develop. Though often considered an ordered, logical world, archives are much more organic than that. We regularly hear stories of documents turning up in archives, found due to a stroke of luck. Most archives contain treasures waiting to be unearthed. They are pregnant with potential.

We might compare the Demarco collection with archives such as the John Rylands Research Institute and Library in Manchester. Opened in 1900, the 'foundational collection' comprised two large collections, one of printed books and another of historic manuscripts. The assemblage has grown in subsequent years and now constitutes one of the finest collections of arts and humanities materials in the UK. Its core mission is to help researchers, curators, conservators and imaging specialists to 'define the human experience over five millennia and up to the current day'. Any visitor to John Rylands soon feels the crackle of intellectual activity that it helps to engender.

Demarco sees his own vast artistic archive as something which will inspire and enthral well into the future. His strongest desire is that it is used by pupils and students as a 'unique academic resource', telling the story of the Edinburgh Festival. Though he hasn't taught in a school for many decades, Demarco still sees himself fundamentally as a teacher. He hopes that the archive will be educating long after he has gone, much as the Festival had acted as a university for him. He wants to see 'students from around the world come and study it and use it'. He intends that a programme of scholarships will assist those using it. Precisely how it is used is something he can't decide. All that he hopes is that it will be used and appreciated.

Demarco knows that, as at John Rylands and other comparable archives and libraries, ensuring that the collection is accessible is absolutely essential. Hence his frustration that it is currently in stasis, with only parts of it 'get-at-able'. This includes the large section purchased by the National Galleries of Scotland in 1995 and which has since been through a process of sorting and cataloguing.[43] Demarco believes that the large part currently at Summerhall is the more important section. It remains largely behind locked doors and has yet to be properly catalogued. This can only happen when it gets moved to a proper research centre.

While having a place where it can be stored safely will be a major step, it's not enough. The small team he currently has which help him maintain and organise the archive will, when it moves, need to be supplemented by teams working on specific aspects of the archive. They will also play a role in continually adding to it, as more material relating to the Festival becomes available. It will become a living resource. Only then can it fulfil its fundamental role, which is to inspire and encourage artistic endeavour among future generations. What really concerns Demarco is the amount that still needs to be done. 'I've hardly begun' – I am still in the foothills… I cannot leave it unfinished.' Hence why communicating the significance of his archive is his current preoccupation. As is fundraising to help him pay his storage costs. Otherwise, some of the artwork will need to be auctioned off.

This pains him as he accepts that coherence will be lost if parts of the archive are lost. Trying to secure a proper future for the archive is something Demarco has committed to as long as he 'remains compos mentis'.

A New Enlightenment

Demarco has always felt uncomfortable in the world of Scottish art. For him, the character of the arts in Scotland has been parochial, insufficiently outward looking. There is, he holds, 'no such thing as Scottish art, only art in Scotland which is part of a European tradition'. Demarco sees the period between the Enlightenment and the arrival of the Festival as something of a dark age culturally.

Demarco's recent collaboration with the Signet Library, as part of its New Enlightenment project, manifested this. The forerunner of the National Library of Scotland, this institution was, as a place for intellectual exchange, right at the heart of the Enlightenment. At this time, Edinburgh was a world-leading place in fields such as medicine, political philosophy and economics.[44]

For Demarco, the Edinburgh Festival represented a reawakening of this spirit, a chance to revivify a slumbering city. Demarco believes that the city's culture remained dormant from the Enlightenment until 'the pure miracle' of the Festival embraced the city. In cultural terms, 'if it wasn't for the miracle of the Edinburgh Festival, Scotland would be intolerable'. It was a 'damp and dismal city' during his childhood. Demarco admits that 'if it wasn't for the Festival', he'd have left Edinburgh in the late 1940s to further his artistic aspirations.

Before the Festival arrived, 'Edinburgh was not a nodal point in world culture'. Edinburgh stood near the periphery of Europe, near the outer edge of the Roman Empire (the Antonine Wall). However, the special character of the light in Scotland was attractive to every creative soul. Similarly, he talks of Edinburgh as itself a 'sculptural' work of art[45]; beautiful enough to inspire any artist or writer.

However, without the Festival it lacked culture. Demarco was overcome with a feeling of gloom and despondency every autumn when 'the circus' left town. Edinburgh returned to being a 'dreich and grey place', shorn of the 'spirit of internationalism'. This, led him to seek out more cultural activity and to study art. Later it inspired him to get involved in the Traverse, in order to help ensure that the Festival spirit lasted longer than three weeks of the year. Demarco proclaims that 'in general, the people that ran Edinburgh at that time tended to hate art'. It was a 'stuffy place of lawyers and bankers' and even Edinburgh cultural institutions were not sympathetic.

The Festival had transformed this marginal city into the European 'capital of culture'. He was excited that international culture was available in Scotland, which became home to 'the world's greatest festival of the arts'.

It gave Edinburgh a 'much needed special dimension' and transformed it into a place of 'cultural pilgrimage'. The Fringe and its key institutions were the product of international figures, such as Jim Haynes and the Traverse, 'not created by Scotland'. The Edinburgh Festival is, in Demarco's eyes, not really a Scottish Festival but a celebration of European and world art and culture. It was in some sense a way to 'Europeanise' Scotland using the language of art as a form of communication.

A Culture Warrior

Another possible charge against Demarco relates to his conception of European culture. His fear about the breaking up of Europe and the decline of its culture does echo public intellectuals and commentators of the right.

Thinkers such as the late Roger Scruton[46] and his many acolytes (most prominently Douglas Murray[47]), believe the defence of European culture is a pressing need to retain social coherence. In trips reminiscent of Demarco's cultural voyages, Scruton regularly travelled to Eastern Europe during the Cold War, teaching, and assisted dissidents fighting political orthodoxy.

Scruton has, since his death, become a lodestar among cultural conservatives. They see European culture under threat from outwith and within, from a relativising cultural elite which has lost faith in its own culture. Demarco's language of the need to 'defend' European culture is certainly echoed by these conservative 'culture warriors'. Like them, Demarco considers himself to be engaged in a 'fight for civilisation'.

Despite the echoes, there are also key differences. For Scruton and those influenced by him, the answer to this lies in embracing a conservative national populism in order to preserve national cultures from 'globalising' forces. In marked contrast, Demarco sees art as inherently international. Further, Demarco's embrace of art with a clear political perspective, notably Beuys', would appal Scruton who would see it as part of a 'politicisation' of culture and a 'flight from beauty'.[48] Demarco also has a much broader and more dynamic conception of culture. From Scruton's perspective, Demarco's championing of the avant-garde would place him among those who have undermined the coherence of European culture. Scruton was generally critical of the 'ugliness' of modern art and often dismissed avant-garde as 'abstract kitsch'.[49]

Culturally, Demarco is a risk-taking radical, encouraging experimentation. While he sees art as a unifying force, this is not in some cuddly, comfortable way. Most of the art he has championed has been 'difficult' and 'broke the rules'.[50] For example, Demarco (and selections from his archive) features prominently in Birrell and Finlay's short history or 'archaeology' of the Scottish counter-culture, *Justified Sinners*.[51] The book couples visual art with the type of political engagement that alarms the likes of Scruton. What Demarco has promoted has not been art which provides simple answers but provokes a questioning and explorative frame of mind. Like Marina Abramović, he is 'thrilled by the unknown'.[52] He seems to exemplify Camus' belief that artists should 'create dangerously'.[53] Demarco often quotes George Lascelles (Lord Harewood), Festival Director 1961–1965, who believed that the Festival ought to aim to give 'the public what it's going to want tomorrow', not what was comforting.

For Demarco, the great achievements of European culture have been forged by this explorative attitude. Demarco's life has been a constant journey, driven by a craving to discover and share great art, especially that on the boundaries of acceptability. The ground-breaking Strategy: Get Arts being the most obvious example. The 'marginal' figures he championed, such as Joseph Beuys and Marina Abramović[54], are now acclaimed and considered ahead of their time. This spirit often led him to turn his back on institutions he helped build. 'I had to get out of the Traverse when it ceased to be avant-garde enough.'

A Man Out of Time?

Demarco himself now finds himself feeling alienated from something he helped build. Like many Edinburgh folk, he has started to chunter about the way the Festival and Fringe inconvenience life in the city. Demarco had mixed feelings when the 2020 Festival was cancelled. He hoped that the pause might offer an opportunity to rethink and 're-charge' the Festival. George Steiner had suggested such a rethink should have occurred at the time of the 50th Festival.[55] Demarco believes this rethink is now long overdue. He is not alone.

The *cri de cœur* is part of the tradition of the Festival and Fringe. Writing in the *Guardian* in 2022, Brian Logan echoed Demarco in writing that this 'world-class cultural crucible' had reached 'crisis point'. However, Logan was talking about the contemporary 'iteration' of the Fringe; as the breeding ground for the next generation of comedy stars. He still believed that it remained 'a jewel in the crown of this country's – and the world's – cultural life'.[56] More recently, the Fringe Society chief executive Shona McCarthy suggested that the Fringe was facing an existential crisis.[57] Again, her conception of the Fringe is very much the contemporary, comedy-dominated version, which repels Demarco. For Demarco, the existential threat has been an evolving one, eating away at the original vision. Demarco feels that it stopped being a cultural jewel during the 1990s. He now sees the Festival as 'irrecoverable', though the original idea remains powerful and 'deserves to be reborn'. Demarco believes that ultimately the Festival failed to 'take root' in the city. Edinburgh continues to have an uneasy relationship with the Festival and Fringe. While a proportion embrace it wholeheartedly, it is seen as a major encumbrance by many. Demarco, sadly, admits to having joined this band of Festival grumblers.[58]

Will Richard Demarco's rich archive become a record of something that has subsequently died, or an inspiration to those seeking to revive it? The final leg of Demarco's cultural voyage is focused on helping to ensure that it is the latter.

As outlined here, Demarco's still burning passion derives from a belief that art is the most important language and one which can bridge social and national divides. His perspective connects to a number of long running debates about the place of culture in society and how to democratise it, while retaining a sense of critical judgement. Demarco's critical sense is most obvious in his views regarding the contemporary Festival and Fringe. His fierce critiques of the current 'iteration' of the Edinburgh Festival and Fringe are imbued with a sense of sorrow.

The moving penultimate scene of Marco Federici's film *Rico* takes place at the Venice Biennale in 2019, where selections from Demarco's Archive were exhibited. Demarco, his voice cracking with emotion, leads a group in a shaky but deeply affecting rendition of 'Auld Lang Syne'. The 'old times' being commemorated are Demarco's hope for a Europe brought together by culture. There is undoubtedly an elegiac, melancholic quality to many of Demarco's recent public pronouncements; a sense of a dream under threat from various forces, political and commercial. And yet, he retains his belief in the power of art.

Art is Long; Life is Short

Demarco's response to Brexit was not to fire off an angry polemic. Instead, he helped plant a tree. The connections between art and nature have been a prominent part of Demarco's life, as expressed in collaborations with the likes of Beuys and Ian Hamilton Finlay. Demarco has long sought out wild places for inspiration. They are, in Demarco's view, more important than galleries and art schools as locations to galvanise artistic endeavour.

The Brexit Tree project, led by Clemens Wilhelm, has deep parallels with Joseph Beuys' 'social sculpture' 7,000 *Eichen*. This was an expression of art's potential to challenge and transform society. The Brexit Tree in Huntly is a weeping willow, a tree which in many cultures symbolises loss and sorrow, but also healing and rebirth. It's also a recognition of the threats to the natural world: 'At the age of 92, I count the blessings of my long life upon this uniquely beautiful and miraculous planet Earth, now rendered most vulnerable by global warming.'

The tree is an attempt to heal the wounds of Brexit by providing a place 'for people from both Brexit camps to meet next to the River Deveron'.[59] Though the Brexit Tree has twice been vandalised and replanted, it continues to grow. It expresses German forester Peter Wohlleben's belief that trees must be respected for their ability to store deep knowledge and survive traumatic change.[60] The Brexit Tree will, as Demarco noted, outlast those who planted it. It manifests Demarco's view that 'art is long; life is short.'

Though largely composed of thin slices of dead trees, Richard Demarco hopes that his archive and the values it manifests will, like the tree, grow and persist long into the future.

PART ONE

RICHARD DEMARCO'S EDINBURGH FESTIVAL

CHAPTER ONE

My Pilgrimage

UNDER THE AEGIS of Edinburgh's Luath Press, I have given myself the daunting task of writing a text expressing my personal memories of every single Edinburgh Festival. I am, therefore, indebted to Roddy Martine, Charlie Ellis and Edward Schneider for adding their insightful texts to my dealing with the complex nature of my relationship with the Edinburgh Festival. Charlie Ellis has written a thought-provoking introduction; Edward Schneider has written a necessary addendum focused on my career as a secondary school teacher at Edinburgh's Scotus Academy, and Roddy Martine has expressed his own extraordinary involvement in the history of the Edinburgh Festival since 1962 when he was a 16-year-old schoolboy at the Edinburgh Academy. I have read his text as someone who, like myself, was inspired by the Edinburgh Festival in his teenage years. Roddy Martine has written his text as a citizen of Edinburgh who understands the difference between the three-week period of the Edinburgh Festival and the 49 intervening weeks when the Festival spirit has 'left Town'.

I have always regarded my ten years, from 1957 to 1967, as Scotus Academy Art Master, as simply a preparation for the self-imposed role I felt obliged to play as co-founder of the Traverse Theatre Club and its transmogrification into what was known as The Richard Demarco Gallery.

Scotus Academy, named after the Berwickshire-born Duns Scotus, the 13th-century Franciscan Friar who became a priest, came into being as a primary and secondary school for Roman Catholic children in Edinburgh. It was located on Corstorphine Hill within earshot of the Edinburgh Zoo. My art room was a small attic space which had previously been the bedroom of Lord Boothby as a child. I was most fortunate to have Arthur Oldham and the four members of The Edinburgh Quartet as my fellow school teachers. Scotus Academy was very much a domestic space within an inspiring pastoral landscape.

It was from this unlikely room that I first planned my programmes for the Traverse Theatre Club Gallery as well as my first contribution to the history of the Edinburgh Festival in the basement art gallery under Jim Haynes' Paperback Bookshop which was of the art of my Scotus Academy students.

I once asked Joseph Beuys what was the quintessential nature of his art. His reply was simply 'My art is my teaching.' I do believe that that is how I would like to be considered in relation to the Edinburgh Festival. Joseph Beuys believed that everyone is an artist; by that, he meant that everyone is born to be creative.

I regard Roddy Martine as a veteran explorer of The Road to Meikle Seggie; he knows it exists to instil the spirit of the Edinburgh Festival well beyond the civic boundaries of Edinburgh, into the farthest corners of the reality of Scotland. Roddy Martine knows well the nodal points and signposts on The Road to Meikle Seggie, leading as it does to Scotland's farmscapes and her historic houses and castles. His experience as an editor and journalist has given him an understanding of the way that the Edinburgh Festival has developed. Recently, he has gifted two important publications to the Demarco Archive Library. One is his history of the Edinburgh Tattoo; the other is the history of The Caledonian Hotel. I was once gainfully employed as the only male receptionist at The Caledonian Hotel and, for two years, I found myself welcoming those who represented the international art world.

In bitterly cold weather, together with Roddy Martine and Terry Ann Newman, we explored the Silverknowes Promenade world of Eddie Tait's Boardwalk Café next to Cramond as a nodal point on The Road to Meikle Seggie. It would, therefore, be linked to other nodal points at Traquair House in Peeblesshire with particular reference to the 17th-century Traquair Library and the Traquair Pavilion containing the 50-year history of the world of Traquair in cultural dialogue with the world of The Demarco Gallery's EDINBURGH ARTS programmes linked to those of Traquair's Beyond Borders Festival programmes.

Another nodal point in the Scottish Borders is the world of the McEwen family at Marchmont House, brought up-to-date by the late Hugo Burge with his artist studios and workshops, linked to the Duns PlayFest created and directed by John McEwen in Duns, Berwickshire. Another key Meikle Seggie nodal point would be Andrew and Helen Threipland's world of Fingask Castle and, in particular, Fingask Castle's Russian Orthodox Chapel. This would be a nodal point linked to that of Glenalmond College focused on the Glenalmond Chapel, as a war memorial, and library. This would emphasise the importance of Perthshire as a key part of the EDINBURGH ARTS expeditions to Rannoch Moor made by Joseph Beuys.

It would also restore the expeditions led by myself, together with Arthur Watson's students from Duncan of Jordanstone College of Art. This explored the world of Shakespeare's *Macbeth* in the Sidlaw Hills, a world inspiring Joseph Beuys to create *Celtic (Kinloch Rannoch) Scottish Symphony*.

This world inspired Shakespeare to link Birnam Wood with that of Dunsinane and therefore to the Whirly Law of the three witches, and Macbeth's Castle atop Sidlaw Hill. It should be noted that this Perthshire world inspired Ronald Craig for 31 years to be the source of his career as a landscape painter whilst Art Master at Glenalmond College (1956–87).

Last year, the Demarco Foundation celebrated The Road to Meikle Seggie as a natural extension of the Edinburgh Festival within the cityscape of Edinburgh. The Demarco Foundation's contribution, therefore, was about the need to explore The Road to Meikle Seggie in 2022, not only in the world of John Calders' Ledlanet Nights Opera Festival but also the Perthshire parish church of Dunning in the heart of Scotland's Pictish Kingdom. At its centre is the Pictish Cross with the Romanesque interior.

Perth is noteworthy as the place associated with the boyhood of two giants of the cultural life of Scotland. They are John Ruskin and Patrick Geddes. The River Tay and its tributary, the River Brann, are associated also with the world of Ossian.

During last year's Edinburgh Festival, I celebrated its 75th anniversary by exploring The Road to Meikle Seggie from Edinburgh to Dunoon's Burgh Hall and the Botanic Gardens at Benmore in the Cowal Peninsula of Argyllshire. It was there that I have recently discovered the world of Clan McEwen. This year John McEwen was officially declared the McEwen Clan Chief.

The Meikle Seggie road also led to the East Neuk of Fife, to the remarkable exhibition in the farmland of the Bowhouse. This expanded my thoughts on the nature of the world's wilderness spaces, a world explored fearlessly by Alexander Lindsay. He uses the cutting-edge of photography to reveal the physical reality of the world's landscapes which resist the presence of man. I have taken the point of departure of The Road to Meikle Seggie as Edinburgh's Signet Library. This library originated in the 14th century. It was the basis of the National Library of Scotland. It is an expression of the Scottish Enlightenment. It should be brought thoroughly up-to-date with the history of the Edinburgh International Festival as made manifest in the Demarco Archive and Library, and *Demarco's Edinburgh*.

It should be noted that the above text was part of the second draft of intent defining what I believe must be regarded as The Alternative Edinburgh Festival, with an accent on the role of 'the artist as an explorer' in the footsteps of such Edinburgh Festival luminaries as Joseph Beuys, Henning Christiansen, Buckminster Fuller, Roland Penrose, Marina Abramović, Magdalena Abakanowicz, Paul Neagu, Tadeusz Kantor, Patrick Heron, Hugh MacDiarmid, Ian Hamilton Finlay, Jimmy Boyle, Sally Potter, Jacky

Lansley, Hamish Henderson, Father Anthony Ross (OR) and Sean Connery.

The Road to Meikle Seggie leads to the European continent, to the farmlands of the Apennine Mountains, the Orcadian and Hebridean Islands, the Arran Islands and those of Bute, and therefore the masterwork of Brâncuși at Targu Jiu in Romania, Kurt Schwitters on Cylinders Farm in Cumbria, to the farmscape of Louisiana Museum in Denmark and that of Giuliano Gori's Fattoria di Celle in Tuscany and Gabriella Cardazzo's The ArtSpace in Veneto, Ian Hamilton Finlay's garden at Stonypath, Dalkeith Palace on the spot from which General Monk ruled Scotland for Oliver Cromwell, and Charles Jencks' astonishing cosmic Carrick Multiverse, created for the Duke of Buccleuch and Queensberry near Thornhill in Dumfriesshire. These are all extensions of the Edinburgh Festival in stark contrast to Mother Nature.

There is no doubt that the Edinburgh International Festival must return to its birthright, to the time when, in its inaugural programme, it defines itself as a 'flowering of the human spirit and a healing balm, healing the wounds of war'.

It was, at its birth, according to John Falconer, the then Lord Provost of Edinburgh, 'in no way a commercial venture'.

According to George Steiner's 50th anniversary celebratory lecture at the Edinburgh Festival of 1996, the Festival has to encapsulate an image in which the world of high culture and that of education on primary, secondary and tertiary levels are 'two sides of the same coin'.

CHAPTER TWO

The Challenge of a Festival in Europe

THE PIETY OF Maria Fusco, my maternal grandmother, and her pride in being born in Italy, gave me, at the early age of six, my first ever experience of what she enthusiastically referred to as a painting, a veritable example of the Italian Renaissance. Art which had helped her in her devotion to Mary, Mother of God. She called it simply 'Madonna and Child'.

She regretted that I could not see its full-scale reality. I had to do with a small-scale, sepia coloured reproduction in the form of a marker for my prayer book, given no doubt to help me prepare for my first Communion.

Her unerring good taste in early Renaissance Italian Art had inadvertently introduced me to the School of Siena, arguably the best possible place for anyone to begin a commitment to the language of art. I had to consider it every day I went to church, and the ineffable truth it embodied of the love between the young mother and divine son. Why was it a work of art? What were its real colours? Where were the reds and golds that my grandmother enthused about? What was the significance of the two haloes intertwining? These were recurring questions when I knelt to prayer.

My mother assured me that my grandmother was right. There was much to be proud of in my Italian heritage. Italy had indeed produced the world's finest artists. From her lips I first heard the names of Michelangelo, the 'world's greatest sculptor' – and da Vinci, the 'world's greatest painter'.

'Pietà' was a word to be taken most seriously, particularly in relation to Michelangelo's last ever work of art: known as *The Rondanini Pietà*. This presents the Mother of God holding in her arms her beloved Son, no longer in the form of a newly born child, but as a 33-year-old man, in the form of a sacrificial victim newly dead.

Imagine the octogenarian Michelangelo near his own death but fighting hard to create another version of the masterwork he had already hewn out of the marble, still resistant to his most valiant efforts, in his determination to go beyond the limitations of the material, and the fact that time was running out on him. Who would not have yearned for the reality of this sculpture, prefiguring as it did, the work of Rodin?

I knew it was not enough to look at it as a black and white photograph in a book on Italian Art and Architecture that I discovered in the studio of Betty Maxton, a young Scottish art teacher and painter. In her studio where I sat as her model, there existed the books on art history which were to intrigue me as she painted a portrait of my 13-year-old face, as typical of those Italian children's faces she had seen in the paintings of Andrea Mantegna. What better way was there to be introduced to Mantegna? It was Betty Maxton who persuaded my parents that I should become an art student. It was she who introduced me to that treasure house of European culture – The Scottish National Gallery.

She kept my hopes high throughout the war years that I would eventually see Milan Cathedral for myself as a hymn in stone, praising Mary, the Queen of Heaven and all the Angels, and St Peter's in Rome, wherein I would see Bernini's high altar with its distinctive corkscrew-shaped pillars. My 20th birthday fortunately coincided with the Holy Year of 1950, and my father took me to see the land of the Demarcos, on a pilgrimage he was determined to make to Rome. He had always taken pains to explain how the Romans had returned to Scotland in the 19th and 20th centuries, in the shape of the Italo-Scots with names such as Marcantonio, Di Rollo, D'Agostino and Demarco. He assured me that I would find all these names on the war memorial in the main square in Picinisco, the town next to Monte Casino from which most Edinburgh Italians began their long journeys to Scotland via France, England, and even Ireland.

He was convinced that the Demarco family was descended from a Roman legionary called Marcus. Such a thought was intriguing, particularly when I imagined that there could have been such a Marcus serving in that famous 9th Legion, the 'Lost Legion', the one that had disappeared north of Edinburgh, somewhere in the Highlands.

The Romans were Pagans, my father warned me – they worshipped false gods. The 20th-century Romans in Scotland were Catholics. It was obligatory to learn the importance of not only the saints whose names defined the city's churches, both Protestant and Catholic, but also the orders of the angels. It was these saints and the angels that would help me to see how Edinburgh and Rome were part of the same world – that of Christendom.

The most memorable names were Ninian and Triduana because they defined the local Roman Catholic Parish Church at Restalrig. They were easily associated with their earlier missionaries: Columba, Fillan, Ronan, Giles and Serf. Their missionary zeal paved the way for the travelling scholars of Scotland's medieval universities of St Andrews, Edinburgh and Aberdeen to extend their studies to the Sorbonne, and then on to Padua and Bologna. Their journeys naturally involved miracles, which helped them on their way.

CHAPTER THREE

Let Us Consider the Romans in Scotland as Pagans and Christians in Peace and War

THE DOORS OF St Peter's in Rome are the Italian equivalent of the Holyrood entry into the House of God. These two thresholds served as proof that Christianity, not the Roman Empire, provided the symbols which seemed best able to link Scotland with Italy. If the Romans had enjoyed the protection of the angels, would they have possessed the power to remain in Scotland?

It was important for me to learn the fate of the pagan Romans. In the National Museum of Antiquities could be seen the battle-worn metal helmets and masks worn by the Roman Legionaires, and there was a particularly memorable effigy of a Pictish warrior, one of their fierce adversaries. He is one of those who painted their bodies and made strange warlike sounds, one of the fearsome 'Painted Ones'.

The land of the Picts lay north of the Antonine Wall among the Ochil Hills and northwards into Strathtay, and beyond into the vast mountain wilderness of the Grampian Mountains. The Romans built forts as far north as they dared, but at Mons Graupius they were forced into the decisive battle which brought them defeat.

One and a half millennia were to pass before the Romans returned to Scotland, in the form of Italian immigrants. They came from those mountainous regions of Italy into which the remnants of the Roman Legions had fled after the fall of Rome. The mountains were located south of Rome in what is now known as Provincia di Frosinone, and north of Rome in Tuscany, west of Lucca, around the exquisite little cathedral city of Barga.

These modernised Christianised Romans were to give a valuable new European dimension to Scotland's social, economic and cultural life. Sadly, Fascist Italy's decision to enter World War II as an ally of Nazi Germany caused great anguish and hardship for the Italo-Scottish community. For the duration of the war, the Italo-Scots were represented as an undesirable foreign presence, undeserving of respect. The presence of 10,000 Italian Prisoners of War in the streets of Edinburgh, survivors of the Desert War, did not help, but the presence of 200,000 Polish Servicemen did.

They provided the proof that being Roman Catholic and Continental indicated a Europe beyond the confines of the British Isles. Thankfully, an informative and detailed account of the Italians in Scotland, in relation to the Italian community in Britain, has been published. Entitled *The Italian Factor*, it was written by an Italo-Scot, Dr Terri Colpi. She gives an incisive view of how this community, numbering a quarter of a million, developed to play a significant role in the cultural life of every part of the British Isles and, in particular, Scotland.

To provide some understanding of what it was like to be an Italo-Scot in 1939, I had been christened Riccardo but, although I was known at home as Rico, my father insisted I became Richard. It was a difficult time to be an Italo-Scots schoolboy in Edinburgh as my older contemporaries such as Eduardo Paolozzi also discovered. We were regarded with suspicion.

Although the Edinburgh of the 1930s for me seemed removed from the European continent, the Edinburgh of the 1940s was, for the most part, about the alarming physical presence of Nazi Germany in the form of the air raids I experienced, including the very first which preceded by many months the Battle of Britain.

This daylight raid on the Forth Bridge nearly caused me to become one of the first civilian casualties. One of the war's front lines became Portobello Beach as the tide was turning, in the tranquillity of my long idyllic Indian summer day on the beach. Building sandcastles by the water's edge was rudely interrupted by a hail of machine gun bullets. They appeared glistening around my feet, fired from the guns of a Spitfire hotly in pursuit of a doomed Junkers bomber which was subsequently shot down over the Lammermuirs.

I attended the funeral of the two Luftwaffe crew members, remembering their terrified young faces in the enormous glass nose of their plane as it flew screaming in its death throes, already on fire, a mere 100 feet above my head.

In my child's mind I had no sense of fear, only sadness when I saw the young airmen's faces again, this time reproduced on the front pages of *The Scotsman* from the photographs found on their bodies. Never did I regard Germany thereafter as a country full of the enemies of Britain but as the country which had involved these young men on a meaningless and foolhardy mission. The irony had not escaped me that if I had died from the Spitfire's bullets I would have personified the madness and confusion of total war. Such childhood memories of wartime serve to remind me how I have travelled far in time from that September day when Edinburgh was regarded as a theatre of world war.

The Edinburgh of the immediate post-war years produced, totally unexpected, the reality of the world's largest International Festival of the Arts. This was to provide the international stage upon which the artists of all the world could demonstrate the excitement and the power of thought-provoking, and often disturbing, ideas.

The Festival placed Edinburgh on the world map of international culture, despite the fact that it was a city with neither an opera house nor a large cosmopolitan population. But it had, in the Usher Hall, an ideal and imposing setting for classical music, and the equally impressive exhibition spaces of the National Gallery of Scotland and The Royal Scottish Academy.

Although the Festival began as essentially committed to music and drama, the visual arts were acknowledged in the form of blockbuster Arts Council of Great Britain exhibitions, celebrating, for the most part, the achievements of masters no longer alive. Gradually, however, modern art was considered a valid subject for such exhibitions.

CHAPTER FOUR

Maison Demarco

MY FIRST EVER experience of an art space was as a seven-year-old in 1937. It was NOT in one of Edinburgh's West End theatres such as the King's Theatre or the Royal Lyceum or the National Galleries of Scotland or The Royal Scottish Academy on The Mound. It was in a large marquee just off Portobello's Promenade and a short walking distance from Maison Demarco on the ground floor of a handsome red stone Arts and Crafts tenement building known as Marlborough Mansions.

This building was in two sections: sadly, the one on the actual promenade was demolished many years ago, along with Maison Demarco, leaving no trace of their existence. Maison Demarco had attracted countless numbers of Edinburgh's citizens because its interior manifested the spirit of a Parisian café such as the Café les Deux Magots and as a smaller version of La Coupole. This interior provided the experience of the Europe of the 1930s. Music was provided by musicians playing in the style of a Palm Court orchestra. The wood panelling came from Paris and the conversation of the proprietors, Gabriel and Cristina Demarco, was a combination of Italian, English and French. This interior had the distinct aroma of French cigars mixed with French coffee.

I lived my childhood as a European within the walls of Maison Demarco. In the 1930s, my father was the manager of both Maison Demarco and its ice-cream-making factory as well as the tented marque theatre. They were popular features of Portobello during the summer months when Portobello's population was increased by tens of thousands of Glaswegian holidaymakers. A magnificent large-scale Art Deco outdoor swimming pool brought a distinct Hollywood glamour to Portobello, together with the County Cinema. Its opening in 1937 coincided with a special premiere of Walt Disney's masterpiece film *Snow White and the Seven Dwarfs*. It was a supreme example of the Art Deco architecture of the 1930s.

The Maison Demarco Theatre attracted many popular entertainers, including Donald Peers with his much-loved tenor voice singing a repertoire of popular songs. In the same theatre space, Maidie Dickson, the wife of Chic Murray, made her Portobello debut. Sadly, this theatre was erected and dismantled for the summer months only but, it introduced me to the experience of an alternative theatrical space.

Of course, it undoubtedly prepared me for the experience of the premiere of Tyrone Guthrie's 1948 Edinburgh Festival production of *Ane Satyre of the Thrie Estaitis*. This late medieval play was presented in the most unlikely setting of the Church of Scotland's Assembly Hall, set dramatically high on Edinburgh's Castle Hill. The audience was introduced to what was then known as the alternative to the proscenium arch-styled theatre. This was a classic 'open-stage' performance, unimaginable in the post-war years of Scottish theatre.

That same year, I was all too conscious that the very first Edinburgh Festival Fringe production was not staged in Edinburgh but in the Romanesque interior of Dunfermline Abbey. It was a production of *Everyman*, a well-known medieval morality play which has ever since stood the test of time as the true spirit of the Edinburgh Festival.

Camera Obscura and Edinburgh Art College

In 1948, I became curator of Edinburgh's Camera Obscura on the Castlehill section of the Royal Mile, and it was here that I met the actor Duncan Macrae. It was he who introduced me to Tyrone Guthrie, director of Sir David Lyndsay's 16th-century masterpiece *Ane Satyre of the Thrie Estaitis*. It was an historic open-stage production in the unlikely setting of the Assembly Hall of the Church of Scotland, virtually next door to the Camera Obscura, a stone's throw from Edinburgh Castle Esplanade and James Court. It was here, in the basement of a Lawnmarket tenement, the Traverse Theatre opened its doors in 1963; and where my career as patron of the visual and performing arts truly began in collaboration with so many friends who shared my dreams of extending the Edinburgh Festival spirit beyond the all-too-short three-week Festival period into the remaining 49 weeks of the year.

I was in my first year at Edinburgh College of Art and was standing in a queue of fellow students when I encountered for the first time John Martin and Douglas Soeder who were to go on to create the immensely successful graphic design practice Forth Studios Ltd. Both of them became my greatest friends and loyal supporters.

The fourth Edinburgh Festival in 1950 provided a creative launching pad. It gave audiences two Scottish plays – *The Queen's Comedy* by James Bridie and *The Atom Doctor* by Eric Linklater. The unforgettable Duncan Macrae gave a memorable performance in the form of the character of Vulcan.

Sybil Thorndike gave a characteristically distinguished performance as Lady Randolph in a production of *The Douglas* supported by a cast which introduced Laurence Harvey to the Festival.

However, the dominating contribution that year was the exhibition devoted to the genius of Rembrandt. It was presented in the National Gallery of Scotland. RA Westwater, as art critic of *The Scotsman,* wrote: 'These 36 paintings give a complete picture of the whole development of Rembrandt's prodigious genius.'

Glyndebourne Opera gave two unforgettable performances in the King's Theatre of *Ariadne and Nexos* by Hugo von Hofmannsthal, preceded by Molière's *Le Bourgeois Gentilhomme* with music by Richard Strauss. Ian Hunter began his five-year directorship of the official Edinburgh Festival programme.

In 1962, when I was given the opportunity to first contribute to the Edinburgh Festival Fringe, it was in the cellar of Jim Haynes' 18th-century bookshop in the centre of Edinburgh University's George Square campus. This was the Paperback Bookshop.

The ground floor contained a small bookshop. This ground floor space provided the Edinburgh Festival Fringe with its smallest theatre space. The audience was restricted to a dozen seated in close proximity to the actors.

In addition, the basement space of this pre-Edinburgh New Town building provided me with my first Edinburgh Festival exhibition space. It was converted into an art gallery in order to exhibit the art works of my senior art students at Scotus Academy. I remember well the private view which was recorded by an article published in the *Edinburgh Evening News*. It was honoured by the presence of Ernest Dinkel, Head of Edinburgh College of Art's School of Design.

One year later, as co-founder of the Traverse Theatre Art Club, I found myself directing The Traverse Art Gallery in a room directly above the Traverse Theatre space. This was located also in a semi-derelict tenement building in Edinburgh's Lawnmarket. It was in the basement area that the Traverse Theatre and Art Gallery were established in what had formerly been a soup kitchen for the impoverished citizens of Edinburgh's Old Town, and a house of 'ill repute'.

This gallery space was designed by my good friend, the architect Gerry Wilson. The exhibition programme was resolutely international and, in its first year of operation, it attracted artists from all over the British Isles and the Continent of Europe.

By 1966, this small gallery became the forerunner of The Demarco Gallery which was to provide much larger spaces in the domestic environment of an Edinburgh Georgian New Town four-storey mansion house in Melville Crescent. This was the Edinburgh equivalent to my favourite London art gallery, which was also established in a Georgian Mayfair townhouse in Dover Street. This was not a commercial art gallery such as those to be found in Cork Street or Bond Street; it was London's Institute of Contemporary Art. It had a distinct educational purpose, founded and directed by Roland Penrose, the personification of a London-based artist and art patron committed to the avant-garde art world of Europe as personified by Pablo Picasso.

The Demarco Gallery was much enlarged for the 1973 Edinburgh Festival. It was extended with a whole row of Edinburgh New Town houses in Melville Street which had recently been vacated by Melville College, one of Edinburgh's long-standing private schools.

This seemed the ideal gallery space for The Demarco Gallery's 1973 EDINBURGH ARTS programme inspired by the Bauhausian spirit of Black Mountain College. It was there that Marina Abramović made her first ever performance in Britain, and Joseph Beuys performed his '12 Hour Lecture'. It heralded the transformation of The Demarco Gallery from the Edinburgh equivalent of a London commercial gallery into an extension of the international world of Roland Penrose.

CHAPTER FIVE

Festival of the Arts 1955–1958

ROBERT PONSONBY SUCCEEDED Ian Hunter as the third Director of the Edinburgh Festival of Music and the Arts in 1955. Chancellors and Rectors were invited to the opening ceremony representing over 30 universities where they heard an oration from Dr Thomas Honeyman, Director of Glasgow's Civic Art Galleries. This was entitled 'The Universities and the Arts'. A hopeful premise. I had finished my National Service the previous year and was wondering what I was going to do with my life. What I discovered when I returned to my home was inspirational.

The Berlin Philharmonic Symphony Orchestra conducted by Eugene Ormandy, The Philharmonic Symphony Orchestra of New York conducted by Dimitri Mitropoulos, The Royal Danish Ballet, The Azuri Kibuki Dance company from Tokyo were in attendance. Laurence Harvey and Madeleine Christie starred in Thornton Wilder's production of *A Life in the Sun,* directed by Tyrone Guthrie. There was a Glyndebourne Opera production of *Il Barbiere di Siviglia (The Barber of Seville)* by Giuseppe Verdi conducted by Carlo Maria Giulini.

The Edinburgh Festival of this year was in particular to be remembered for an outstanding exhibition devoted to the paintings of Paul Gauguin. David Baxandall, as Director of the National Galleries of Scotland, considered this exhibition to be 'the greatest Festival exhibition of the series'.

He continued, 'The full range of Gauguin's work has never before been shown in Britain. There have been big exhibitions in Paris and Basel, but these did not show the gradual development, the long struggle to learn how to say what he felt he had to say nearly so well as can be seen in Edinburgh.' The exhibition contained 78 drawings.

Vittorio de Sica attended the Edinburgh Film Festival showing of his film *L'Oro di Napolia,* and made a speech in which he prophesied a revival of what he termed 'Neo-Realismo', referring to the success of his film *Umberto D.* That same year, the Japanese entry *Ugetsu Monogatari* received the Selznick Golden Laurel Award. The Japanese also presented *Children of Hiroshima,* a most moving account of the aftermath of the Atom bomb being dropped on Hiroshima on an unprepared civilian population.

In 1958, the movement of Modern Art was properly manifested in the Edinburgh Festival's Moltzau collection, housed in The Royal Scottish Academy, entitled *From Cézanne to Picasso*. Ragnar Moltzau was Norwegian, and his nationality provided evidence again of the important role which William MacTaggart, President of The Royal Scottish Academy, and Lady MacTaggart, were to play through their commitment to a Scottish–Norwegian cultural dialogue.

In the catalogue, David Baxandall, as Director of the National Gallery, traced succinctly the history of the Modern Movement, which was born out of Cézanne's perception of the reality that underlies the obvious surface of things. There was a masterwork by Maurice de Vlaminck to express the power of Fauvism and, of course, Edvard Munch was represented along with Gauguin, Van Gogh and Soutine. There was a whole battery of images by Matisse, Léger, Modigliani, Braque and Picasso.

Onwards to the Traverse Theatre and The Demarco Gallery

How could I be so fortuitous to be introduced to the Modernism of Bonnard and Vuillard alongside the best possible expressions of post-war performance art! How could I be living in a city revitalised by the presence of Wilhelm Furtwängler, Bruno Walter and Kathleen Ferrier, as well as Jean-Louis Barrault? The dark veils over wartime Edinburgh had been lifted by the sights and sounds of the most sublime manifestations of art, giving a new dignity to the concept of Europe.

So it came to be that among like-minded friends, mainly associated with Edinburgh University, the idea of a permanent arts club, inspired by the example of the Festival Club, should be born outside the all-too-short three-week Festival period.

There was many a gathering, many a party, many a lunch and dinner where friends gathered, coinciding with the arrival of Jim Haynes, heavily disguised as a member of the United States Airforce. He transformed Edinburgh with his Paperback Bookshop. I shall not forget the night I took David Buck, Roy Dotrice and Peter McEnery to form an audience of five, including myself and Jim to see a Paperback play performed by three actors, inspired by the writings of David Hume. The Traverse Theatre was simply the enlarged version of this improbable miniature theatre space in 18th-century Charles Street.

Jim Haynes and I had met appropriately enough in 1957 on the corner of the High Street and Blackfriars Street immediately after we had both been to see Ugo Betti's play *Corruption in the Palace of Justice*. This took place in a converted church in the Canongate, known as Cranston Street Church Hall, which served as Oxford University's Dramatic Society Theatre.

How could I have ever imagined at that first meeting that it would lead to a building then used by Lindsays the Printers, and that this building would house two theatres presenting a total of 56 productions and events for the 1992 Edinburgh Festival under the aegis of an institution best known as a Gallery of Modern Art?

I wonder now just how these 56 productions would have affected the concept of the Festival Fringe as it was then – in an altogether smaller and more manageable form.

It seemed inevitable that Jim Haynes should stay on in Edinburgh to operate his bookshop for six eventful years in the early 1960s and meet John Calder, the publisher, friend of Samuel Beckett, and founder of Scotland's answer to Glyndebourne, Ledlanet Nights, and inevitable too that the Edinburgh Festival should be tested to breaking point with the Writers' and Drama conferences of 1962 and 1963 organised by John Calder with the help of Jim and his friends, including Allan Kaprow, the artist who arguably was the first artist to introduce the concept of 'The Happening' to the United States. Mark Boyle, Charles Marowitz and Ken Dewey were also there in 1963 to help Edinburgh Festival-goers contemplate a decorous glimpse of nudity for the first time on a Festival stage.

These two conferences gave the Edinburgh Festival a new meaning, and the world of international theatre and literature was personified for me in the bulky figure of JB Priestley sitting happily in my little white Mini, earnestly discussing the merits of DH Lawrence with Lillian Hellman. I was driving them back to their Edinburgh hotel from a party thrown by Jimmy and Yves Walker in their house in Eskbank, which it seemed every imaginable literary figure of note had decided to attend. I remember thinking what a pity it was that Lawrence had not lived to enjoy it, or John Calder's vigorous legal defence of *Lady Chatterley's Lover*.

The heavy whiff of avant-gardism was in the air by the time the Traverse Theatre Club was born in January 1963 with a restaurant and gallery to bolster the slender income anticipated from a 59-seat theatre presenting an unrelieved programme of experimental theatre.

As Vice-Chairman of the Founding Committee, I worked with Jim in his many roles as Chairman, as the Traverse Artistic Director, as impresario, as enabler, and above all, lover of life and people – and I observed with deep sadness Edinburgh's incapacity to deal with his genius.

In 1966, after a historic Traverse AGM in the Old Pollock Halls, attended by 400 Traverse club members, a new committee was formed to replace the one that had virtually founded the Traverse. Jim had persuaded this new committee to commit themselves to his concept of the Traverse's future, but much to his surprise and anguish, they proved to be totally unsympathetic to his ambitious plans. Within a few months he had no alternative but to leave Edinburgh and devote himself to London's cultural life, much in need then of his spirit of internationalism.

The time had surely come for The Traverse Art Gallery to move into its own premises provided by three of the original Traverse Committee: John Martin, Andrew Elliot and James Walker. The new premises was in a splendid Edinburgh New Town house, just big enough for the Gallery to present aspects of the performing arts and indeed, its first new exhibition was not of painting but of sculpture – it was in a new art form born out of the German and French Fluxus Movement, and certainly out of Allan Kaprow's Festival Happening in the shape of an auto-destructive sculpture by Ivor Davies which literally blew itself apart in the Gallery's basement area.

Alas! The new Traverse Theatre Committee would not allow the Gallery to have the Traverse name and so it came to be, after much heart-searching, that it should NOT be called the Scottish Contemporary Art Gallery, The Melville Crescent Gallery, The Demarco, Elliot, Martin and Walker Gallery, but simply The Richard Demarco Gallery, to prove that there was, by the early 1960s, one Italo-Scot who wished the Italo-Scottish community to be identified with the concept of Modernism then burgeoning in Italy and led by such artists from Italy, West Germany and France as Yves Klein, Luigi Fontana, Mimmo Rotella, Günther Uecker, Enrico Baj and Piero Manzoni.

In this building, The Demarco Gallery's programme could honour aspects of theatre which the Traverse did not wish to consider, those which blurred the perimeters separating the visual and performing arts. The history of The Demarco Gallery's 850 art exhibitions in Edinburgh and elsewhere has been well enough recorded, but not so its programme of theatre, music, dance, and particularly in relation to performance art in all of its multifarious expressions, with the use of video, film, dance, theatre and music in sometimes thought-provoking and ever shocking ways.

From the beginning, indeed the very first exhibition at the 1966 Edinburgh Festival, The Demarco Gallery promoted a programme representing singers, dancers, actors, poets and performance artists such as Tony Coe, Russell Hunter, Caroline Blakiston, Lindsay Kemp, Kevin Anderson, Roger McGough, Mike McGear, John Gorman, Adrian Henri, Stuart Hopps, John Godber, Leonard Friedman, Harrison Birtwistle, Keith Critchlow, Alan Hacker, Miriam Raducanu, Gigi Căciuleanu, Richard Stilgoe, Clive

James, Dinah Stabb, Max Stafford-Clark, Charles Lewsen, Marin Sorescu, Stephen Rea, Julie Covington, Tony Buffery, Pete Atkin, Nancy Meckler, Isla St Clair, Jean Redpath, The Bernicia Ensemble, The Edinburgh Quartet, Józef Szajna with the British premiere of his Theatre Replique, Friedhelm Döhl, Nancy Cole, Mauricio Kagel, Paul Neagu, Tim Jones, Ferdinand Kriwet, Bogusław Schaeffer, Zbigniew Warperchowski, Norman MacCaig, Liz Lochhead, Edwin Morgan, Michael Horowitz, Lizzie Higgins, George Melly, Tina Brown (with her first ever play *Under the Bamboo Tree*), and the White Mountain Dance Company from New Mexico. I will always remember Sandy Dunbar, the then Director of the Scottish Arts Council, participating in their dance masterclasses.

Not all of the performances were at The Demarco Gallery. Some were at Forrest Hill Poorhouse in which Tadeusz Kantor and his Cricot 2 Theatre first appeared alongside Joseph Beuys, and some took place at Melville College and Edinburgh College of Art.

CHAPTER SIX

The Forrest Hill Poorhouse

THE MOST CHALLENGING Edinburgh Festival space used by The Demarco Gallery, even more so than the classrooms and gymnasium of Melville College, was that which was defined in 1972 as Edinburgh University's Forrest Hill Poorhouse. It was, in fact, a derelict plumbers' workshop, disused for a lengthy period of over 20 years. It comprised the ground floor and basement of a historic 18th-century five-storey tenement building, abutting the medieval graveyard surrounding Greyfriars Church, the Edinburgh centre of the followers of Saint Francis. During the reign of Queen Victoria, this churchyard became world famous for the heart-rending story of Greyfriars' Bobby. In its long history, the Poorhouse once provided a home for Edinburgh's destitute poor; it was also known as Edinburgh's equivalent of London's Bedlam. It was in stark contrast to the concept of Jay Jopling's London-based White Cube Gallery.

The Poorhouse identified this area of Edinburgh with the poor and disadvantaged in Edinburgh's society since the early Middle Ages. The Franciscan Order followed the example of Saint Francis of Assisi, tending to the poor, the sick and the dying in society. At one time, it was associated with a place for public and religious dissenters. It was, therefore, where the 17th-century Covenanters died in large numbers in what was virtually a prison. It would not be considered as a fit place for a 20th-century Edinburgh Festival venue.

In 1972, when The Richard Demarco Gallery in Melville Crescent was an acceptable space for cultural events, Forrest Hill Poorhouse stood in dramatic contrast as a virtually uninhabitable slum. I was attracted to its physical nature; its stone walls and flagstone floor paving could be easily identified with those unfortunate souls who had suffered there. It was also a place of healing, a Franciscan poor house and hospital. I could easily associate it as the Edinburgh version of Tadeusz Kantor's concept of a poor theatre and Joseph Beuys' exhortation to his students and fellow artists of 'Show your wounds'.

It was certainly the ideal place for Jimmy Boyle to be introduced to Joseph Beuys when Jimmy Boyle, serving life imprisonment, was released for one day. He introduced himself to Joseph Beuys in The Poorhouse with the words 'Hello, Joseph. I am the Coyote', referring to Joseph Beuys' decision to be in dialogue with an American coyote in René Block's New York gallery. The coyote was an outcast from 20th-century society in the United States. It was certainly the ideal space of inspiration for Joseph Beuys to meet Buckminster Fuller and reconsider the folly of relying upon non-renewable fossil fuels and imagine a future for Scotland entirely dependent on North Sea Oil.

The Poorhouse attracted not only Joseph Beuys but a host of artists and teachers and art teachers – art students under the aegis of EDINBURGH ARTS 1973. Among them are the names of Lord (John) Bute, Michael Spens, Richard Eyre, Alvin Balkin, Fr Anthony Ross, Patrick Reyntiens, Bill Beech, Colette Colbert, Tadeusz Kantor, Wiesław Borowski, the members of the Cricot 2 Theatre Company, Sally Potter, Jacky Lansley, Jane Alexander, Jay Jopling, Paul Neagu, Charles Stephens, Jenny Agutter, Sean Connery, Tina Brown, Earl of Haddington (Lord Binning), John Calder, Michael Meyers, Sandy Nairne and Mark Francis.

The Jimmy Boyle blackboard diptych is now in the collection of the Museum of Art in Mönchengladbach. This museum was the result of the collaboration between Johannes Cladders, the Director of the Museum, and Hans Hollein, the Austrian sculptor-architect. I well remember the opening of that Museum and Joseph Beuys actually making a work of art during the opening with fresh red roses and carnations added to an upright piano. The diptych in the form of two blackboards which Beuys entitled Jimmy Boyle Days is exhibited within sight of the sculpture which Beuys entitled A New Beginning is in the Offing. It is, in fact, inspired by Forrest Hill Poorhouse. It is a perfect symbol of that space which inspired Beuys to make three masterworks. I regard this sculpture as a perfect example of an *objet trouvé*. It consists of the actual weather-beaten doors of the Poorhouse of 1981. The Jimmy Boyle Diptych is inseparable from the Poorhouse doors. You can still see weather-beaten remnants of posters advertising the three days of The Black and White Oil Conference and posters advertising the two masterworks of Tadeusz Kantor performed within what he regarded as the ideal space for him to work and perform.

Therefore, when I think of how Joseph Beuys collaborated with Tadeusz Kantor and in his Cricot 2 Theatre interpretation of *Lovelies and Dowdies* during the 1973 Edinburgh Festival, I can find it impossible to forget how Joseph Beuys celebrated his love of Polish culture by gifting 1,000 art works to Ryszard Stanislawski as Director of the Muzeum Sztuki in the city of Łódź. This means that I cannot separate the reality of The Demarco Gallery housed within the walls of Forrest Hill Poorhouse from the walls of the Mönchengladbach Museum of Art and I must add the fact that the Mönchengladbach Museum is dominated by the sculptural reality of the negative spaces of the void created by the underpass of a section of a New York motorway. Frank Lloyd Wright questioned the nature of an art museum when he designed the Guggenheim in New York and so did Frank Gehry when he designed the Guggenheim in Bilbao. But, when I think of these remarkable manifestations of 20th-century architecture, I cannot separate them from the space of Forrest Hill Poorhouse which remains in my mind as a space which questions the housing of art in modern times. I cannot forget that the Poorhouse was the property of Edinburgh University and they allowed it to be developed as luxury housing. Forrest Hill Poorhouse is now a roofless garden space but its walls are still withstanding the passage of time and contain the monuments of celebrated Edinburgh citizens buried within Greyfriars churchyard. I must not forget that the art of Joseph Beuys was made manifest within the walls of Forrest Hill Poorhouse. Paul Neagu is now honoured by Tate Modern. He made good use of the interior of the Poorhouse and also the churchyard as a member of the faculty of The Demarco Gallery's EDINBURGH ARTS 1972, 1973 and 1974, the Edinburgh Festival summer school. Paul Neagu, Joseph Beuys and Tadeusz Kantor were prominent members of the EDINBURGH ARTS faculty as artist-teachers. The students of EDINBURGH ARTS were therefore fortunate to be involved in what was part of the official Edinburgh International Festival programme.

Special mention has to be made of the way in which The Demarco Gallery presented much of the theatre under the aegis of its annual experimental summer school. This was perhaps too inaccurately called EDINBURGH ARTS. It involved mainly university and art school students and their teachers from not only Britain but North America, with the healthy addition of East European highly professional avant-garde artists. I shall not forget Melville College, in what had been the school gymnasium, giving Edinburgh Festival-goers an undiluted dose of performance art. They were led by the young Marina Abramović on her first ever visit to Britain, supported by Raša Todosejević, George Urkum, Zoran Popovic and Neša Paripović, and the team A3-For Action and Anonymous Action led by Slavko Timotijević from Belgrade.

As a result of this, and the fact they observed Joseph Beuys perform his '12 Hour Lecture' in the same space, Joseph Beuys was invited to Belgrade a few months later. Serbia's capital could well do with his presence now. In 1973, his 'Lecture and Action' at Belgrade International Student Centre was already about the need for Europe to come together culturally and politically.

In St Mary's Episcopal Cathedral, The Demarco Gallery organised a recital by American contralto Beverly Malmstad, a performance very much in contrast to those which took place on Lochgilphead Beach in Argyll where Jacky Lansley and Sally Potter directed the EDINBURGH ARTS modern dance classes, continuing a tradition The Demarco Gallery had begun in 1972 with Stuart Hopps, then the Deputy Director of Scottish Ballet.

EDINBURGH ARTS was even prepared to move behind the high-security walls of the Special Unit of Her Majesty's Barlinnie Prison to reveal the talents of Jimmy Boyle as a sculptor and Larry Winters as a poet, in collaboration with artists Bill Beech, Steve Whiteacre, Michael Meyers and Phil Hitchcock, representing the art schools of Sheffield, Kansas City and Chicago, and with Mark Francis, then an Oxford University undergraduate who became the Director of The Andy Warhol Museum in Pittsburgh. What a pity Andy Warhol was not there alongside Joseph Beuys and Buckminster Fuller helping to question the inadequacy of Scotland's penal system.

1974 was also the year when The Demarco Gallery took over the derelict building of 142 High Street, before it became Edinburgh's Wax Museum, where apart from the exhibitions were the Gallery's *Oxford Review* by Peter Wilson and Richard Sparks, and nearby at St Cecilia's Hall there was the piano recital by Peter Williams and a violin recital by Leonard Friedman.

Writing in *The Times Educational Supplement*, the journalist Juliet Clough was obviously amused by the latest development on the Edinburgh Fringe. I had imported 50 students mostly from the United States for EDINBURGH ARTS '74, a six-week course run in conjunction with Edinburgh University and based in Edinburgh, Stirling and Argyll in negation of the popularly accepted summer school idea.

> The work produced on the course all stemmed from the students' reactions to Scotland. There was bicycle dancing, and hand-outs of flowers in Edinburgh streets, Arthur's Seat was outlined in light, mirrors flashed from the battlements of Doune Castle. There was plainsong in Dryburgh Abbey. Someone sculpted in mud. Another wrote a project on the theatre; someone else constructed a pair of shoes for climbing Arthur's Seat, complete with curly horns to reassure the sheep grazing on its grassy slopes.
>
> Few of my friends escaped. One found his two-mile avenue of trees turned into a happening ground; a farmer was roped in for discussion on everything from pesticides to what it must be like to own 400 acres in which to exhibit sculpture. Lectures ranged from Scottish social history to the Edinburgh Police Force, and there were evening entertainments from Gaelic singing to posh dinners at the historic Beehive Inn in Edinburgh's Grassmarket.
>
> Innocent sightseers at Scottish castles and stately homes were

occasionally startled to see a bus load of young people turn out and form a ring round someone's instant interpretation of, say, the feudal system. 'We are using the dance form as a comment,' explained Sally Potter and Jacky Lansley, alias The Limited Dance Company in charge of the dance workshop. 'The course is structured flexibly round the working process, relating all the time to the specific environment. The kids are responding terrifically well. Taking action seems to liberate them in a positive way.'

In the theatre workshops, we used Scottish myths, Edwin Morgan, or anything else the students felt like doing. The corruption of innocence seemed to be emerging as the dominant theme – a well tried one for Americans in Europe.

Henry James? 'Thank goodness no-one has mentioned him as yet,' said John McRae, Director of Theatre at Nottingham University. 'We've been working with Noddy books; we haven't got onto Adam and Eve yet!'

As a variable on the same theme, three days at the end of the course were devoted to an oil conference in Edinburgh. The students had been taken to see 'some big hole in the ground by Loch Carron' and were able to talk to everybody from politicians to the Westminster Government's Under-Secretary of State for Energy.

The visual arts side of the course concentrated on using the Scottish environmental qualities listed by Steve Whitacre, who held the Chair of Foundation Studies at Kansas City Art Institution as 'light, dark, mysticism, poetry and medieval reality'. The purpose was to 'celebrate and represent to the people of their own environment'.

At Barlinnie prison, artists and inmates exchanged work. 'We celebrated our meals together, found creative ways of getting round the problems of not being allowed to show faces in our visual record of the meetings and discussed the line between creativity and destruction,' recalled Professor Whitacre.

'For the students themselves EDINBURGH ARTS '74 was certainly not providing a rest cure', wrote Juliet Clough. One described the experience as 'being sucked along by a tornado'; another said it made him feel more tolerant. One girl, replying to Juliet's insensitive enquiry about whether she had enjoyed herself, said that it was like being introduced to religion. 'Mr Demarco has been reading to us about Saint Columbus. It's just like that!'

By living we learn. Learning through the Scottish experience uniquely based on the Celtic tradition which is the key to Europe. I had been trying to get the students to feel their roots and show them for the first time some of the alternatives to the rational processes of thought which lead us to be defined as educated. I believe that art is the only language we can resort to if we want to bring in the element of love and not merely information to our understanding.

Eventually, in 1975, The Demarco Gallery moved to the Royal Mile's Monteith House, and there it enlarged its theatre programmes to present Dublin's Project Theatre Company's memorable production of William Butler Yeats' *On Baile's Strand* directed by the yet to be celebrated Oscar-winning film director Jim Sheridan.

It was at The Demarco Gallery Theatre that Neil Bartlett first presented his deeply radical concepts of theatre as did Marcella Evaristi, and where Joan Bakewell performed her one-hour version of the lives of the Brontë sisters, and Diane Cilento introduced her film work *Turning*, inspired by sacred Dervish dancing. It was there that Ruby Wax directed and performed in her adaptation of Genet's *The Maids*, and Eiza Ward sang Brecht, directed by Max Stafford-Clark, and Lily Eng's dancing became the best possible example of Canadian performance art, and Andrew Visnevski's Cherub Company presented their compelling brand of Shakespeare, and Neil Cunningham performed Heathcote Williams' *The Immortalist* with dynamic energy.

The Demarco Gallery's EDINBURGH ARTS exhibition programme in 1975 found itself presenting Polish performance artwork by Barbara Kozłowska and Zbigniew Makarewicz, both on the beaches of Malta, alongside the English artist Paolo Patelli and the English artist Bryan MacDonald, and at the recently vacated Edinburgh Fruitmarket building which was many years later to become the City Art Centre Gallery. This enabled The Demarco Gallery to take the opportunity of presenting a performance by Marina Abramović in which she put herself in great physical danger, from the extreme heat and cold that she was prepared to submit herself. This was presented alongside two other seminal works, one by Nigel Rolfe, and the other by the Ting Theatre of Mistakes in another building originally built as part of Edinburgh's Market Street Fruitmarket.

In 1974, this building had been converted into a gallery run by the Scottish Arts Council and The Demarco Gallery was able to rent it. Both of these productions were transferred under The Demarco Gallery's name, northwards to St Andrews to make a lasting impact on the bi-annual St Andrews Festival programme which until 1977 had resisted performance art.

When The Demarco Gallery lost its lease on Monteith House in 1980, it used Edinburgh's Celtic Masonic Lodge, St Margaret's School for Girls and the RC Cathedral Hall as Edinburgh Festival Fringe venues. There, memorable productions of companies from Bryanston School with Olwen

Wymark's play *Find Me*, directed by Bernard McLeod, Indian Classical Dance with Alpana Sengupta and musicians, Mama Lu's Harlem Break dancing, and Alfredo Michelson's brilliant performance in *Moscow Circles,* Charles Lewsen's electrifying two-and-a-half hour tour de force – *In the Seventh Circle*. Eton College was represented from 1982 to 1984 with the Blue Sunday Company's *Macrune's Guevera,* Fleur de Lys Productions' *The Body Show* (1985), Jonathan Rigby's Free Shakespeare Company's productions of *Othello* and *King Lear,* and James Marriot's Circus Company with a remarkable new play *Voyages from a Black Room,* which received deserved praise from *The Sunday Times* drama critic Harold Hobson.

Other schools such as Marlborough College and Fettes College revealed The Demarco Gallery's commitment not just to universal theatre but also to school theatre. They were presented alongside productions from the universities of Oxford, Cambridge and Rhode Island, under the energetic and dedicated direction of Kimber Wheelock, and all of them were presented and judged alongside the scintillating professionalism of Fascinating Aïda, and a new play entitled *Cressida* written by Morwenna Banks and performed by herself and Tony Slattery, and a performance which more than deserved its Fringe First Award by Miriam Margolyes in a play on the life of Gertrude Stein. There was Cambridge University's Opera Society's *Fidelio,* and a new opera by Terence Sinclair, *The Terrorist,* and the Peter Maxwell Davies opera *The Lighthouse*.

There were always strong contrasts, such as the juxtapositions in the same programme of Peter Gales' spiritually enlivening *Life of Gerard Manley Hopkins,* and the light-hearted Parisian Revue, *Les Ginettes,* and John Kendrick's sombre play, *Third Class Carriage*.

John Kendrick was delighted one night to find himself performing to Sean Connery sitting a few feet from the stage as a member of the audience. Sean had made a point of supporting The Demarco Gallery during its Festival programmes from 1972 to 1982. That was a moment to be compared to Clive James realising that he was performing his 1973 Cambridge Footlight-style review at The Demarco Gallery with Laurence Olivier sitting in the front row as part of a small but obviously select audience.

And there were other diversions. Don McGovern, the American playwright, collaborated with The Demarco Gallery to form a company capable of taking over St Martin's Church in the Gorgie district of Edinburgh to present an ambitious new play entitled *Cross Purposes* – a rare event on the Fringe in the 1980 Festival when venues were by then no longer conceived as temporary theatres prepared to present a complicated production with a stage set that could not be dismantled or shared with any other production.

Even in 1981, when The Demarco Gallery was denied its annual grant funding by the Scottish Arts Council, it managed to present in collaboration with Festival Theatre USA – a musical *You're a Good Man, Charlie Brown* and a Rock Opera (*Tommy*), and six other productions involving the highly committed and talented students of the University of California's School of Dramatic Arts in Los Angeles.

The spacious Roman Catholic St Mary's Cathedral Hall was the setting for The Theatre of the Eighth Day's *Auto Da Fe*, a play in defence of the then banned Solidarity Movement in Poland. This was also the year Zofia Kalińska presented her Polish Akne Theatre production of Genet's *The Maids* in the boiler room of the now semi-derelict James Clark's School in the Pleasance, accompanying Akademia Ruchu, Poland's leading exponents of performance art, and Paul Bradley's Babel Theatre presentation of what he called *A Humdrum Plan*, which re-awakened the images first brought to Edinburgh by Jerzy Grotowski.

In 1986, The Demarco Gallery used another school, this time that of George Heriot's School, to present Arnold Wesker's *The Merchant*, his undervalued play inspired by Shakespeare's *The Merchant of Venice*, and Angela Pleasence and Leonard Fenton in a John Calder production of a new Beckett play.

There was also the world premiere of a new play by Roger Firth on the life of John Clare, masterfully interpreted by Freddie Jones under the direction of Patricia Garland, and the Catherine Carnie production of *It's Different for Girls* which gave Annabelle Apsion an opportunity to shine as a young actress. The National Student Theatre Company produced *Skylark*, a musical play on the life of Billy Bishop, the Canadian World War 1 air ace, a one-man show tour de force by a remarkable student actor, Jonathan Lewis. He played 14 separate characters with Jason Carr providing the piano accompaniment in a style reminiscent of vintage Noel Coward.

However, the most memorable and controversial production at George Heriot's School was that of the Scipion Nasice Sisters Theatre from Ljubljana, performed in a tent. It was sadly closed by fire regulations after only four performances, the audience recognisable only by their heads protruding from holes in the stage, juxtaposed with flaming torches.

James O'Brien's Giro Theatre first appeared on the Edinburgh Fringe with their unique production of political protest, questioning the gross miscarriages of British justice in their unique production of *Prosser*. The Demarco Gallery also collaborated with T Flynn Productions using a temporary theatre space in Edinburgh's West End to present two new plays by Sean Mathias, *A Prayer for Wings*, directed by Joan Plowright, and

Infidelities, directed by Richard Olivier, with actors of the calibre of Patty Duke and Jill Bennett, Anne Mannion, Jason Carter, Peter Kelly, Kevin Allen and Michael Shaw.

I shall always be indebted to Ian McKellen for suggesting that this example of London's professional theatre should be presented at the Edinburgh Fringe.

CHAPTER SEVEN

A Visual Explosion

IN 1962, THE dialogue between The Royal Scottish Academy and Norway had again born fruit. The collection of paintings from Oslo, collected by the film star and skating champion Sonja Henie and her husband Niels Onstad was presented as the Edinburgh Festival's main visual arts offering. Once again Picasso, Matisse, Bonnard and Léger were made welcome in Edinburgh in the form of their paintings, and with the welcome addition of those by Serge Poliakoff, Pierre Soulages, Maria Helena Vieira da Silva, the doyenne of Portugal's art world, as well as Max Ernst, Joan Miró, Jean Bazaine, and Jean Dubuffet. The fact that not even one of these modern masters was invited to attend the exhibition seems to suggest that they all had good reasons for being elsewhere in Europe, even at Festival time.

In the early 1960s, the Edinburgh Festival was marked by the Festival Director Lord Harewood's concern for all the arts and in collaboration with Richard Buckle, he had shown how a great 20th-century sculpture could be seen to great advantage in a temporary space, not normally associated with art.

Together, they transformed Edinburgh's Waverley Market, which in those days was much in need of love, to present a retrospective exhibition celebrating the life of Jacob Epstein. In collaboration with the architects Graham Law and James Dunbar-Nasmith, they created an environment which allowed a lifetime's work to be properly honoured in a way that attracted the attention of those Festival-goers who might normally not be attracted by the contemporary visual arts.

Twenty-four spacious rooms were created and imaginatively lit, and 200 examples of Epstein's genius were revealed to their best possible advantage. High above the entrance, the public were confronted by the image of St Michael and the Devil, preparing for the experience of Jacob wrestling with the Angel within.

Richard Buckle had already proved that the visual arts could attract large audiences by the imaginative use of buildings not normally considered as galleries. He repeated his great Diaghilev exhibition with an exhibition celebrating the 400th anniversary of William Shakespeare's birth in 1964.

Shakespeare themes were treated by Kokoschka, Sidney Nolan, Keith Vaughan, David Hockney, Peter Blake and once again Waverley Market became one of the Edinburgh Festival's key venues. At the same time, in The Royal Scottish Academy, there were 201 paintings by Delacroix.

In stark contrast to the exhibition of classic masterworks, the disturbing spirit of the avant-garde was to be found in another converted space – in a building normally associated with the Bank of Scotland's Documentation Centre in George Street.

The exhibition was entitled simply *International Contemporary Art*. There were seven artists, one Scot, Mark Boyle, one Swede, Oliver Herdies, one Spaniard, Xavier Corberó, one Canadian, William Featherstone, and three Americans, Allen Leepa, Esther Gentle and Abraham Rattner, who had been a close friend of Henry Miller and the inspiration for *The Air-Conditioned Nightmare*.

This exhibition came into being as the first, most ambitious avant-garde visual arts contribution to the Festival Fringe programme. It was presented, not strictly speaking, under the aegis of a gallery but designed to prove the truth of Herbert Read's words in *The Meaning of Art*. 'The simple word 'art' is most usually associated with those arts we distinguish as 'plastic' or 'visual', but properly speaking it should include the arts of literature and music.'

These words were used as the introduction to the catalogue made by those responsible for the exhibition programme of the Traverse Theatre Club. Douglas Hall, as Keeper of the National Gallery of Modern Art, in his introduction wrote:

> There should be room in an Edinburgh Festival to show the work of every
> kind of artist, the great ones of the 19th and 20th century art, and Scottish
> artists, both established and aspiring. It is beginning to be that one may
> have a choice of exhibitions throughout the year. But what is so seldom
> seen in Edinburgh, in Festival or out of it, is the work of lesser-known artist
> from the world at large.

Working in an idiom which is internationally accepted, but is still perhaps unfamiliar in Scotland, this is such an important omission that any exhibition which promises to repair it is welcome. He ended with the sentence, 'If it is successful, it could lead to a regular exhibition of contemporary art at every Festival.'

His words were to prove prophetic.

After my studies at Edinburgh College of Art, and National Service in the King's Own Scottish Borderers. I taught at Scotus Academy, Edinburgh's first ever independent school for Roman Catholic boys. As a teacher, I was to meet the incomparable Jim Haynes, the cosmopolitan arts catalyst heavily disguised as an American Airforce radar operator. He managed to personify the life of the ideal American abroad.

Jim was never to be seen in military uniform. He identified himself totally with the population of sophisticated and charming young Americans whose lives were in sharp contrast to those serving in the US Airforce base at Kirknewton on the outskirts of Edinburgh.

These students were to be found instead in the city's centre, busily studying in their 'Junior Year Abroad', and preferring Edinburgh University to Oxbridge because of their claims to Scottish ancestry. One of these students was Jane Quigley, who persuaded Jim to become involved in the life of Edinburgh University's Dramatic Society. She became the renowned actress Jane Alexander.

Naturally it was the Edinburgh Festival which had brought about my first meeting with Jim Haynes. We met on the Royal Mile, after having both been to see an Oxford University Dramatic Society production of Ugo Betti's play *Corruption in the Palace of Justice*. It was mid-August 1957. Within three years, Jim had opened Britain's first Paperback Bookshop, and made contact with John Calder, the publisher and friend of many world-renowned writers and playwrights.

The Paperback Bookshop provided the nodal point in Edinburgh to bring together the worlds of academe and avant-garde culture. Eventually, the Paperback was to serve also as a theatre space for the 1961 and 1962 Festivals. In this miniscule theatre, with a maximum audience of no more than a dozen, the life of Edinburgh was to change irrevocably for the better. The first production was inspired by the philosopher David Hume's *Dialogues concerning Natural Religion*. The Paperback also served as a Gallery, and there I presented the art work of my students at Scotus Academy.

The Paperback became Edinburgh's much-needed International Salon. Its energy flowed naturally towards Ledlanet Nights, Scotland's small-scale version of Glyndebourne housed in a Victorian hunting lodge set on a hillside near Milnathort in the heart of the Fife and Clackmannan hills. Ledlanet was the family home of the publisher John Calder who had made his name by fearlessly publishing Samuel Beckett, William Burroughs, Alain Robbe-Grillet and Marguerite Duras. He had met Jim in the Paperback Bookshop because of their mutual love for books. Their friendship strengthened and Edinburgh's cultural life was to alter radically as a result.

This friendship led to the highly successful Writer's Conference of 1962 and to the Drama Conference of 1963, which ended with an 'action', defining a revolutionary work of avant-garde art. The world's press saw it as an infamous incident because it involved the brief appearance of a semi-nude young woman. Allan Kaprow, Charles Marowitz, Ken Dewey and Mark Boyle were some of the names associated with this scandalous manifestation of the avant-garde. The Edinburgh Festival was shaken to its foundations. Lord Harewood, its director, was obliged to resign.

In the same year, in a dilapidated 300-year-old tenement in Edinburgh's Lawnmarket, Cambridge undergraduates presented an alternative revue to the Cambridge Footlights in what they called the Sphinx Club. It had been my responsibility to put the Cambridge undergraduates concerned into contact with the tenement's owner Tom Mitchell, who was prepared to play the role of an arts patron.

One year later, he gave his blessing and support for what was to become the Paperback Theatre enlarged. It was the Sphinx Club reborn. Its stage area measured no more than 14 x 10 feet when 59 seats were installed. With the stage traversing them, the audience and actors were brought almost into physical contact with each other. It was to become known as the Traverse Theatre Club. As one of its founders and as Vice-Chairman of the Board of Directors, I made sure that it was not just about Theatre, but also about the provision of a gallery space.

The Drama Conference had revealed the power of avant-gardism as evidenced at this time in the cosmopolitan cultural centres of Paris and New York. The artists who had initiated the concept of performance art, known then as 'actions', were led by Allan Kaprow in America, and by Yves Klein in Paris. The world's press chose to concentrate on a Yves Klein Action in which he caused paintings to come into being in collaboration with two nude female assistants, and a quartet of classical musicians.

All those involved with the art gallery at the Traverse Theatre devoted all of their energies to the defence of Modernism. It seemed perfectly natural to give Mark Boyle his first one-man show, and for Jasper Johns to exhibit his 'Numbers' paintings for the first time ever in Scotland in a University premises just off the Royal Mile, in what is now the High Street Hostel in Blackfriars Street. Little did I imagine that in 1992, this same building would be the one that sat opposite the premises of The Demarco Gallery.

1963 and 1966 were to be halcyon years for me: they represented a new era, a time of freedom of expression which caught Scotland unaware. Support for the Traverse Theatre came with the programme of British and world premieres of plays by Fernando Arrabal, Jean-Paul Sartre, Eugène Ionesco, Jean Genet, Sławomir Mrożek, Michel de Ghelderode, John Antrobus, Saul

Bellow, Harold Pinter and Edward Albee to emphasise the Traverse's policy to internationalise the Scottish World of Theatre.

The Traverse Theatre was, in its essential nature, a meeting place for actors, musicians and artists, and so it had a gallery from its opening day. The Traverse Gallery was fortunate to receive patronage from the doyenne of Scottish artists, Anne Redpath, with her cosmopolitan view of the world and love of Europe. However, the most significant source of support came from the artists themselves, who were more than anxious to be part of an international exhibition programme, long overdue in Scotland.

Artists from all over Britain, Spain, Australia, Canada and the USA came to Edinburgh including the ex-patriate Scottish painter William Crozier, for his first one-man exhibition in his native land. He found it natural to be associated with Catalan artists from Barcelona: Xavier Corberó and Iago Pericot, also Americans, Canadians and Australians: William Wright, Bill Featherstone and Abraham Rattner.

The story of how Jim Haynes was forced against his will to leave Edinburgh for London, and how the founders of the Traverse felt obliged to transfer their patronage to the concept of The Demarco Gallery, is too long and deserves to be told in another context. However, if The Richard Demarco Gallery was to define its *raison d'être*, it could not be more simply expressed than in the short introduction to the gallery's inaugural exhibition. This was signed by the three founding-members of the Board of Directors who had transferred their invaluable patronage from the Traverse Theatre to The Richard Demarco Gallery with Jim Haynes' departure from Edinburgh. They were John Martin, Andrew Elliot, James Walker and myself. This was their Statement of Intent issued to accompany The Richard Demarco Gallery's *Inaugural Exhibition of Paintings, Sculptures and Prints*, August 1966.

It probably seems to the art-conscious Londoner, New Yorker or Parisian that Edinburgh, in spite of its decades of International Festivals, is a 'provincial' city, an opinion which until recently was perhaps justifiable. But the success of ventures such as the Traverse Theatre (in the establishment of which we were all closely involved) has led us to believe that Edinburgh is ripe to regain the place she held in her 'Golden Age', when she was a centre of thought and Culture in Europe. While music and drama of an International standard have been brought to Edinburgh through its Festival, there has been no 'Biennale.' No serious attempt has been made to present to the people of Edinburgh and her many visitors the international contemporary art scene. And in a pioneering way, the exhibitions of this, The Demarco Gallery, hopes to rectify such omissions.

CHAPTER EIGHT

Edinburgh in Relation to Scotland and Europe

EDINBURGH'S CITYSCAPE, WITH surrounding landscape and seascape, is arguably the most beautiful and awe-inspiring in all of Europe. However, it is necessary to consider Edinburgh and its setting within the context of Scotland's landscape. Certainly expatriate Scots, thinking of the land of their forebears, dream of its beauty as unparalleled in all the world. They know it expresses what is probably the quintessential essence of Europe's north-western extremity, in the form of a virtually unspoiled wilderness.

Embedded within the landscape of myriad islands, mountains, moorlands, lochs and glens, are the age-old Gaelic and Pictish cultures. They survive from pre-history and the 300 years of Roman occupation, and that period which produced the Celtic Christian missionaries. Their cultures continued, underpinning the rich history of Scotland in the Middle Ages, under the banners of the Crusaders and the emblems of the medieval Guilds.

A medieval network of monasteries, schools and universities linked Scotland in the Auld Alliance, chiefly to France and the Low Countries. Scotland was thoroughly Europeanised by the time Robert Carver was writing his music for the choristers of St Andrews Cathedral, the second largest church in Christendom after St Peter's in Rome.

John Purser's scholarly history of Scottish music-making *Scotland's Music*, described the blossoming of a musical heritage which in its pre-reformation manifestations, successfully interwove the elements of indigenous Scottish traditions with influences from the Continent. He wrote convincingly of how the early stages of part-writing, originating in Notre Dame in Paris, took on a Scottish character.

The Courts of James IV and V established a golden age for musicians led by Robert Carver, who was trained as an Augustinian Monk at Scone and, prior to that, at Louvain. English musicians could not benefit in this way because of England's warlike attitude to France.

The dialogue with Europe weakened with the reformation, and the resultant Union of the Crowns. The sad but romantic failure of the Jacobite Uprisings led unexpectedly to Edinburgh's Age of Enlightenment, and the resultant Industrial Revolution made Glasgow the Second City of the world's most powerful empire.

Scottish culture became associated with dreams of Empire building in a White Anglo-Saxon Protestant tradition, and not in harmony with a Latin-speaking Roman Catholic Church centred on Rome. This contributed for both good and ill to Scotland's present ideological, political and cultural identity.

The story I feel obliged to tell of internationalising processes in Scotland's cultural life encapsulates all these aforementioned facts and thoughts. They should be taken into account when endeavouring to make sense of the role which the English-speaking peoples of the world must play within the new systems, structures and concepts which have come into operation in recent years.

All over Britain, most institutions concerned with the world of education have been tested and found wanting. For a truly united Europe, and world community, education and culture are also two sides of the same coin.

World War II ended and the Cold War began, but before the full intensity of the cold could be felt, in the brief immediate post-war period, Rudolf Bing came to Edinburgh with his dream of extending his beloved world of Glyndebourne to Scotland.

As an Austrian Jew, Bing represented the full brunt of the agony of Nazi persecution. Together with Tyrone Guthrie and supported financially by Lord and Lady Rosebery, their ideal concept was accepted of a great International Festival of the Arts to celebrate the hard-won peace. It was to give Edinburgh City Council the role that even its most cultured members could not have envisaged for themselves as patron of the world's leading exponents of music and drama.

Perhaps they were caught unaware, perhaps flights of angels intervened to allay their natural misgivings and fears. The fact is they took the undeniable risk of making Edinburgh a world capital of culture for three weeks in the autumn of 1947. This decision was to transform the lives of all Edinburghers who were to regard the three weeks of the Festival as the natural and necessary climactic note sounding the importance of the arts in Edinburgh's life. Those fortunate schoolchildren of Edinburgh studying French were given the opportunity to experience Louis Jouvet, performing the Molière masterpiece *L'École des Femmes*.

In the following years, 1948 and 1949, schoolchildren such as myself, had the opportunity to experience the full impact of what was to be known worldwide as 'open-stage theatre'. It took place in the improbable setting of the Assembly Hall of the Church of Scotland. This was to prove itself the ideal setting for Tyrone Guthrie's masterly production of *Ane Satyre of the Thrie Estaitis*, written by Sir David Lyndsay of the Mount as an attack on the corruption rife among 16th-century pre-Reformation Scottish Church leaders. It gave Scotland's actors the opportunity to prove themselves using the auld Scots tongue. Duncan Macrae dominated in his role of 'Flatterie'. Through my friendship with him I was able to attend rehearsals and matinee performances as his guest. This enabled me to make drawings of all the actors re-creating the Scotland of James v.

During these early Festivals, I was mesmerised by the acting of Jean-Louis Barrault and the dancing of Roland Petit and Zizi Jeanmaire with the Ballets des Champs-Elysées. Through the experience of seeing Zizi Jeanmaire's *Carmen* in both the Théâtre Marigny in Paris and the Empire Theatre in Edinburgh, I knew that, through the language of art, Edinburgh and Paris were entwined, at least for three weeks of every year. The youthful Richard Burton and Claire Bloom were to perform on the stage of the Assembly Hall as the very personifications of Hamlet and Ophelia.

The Road to Meikle Seggie

Of course, Inchcolm Island does not represent the usual cityscape of the basically urban ambience of Edinburgh Festival Theatre productions. As a place for theatre, it signifies the quintessential nature of Meikle Seggie and the EDINBURGH ARTS journey. Meikle Seggie's road beckons to anyone wishing to explore those most mysterious regions of Scotland where history and mythology become as one. The road leads to these ancient stones and pagan ways of worshipping the Earth. It extends by way of Corstorphine Hill on that pathway which led Robert Louis Stevenson's heroes, David Balfour and Alan Breck safely back from their Hebridean adventures in *Kidnapped*, eventually to Queen's Ferry, where David Balfour was indeed kidnapped.

It leads to the Medieval Carmelite Chapel which accurately marks the site of the Queen's Ferry to this day – associated with the Queen who first came to Scotland as Margaret, Princess of Hungary to become King Malcolm's bride and successor as Queen of Scots to Shakespeare's infamous Lady Macbeth.

In the reign of Malcolm and Margaret, the royal court was located in both Edinburgh and around the spiritual capital of Scotland, centred on Dunfermline's Royal Palace. The road between involved the crossing of the Forth at Queensferry. It was from Queensferry that the Festival-goers who experienced La Zattera di Babele's *Macbeth* embarked for Inchcolm – to begin the voyage on which they were assailed by the sight and sound of Macbeth's witches.

It seems appropriate to quote from the introduction I wrote for the catalogue of the 1999 exhibition entitled *The Road to Meikle Seggie*. This involved three French artists – Jean-Sylvain Bieth, Pascal Barbe and Françoise Vergier. Their contribution was shown at The Demarco Gallery in relation to an exhibition presented at the Scottish National Gallery of Modern Art and the French Cultural Institute. This caused 36 French artists, art critics, gallery directors and administrators to travel to Meikle Seggie, on an ideal April day full of bright sunshine.

They personified all the visitors to Edinburgh who should be encouraged to explore Scotland beyond Edinburgh. The road revealed to them the ancient pagan powers and rituals, defining the time-honoured worship of the Earth Mother and her consort The Green Man.

Every year – even now – he appears as the Berry Man of Queensferry. He is part of the mythology which has helped keep alive the legend of the Dragon of Dunning down through the centuries, since the time of St Serf, coming from Rome as a dragon slayer and missionary to impose the Roman Rite of the early Christian Church upon the stubborn defenders of the Celtic tradition, practised on Iona and throughout the Hebrides.

My introduction began thus:

Meikle Seggie does not exist geographically as a village or a town. However, it does indeed exist as a place-name defining a lost settlement on a road that leads across ancient ways travelled by those witch hunters who caused the deaths of so many 16th and 17th century Scottish women (and indeed, men).

The Road to Meikle Seggie leads you across the waters of the Firth of Forth taking into account the Island of Inchcolm at Queensferry, and the Chapel of St Bridget, another personification of the female nature of the Earth. Beyond Fife lie the Ochil Hills where you discover Dunning with its monument dedicated to Maggie Wall, burnt as a witch in 1657.

Thereafter you pass through the Yetts o' Muckhart to Dollar Glen, the 'Vale of Douleur' to that point, beneath the precipitous slopes upon which stands Castle Campbell (aka Castle Gloom), where two small rivers meet. They are called by tradition, the Burn of Sorrow and the Burn of Care. The point at which the waters of Pain and Love co-mingle is defined by seven waterfalls, each with a Gaelic name. The sight and sound of these waters inform you loud and clear that you are in the presence of the Earth Goddess, Mother Nature presenting herself to you in all of her beauty, majesty and sensuality.

Leaving Dollar, you can find yourself moving northwards on the road to Stirling Castle, with its memories of the Scottish patriots, William Wallace and Robert the Bruce, towards the sacred island monastery of Inchmahome, set magically amidst the waters of Scotland's only lake, that of Menteith. By way of the Trossachs, so clearly identified with Sir Walter Scott's Waverley novel *Rob Roy*, you soon find the road which will take you deep into the heartland of the Celts and the Picts, into a landscape of innumerable mountains and lochs, along the banks of Loch Lubnaig and Loch Earn to within sight of Edinample, arguably the most beautiful of all Scotland's castles.

The Road to Meikle Seggie, of course, inevitably leads to that land which the Celts call the 'Land of the Ever Young', to the Kingdom of Dalriada to the valley of Kilmartin and the Hebridean island-world where the midsummer sun has difficulty in setting. This marks the final north-western frontier of Europe. There the road will lead you back into the European heartland, to France, Italy, Poland, Hungary, and inevitably towards the studios of those artists who have wished to reconsider Europe by travelling the road in the spirit of The Artist as Explorer.

Two European Revolutions

The development of the Off-Off Broadway movement in New York compelled Ellen Stewart, founder of New York's La Mama Theatre to join forces with the Traverse Theatre in Edinburgh. Everything seemed possible until 1968 when the Russian tanks entered Prague. The 1960s turned out not to be the time of revolution powerful enough to bring down the Berlin Wall. However, in the aftermath of the dramatic collapse of communism, there appeared, again, a true possibility of revolution in cultural, economic and political terms.

Pre-war Edinburgh was a city virtually disconnected from the mainstream of those modern art movements originating in the spirit of the Communist revolution. The art schools of Scotland were hardly, if at all, affected by Vladimir Tatlin and Kazimir Malevich and their revolutionary brethren, or the urgent desire for change in art education as evidenced in the Bauhaus. Scotland's artists had fixed their eyes firmly on the School of Paris, beguiled by its tradition of *La Belle Peinture*. They ignored the revolutionary spirit of the Italian Futurists, the Dutch De Stijl vision of Utopia, the French Cubists and Dadaists. These movements were born from a Europe in ferment, suffering from the ill-considered Peace Treaty of Versailles, but looking forward to a modern reconstructed world.

The failure of Scottish artists to engage in what was tantamount to a European *cri de cœur* affected all aspects of Scotland's cultural life. Scottish artists did not follow the example of those on the Continent who worked instinctively to bring the worlds of the visual and performing arts and literature together. There were, of course, notable exceptions in the support that William McCance received, as a Scottish Cubist, from Hugh MacDiarmid. The spirit of the Scottish Colourists did not take on board the more sombre palette and subject matter of Braque and Picasso. During his career teaching in the 1930s at Edinburgh University, Herbert Read, that fearless defender of 20th-century Modernism, found great difficulty defending the sculpture of Brâncuşi.

The problem lay in the absence of an art gallery world, and a Scottish equivalent of the dealers and collectors who gathered together in the more cosmopolitan London art scene. There was little evidence of an Edinburgh-London dialogue. Indeed, Edinburgh did not have the will to take on board the achievements of The Glasgow Boys and the Modernist attitude of Charles Rennie Mackintosh, which introduced the spirit of the Austrian Succession to Scotland. This spirit was not to be nurtured in Edinburgh, and for that matter, as the century progressed, it was not to be nurtured as it should have been in Glasgow.

There was no equivalent of the Tate Gallery collection of modern art in all of Scotland, with the possible exception, on a much smaller scale, of the Aberdeen City Art Gallery. It was difficult to find a permanent exhibition space welcoming 20th-century artists and movements from abroad. It so transpired that it was the responsibility not of a National Museum or Gallery, but of the Society of Scottish Artists in their annual exhibitions at The Royal Scottish Academy, to make the first sporadic attempts to bring the reality of contemporary foreign art to Edinburgh.

When this Society celebrated its 100th Anniversary, the eminent art critic Cordelia Oliver, with her customary erudition, in her introduction to the exhibition catalogue, reminded the Society's members that evidence of Symbolism first appeared in Scotland in the Society of Scottish Artists' exhibition of 1909, with a painting by Gustave Moreau, and in 1913, there appeared a few examples of Post-Impressionism, with works by Cézanne, Gaugin and Van Gogh. She pointed out that one single invited work, by Gino Severini, most probably accounted for Stanley Cursiter's all-too-brief involvement with the spirit of Futurism.

In 1931, due to the efforts of William MacTaggart and his Norwegian wife, 12 major paintings by Edvard Munch dominated the Society's annual exhibition, causing, naturally, great controversy. Letters to *The Scotsman* revealed a fear that Munch's influence could do no more than cause harm to the minds of young artists. A number of the Society's Lay members felt obliged to resign in protest.

In the late 1930s, Jim Ede, the then indefatigable young Tate Gallery curator, and collector of 20th-century art, lent a group of sculptures by his beloved Henri Gaudier-Brzeska, and again, through the intervention of London-based initiatives, represented by the Directors of the Meyer and Zwemmer Galleries, a few examples of uncompromisingly modern painting by Di Chirico, Picasso and Léger found their way to Edinburgh.

Immediately after the war, with John Maxwell and Anne Redpath as influential Society of Artists Council members, the School of Paris was celebrated in works by Rouault, Ménessier, Marquet, Valadon and even Picabia. It was only with the beginning of the 1950s that the SSA focused upon the alternative, basically Germanic, art of Karl Schmidt-Rottluff, Lyonel Feininger, Ernst Ludwig Kirchner, Max Beckmann, Franz Marc and Oskar Kokoschka. As the 1950s came to an end, under the Presidency of James Cumming, aspects of abstract expressionism and Tachisme were presented in work by Appel, Jorn, Riopelle and Tàpies. The fleeting nature of the Society of Scottish Artists exhibitions could not help to establish patronage for any of the undoubtedly important artists represented by all too few examples of their work. The artists, themselves, of course, with the notable exception of Kokoschka, were not given the opportunity to experience the reality of Scotland and her artists.

CHAPTER NINE

Strategy: Get Arts

THE DEMARCO GALLERY's efforts to help strengthen the dialogue between East and West Europe began in the early 1970s with the Germans, Romanian and Polish exhibitions seemed to come to naught in the early 1980s when Nicolae Ceaușescu succeeded in making the whole of Romania one enormous prison house, and when martial law was declared in Poland.

At this difficult and depressing time, it seemed to be fitting and right that Scotland could again provide the neutral ground where the artists from East and West could meet. However, with denial of financial support from the Scottish Arts Council, Scotland could not provide the setting for what was probably the most life-enhancing and reassuring exhibition presented in 1983.

Writing about it in *Studio International,* I defined it as important in terms of the development of international dialogues taking place in the summer at the Venice Biennale and dOCUMENTA. The exhibition took place at the Musée d'Art Moderne de la Ville de Paris. Its full title was *Échange Entre Artistes, 1931–1982, Pologne – USA: Une Experience Museographique.* This title indicated its unique nature and its historic value.

The exhibition was literally about an exchange of artworks by Polish and American artists who felt deeply the need to develop close cultural ties between Poland and the USA. It resulted, in effect, from a dialogue that had developed over many years between Ryszard Stanislawski, Director of the justly celebrated Museum of Łódź , and two of his good friends who had long admired his work. Pontus Hultén, formerly Director of the Centre Pompidou, and in 1983 Director of the Museum of Contemporary Art in Los Angeles, and Suzanne Pagé, then the Director of the Musée d'Art Moderne de la Ville de Paris.

Suzanne Pagé and Pontus Hulten had long respected Ryszard Stanislawski, knowing his capacity to defend the most difficult trends in contemporary art and relate them to the truth embodied in the unique and invaluable permanent collection at the Łódź Museum which was to a great extent created through the 1930s dialogue between Polish artists and their contemporaries: Arp, Van Doesburg, Mondrian, Seuphor and Vantongerloo. The Polish artists were avant-gardists associated with groups such as Artistes Révolutionnaires, Grupa Krakowska, Praesens and Blok. Their names should be much better known throughout the art world; Władysław Strzemiński, Katarzyna Kobro, Stanisław Witkiewicz, Leon Chwistek and Henryk Stażewski. They were all in direct contact with Malevich and Mondrian and the international avant-garde represented by the groups Cercle et Carré and Abstract Creation. Anka Ptaszkowska played a lead role in bringing the exhibition into being. She had lived in Paris since 1968 and along with Wiesław Borowski and Mariusz Tchorek, she had helped to found what must be seen as the most important independent art gallery to have come into being in post-war Eastern Europe. This gallery, known as the Foksal Gallery, opened its doors in two small rooms in the pavilion of the Foksai Palace in Warsaw, and although Mariusz Tchorek and Anka Ptaszkowska felt obliged to leave Poland, Wiesław Borowski remained as an intrepid and courageous gallery director.

Through his spirit of internationalism, artists such as Allan Kaprow, Tam MacPhail, Ian McKeever and David Mach were able to present their work in Warsaw, even in the most politically volatile conditions.

Determined as I was to see the exhibition made manifest in the land of the Celts, and knowing that Scotland would not be able to provide a Museum space as prestigious as the Musée d'Art Moderne, I advised Anka Ptaszkowska to work with Ted Hickey, Director of the Ulster Museum in Belfast. The Arts Council of Ireland provided the financial support lacking in Scotland, and when the exhibition opened, it was seen as an historic event, which not only gave the art community of Belfast hope for the future of East–West relations in Europe, but for their own conditions of life and work in their own world divided by sectarian violence and political impasse.

In fact, every imaginable aspect of the avant-garde in the late 1960s and early 1970s had to be taken into account without delay, but none more so than that revealed in what was to be the most important and historic exhibition which would change the image of the Edinburgh Festival.

This was proven conclusively that New York was no longer the world capital for the visual arts. The Strategy: Get Arts artists from Düsseldorf were not all German. There were George Brecht and Dorothy Iannone from America, André Thomkins from Switzerland, Daniel Spoerri from Romania, Mauricio Kagel from Argentina, Henning Christiansen from Denmark, Robert Filliou from France and Tony Morgan from England.

My one and only contact with the German art world was at the time Günther Uecker. Our friendship had begun in Dublin at the first ROSC exhibition in 1967. It was to be one of the most enduring and fruitful friendships spanning several decades. Without this friendship there is no doubt that The Demarco Gallery might not have been able to enter into the post-war history of German art.

Even at our first meeting I recognised that such was Günther Uecker's youthful grasp of the immediate post-war European cultural heartbeat, that his name became naturally associated, for me at least, with the vitally important initiatives of the New Realists, and the manifestations of Group Zero. In the years just after The Demarco Gallery opened in 1966, his was among the names of artists which gave me hopes of a European cultural revival unyielding to a North American Cultural Imperialism. It was Günther Uecker more than any other artist who reassured me that the spirit of Yves Klein was continuing undiminished. After all, he was Yves Klein's brother-in-law and good friend.

It was in the studio of another friend, Gerhard Richter, that I knew Günther Uecker was fully prepared to support the concept of the very first German exhibition ever to take place in Britain and, indeed, the first German exhibition to take place post-war outside Germany. The artists included Erwin Heerich, Konrad Klapheck, Dieter Roth, Günter Weseler, Sigmar Polke, Bernhard and Hilla Becher, Friedhelm Döhl, Karl Gerstner, Gotthard Graubner. Ferdinand Kriwet, Adolf Luther, Heinz Mack, Eric Reusch, Klaus Rinke, Blinky Palmero, Reiner Ruthenbeck, Franz Erhard Walther, and Stefan Wewerka.

The preparedness of Joseph Beuys to participate helped considerably to encourage what turned out to be a team of 37 artists.

Edward Lucie-Smith, writing for *The Sunday Times* touched on the true value of the exhibition:

> The Demarco–Düsseldorf show is shock tactics; it makes English artists
> look provincial. It even makes the New York avant-garde look tame. Its
> importance does not lie in the fact that one is confronted with masterpieces,
> whatever that word might now mean, but rather that it calls the whole
> direction being taken by the visual arts into question. That surely is
> a healthy rather than an unhealthy thing. At a secondary level, it re-
> establishes the dialogue between American and European art.

Strategy: Get Arts brought East and West German artists together; it seemed necessary, therefore, to follow Strategy: Get Arts with East European exhibitions as part of the official Edinburgh Festival programme, and so the Romanians Horia Bernea, Ion Bitzan, Radu Dragomirescu, Serban Epuré, Pavel Ilie, Ovidiu Maitec, Paul Neagu, Ion Pacea, Diet Seyler, Vladimir

Şetran, Radu Stoica, and the Group Sigma One from Timisoara, followed hard on the heels of the Düsseldorf artists.

The Poles followed one year later in 1972, led by Tadeusz Kantor and his Cricot 2 Theatre colleagues, who included Maria Stangret and Zbigniew Gostomski. They were supported by Magdalena Abakanowicz, Kōji Kamoji, Teresa Pągowska, Roman Opałka, Edward Krasiński, Bogusław Schaeffer, Józef Szajna, Jerzy Bereś, Stanisław Dróżdż, Zdzisław Jurkiewicz, Wanda Czełkowska, Wojciech Bruszewski, Jan Chwałczyk, Ireneusz Pierzgalski, Maria Michałowska, Wanda Gołkowska, Jerzy Nowosielski, and Grzegorz Koterski.

In 1973, Austria and France had to be taken into account, with artists such as Jean Le Gac, Gérard Gasiorowski, Gérard Titus-Carmel, Christian Boltanski, Henri Martin, and Vladimir Veličković, in relation to Arnulf Rainer, Hans Hollein, Anton Pichler, Hermann Nitsch and Karl Prantl.

It is important to note that, without the willingness of the Edinburgh Festival directors to accept all The Demarco Gallery's Festival exhibitions as part of the Festival's official exhibition programme, these exhibitions would not have received the vitally important patronage they required usually from the ministries of Culture or National or Civic Galleries representing their national identities.

For this reason, I was indebted to Peter Diamand and his deputy director Alex Schouvaloff who were the first to agree that The Demarco Gallery should help the Edinburgh Festival present contemporary art. John Drummond and Frank Dunlop, as Peter Diamand's successors, were also generous in their personal support despite the fact that the Edinburgh Festival's budget was severely restricted.

More often than not, The Demarco Gallery had to find patronage elsewhere, usually abroad. Throughout the period of the early 1970s, the dialogue with Italy had also to be strengthened in collaboration with four outstanding patrons of contemporary art. The first contact was made with Gabriella Cardazzo at the 1968 Venice Biennale. She represented the Galleria del Cavallino. Her legendary father Carlo Cardazzo, who had established their gallery in Venice under the wartime conditions of 1942, died tragically young in 1964.

Under his inspired direction, his gallery had become the place of patronage for a great family of international artists, including Jackson Pollock, who was given his first one-man exhibition in Italy in 1953. Carlo Cardazzo was the collector, dealer, poet upon whom young and experimental artists could depend. He brought together Lucio Fontana and Alberto Burri with leaders of the Venetian School as up and coming artists, together with Asger

Jorn, Serge Poliakoff, Georgio de Chirico and Georgio Morandi. Under the direction of Gabriella and her brother Paolo, the Galleria de Cavallino has now presented well over 1,000 exhibitions from all over the world.

Through the Cavallino, it seemed natural to find the worlds of Luigino Rossi at Stra, in the area of the Veneto known as a centre for the design and manufacturing of shoes. Rossimoda is now a world-renowned name for Italian shoe design. Into this world, Luigino Rossi warmly welcomed artists and EDINBURGH ARTS participants.

Varese is three hours distant from Stra, near to Lago di Como. There, in the hilltop village of Biumo, now a district of Varese, there is to be found the Villa Litta, and a pivotal exhibition of world importance, with a heavy commitment to America artists. The collection began when, as a young businessman, Giuseppe Panza travelled in Europe and the United States.

He was among the first to collect the work of Robert Rauschenberg, and the leaders of the New York School to be found in the gallery of Leo Castelli. The Villa Litta with its 18th-century architecture, became the ideal, if unlikely place in which to experience the full power of American contemporary art. Here, Giuseppe Panza created a place for art equal in its purity of intention to that of the Angelico's Convento San Marco. Giuliano Gori was a friend of Giuseppe Panza, and his world is located 15 miles from Florence on a hillside near Pistoia, in and around the Villa Celle. In an arcadian English-style garden, and in the extensive vineyards covering the classical Tuscan hillsides, beside man-made lakes, streams and waterfalls, in woodland and in meadowland, can be enjoyed well-nigh perfect examples of site-specific artworks, including a maze built in Carrara marble by Richard Serra, and an observatory built by Dennis Oppenheim, as well as a giant astrolabe-like form by Alice Aycock.

Through these outstanding patrons of contemporary art, it was possible to develop dialogues with Cavallino artists such as Paolo Patelli, Remo Bianco, Piccollo Sillani, Giancarlo Venuto, Guido Sartorelli, Iginio Legnaghi, and Giorgio Teardo, and at the Villa Celle, other Italians such as Mario and Marisa Merz, Giuseppe Penone and Giulio Paolini, and the Israeli sculptor Dani Karavan, as well as the Americans James Turrell and Robert Irwin, and Lawrence Weiner at the Villa Litta.

Having good friends in Italy enabled The Demarco Gallery to help bring about its long cherished dream to present a Scottish presence at the Venice Biennale. Under the aegis of the Scottish Sculpture Trust, three Scottish artists created an open-air pavilion in the heart of the Biennale's Giardini. Arthur Watson, Kate Whiteford and David Mach were selected to represent Scotland at the 1990 Biennale. This they did to dramatic effect despite a shortage of funds and time. There is no reason why there should not be a Scottish presence considering Scotland's desire for Devolution but alas those driving political agendas have always had a tendency to misunderstand art.

It was unthinkable, in dealing with Italy, to leave out the nearby world of Yugoslav art, with artisans of the calibre of Marina Abramović, Radomir Damnjanović Damnjan, Julije Knifer, Braco Dimitrijević, Ida Biard, Sanja Iveković, Dalibor Martinis, Neša Paripović, Nuša and Srečo Dragan, Zoran Popovic, Raša Todosijević, Vjenceslav Richter, Gabrijel Stupica, Gergely Urkom, Goran Trbuljak, Slobodan Tadić , Boris Bućan and Jagoda Buić.

The 1970s expedition to Yugoslavia led inevitably in the 1980s to the young Slovenian artists constituting the Irwin Group as stout defenders of Slovenian independence. Marijan Susovski and his colleagues at the Zagreb City Art Gallery were to prove to be invaluable in the ways in which artists from all regions of Yugoslavia could be assessed.

At the time when EDINBURGH ARTS came into being, the dOCUMENTA 5 exhibition was under the direction of Harald Szeemann. He was a unique figure in the development of European Art through the 1970s, with the intellectual power to question the post-war ascendancy of the North American art world. 'When attitudes become Form' had struck the British Isles with the same impact as that of Strategy: Get Arts.

In 1983, as Contributing Editor of *Studio International*, I wrote a review of Harald Szeemann's arguably most important exhibition, which seemed to touch upon the ideals and initiatives of EDINBURGH ARTS. The review was entitled, 'Towards the total Artwork – Europeans in search of Utopia'.

The exhibition itself was entitled *Der Hang zum Gesamtkunstwerk*. It was sponsored by the Kunsthaus in Zurich, and therefore it could easily be seen as the inevitable successor to Harald Szeemann's Monte Verità exhibition, presented in Zurich in 1978.

The exhibition catalogue of *Der Hang zum Gesamtkunstwerk* was an impressive and weighty document. At 509 pages, it covered most thoroughly every aspect of the European search for Utopia from the 9th century onwards. The most eye-catching painting was Anselm Kiefer's *Heroes of the German Spirit from Wagner to Beuys*, indicating clearly that the exhibition intended to lead you from the world of Wagner and King Ludwig and their contemporaries to that of the late 1970s in a way which was essentially open ended. It never reached London, perhaps because it was predominantly planned from a German-Swiss viewpoint.

In the large ground floor space leading off from the entrance hall, there was a spectacular model of Gabriele D'Annunzio's Vittoriale Degli Italiani, which invited you to consider making the journey to the Western slopes of

Lake Garda to see it in reality, now that it is quite rightly becoming a place of pilgrimage for all those interested in the concept of total art.

The exhibition had the power to attract the widest imaginable variety of interests. It provided a unique experience for the architect, the stage designer, the film maker, the art historian, the sociologist, and, to anyone with a particular interest in the work of that pivotal figure in the development of the modern movement, Kurt Schwitters. He was represented by over 100 works, including his masterwork in the form of a complete one-to-one reconstruction of *Merzbau mit der Kathedral des erotischen Elends* – The Cathedral of the Erotic Misery.

Begun in 1923, the original was tragically destroyed when an allied bomb devastated the two floors and cellar which contained the work in Schwitters' own house in Hanover. It is a world in miniature, a container of memories, and at the same time a church-like space dedicated to his friends, Mondrian, Arp and Richter, and all to the heroic works of the past which had animated his creative spirit. It acknowledged pain and sinfulness interlocked forever with ecstasy and sanctity, a space for the brutalised industrialised townscapes of the Rhine-Ruhr Valley. It contained a Murderer's Cave, contrasted with a Love Grotto.

The contribution of Schwitters and those artists who wished to relate to the history of events, such as Duchamp, Kandinsky, Mondrian, El Lissitzky, Klee, Malevich, Schlemmer, does much to counteract the impact of so many monuments to personal obsessions which crowded in upon the visitors in the upstairs galleries. In fact, the exhibition's success depended upon the fine balance which allowed you to relate the excesses of Ferdinand Cheval (presented by the model of the Palais Ideal as a *coup de théâtre*) to be related to the nearby installation of a reconstruction of Duchamp's *Large Glass*, a work totally dependent upon controlled intellectual thought.

A positive note of optimism was struck and maintained by the commitment to the future revealed in a variety of images, and perhaps the most enduring is that of Vladimir Tatlin's *Monument to the Third International*, here represented by a splendid model measuring 420 x 300 cm.

This could be seen in relation to the reconstruction on a scale of 1:2 of Moholy-Nagy's model of the film set of Alexander Korda's 1936 film version of HG Wells' novel *Things to Come*. Another reconstruction allowed Marcel Broodthaers to be represented by his *La Salle Blanche* of 1975. This installation stood on its own outside the main exhibition area. It had, indeed, a calm independent life. A surreal room in which all thoughts of the future became inextricably inter-woven with our dreams and memories.

The exhibition was memorable for its effective interplay of reconstruction, relating art works to what could be construed as architect's models assuming sculptural forms, such as the *Hängemodell fur die Lirche der Colònia Güell* on a scale of 1:10. This provided a new and unexpected view of Antoni Gaudi, who was surprisingly not represented by the Cathedral of the Sagrada Família. The model defined the point where architecture and sculpture intersect in a thrilling, unique and totally perverse structure.

There were further relationships and dialogues to be discovered: Arnold Schönberg's debate with Kandinsky; John Cage's indebtedness to Marcel Duchamp exemplified in the suite of lithographs published in 1969. 'Not wanting to say anything to Marcel', and, more surprisingly, his interaction with Thoreau in the 1978 suite of lithographs entitled '17 drawings for Thoreau.'

And so the most advanced ideas of art were defined as conversations between the living and the dead, breaking down all the concepts of the modern movements as something existing apart from such events and activities as are normally considered to be in the realm of non-artistic endeavour. One of the main functions of EDINBURGH ARTS was to focus upon such exhibitions, and upon the artists whose art incorporates the history of ideas, and who utilise every imaginable aspect of artistic endeavour.

The Visual and Performing Arts: Points of Intersection

The list of artists crosses the boundaries normally separating the visual arts from music, theatre, dance and architecture, to include James O'Brien's Giro Theatre from Wales, Yvette Bozsik and György Árvai of Hungary's Collective of Natural Disasters, Krzysztof Borowiec and Jan Luzynski of Poland's Grupa Chwilowa, Zofia Kalińska of the Akne Theatre, Mladen Materić of Sarajevo's Stage Obala, Laura Curino's La Zattera di Babele from Rome (with their production of *Macbeth* on Inchcolm Island), Henryk Kowalczyk of Lublin's *Scena Six*, The Theatre of the Eighth Day from Poznan, The Lothe-Lachmann Theatre from Warsaw, and the 'performance artworks' of Lyndall Jones from Melbourne, John Cousins from New Zealand, Alastair MacLennan from Belfast, and Bobby Baker from London, as well as Rosemary Butcher's Dance Company also from London.

There were many unforgettable productions in that European tradition which blurs the lines of demarcation separating more orthodox expressions of theatre from performance art. Notable amongst these were Richard Crane and Faynia William's production of *Rolling The Stone* from London, David Farr's production of *Talking Tongues* from Cambridge University,

R.S.9 Studio Színház productions from Budapest of Gombrowicz's *Operetka* and Wyspiański's *The Wedding* (both British premieres), and, of course, John Bett's production of *Macbeth* on Inchcolm. The Demarco Gallery's preparedness to present theatre as a total artwork is best defined in the introduction I wrote to the catalogue to La Zattera di Babele's *Macbeth*:

> Each project of La Zattera di Babele involved the coming together of artists, poets, actors, singers, philosophers, musicians, dancers and even, when necessary, acrobats. Each project provided the basis for one that is to follow. *Towards Macbeth – A Prologue* was their latest project. It therefore contained within itself the work of all their projects over almost a quarter of a century.

Establishment Censure

The 1980s revealed the inevitability of an ever-widening gap between my concept of Art as a 'Gift' unencumbered by a price tag, and the Scottish Arts Council's concept of art as the producer of an Industry. During the Edinburgh Festival, the Scottish Arts Council decided to remove its annual support of The Demarco Gallery. The Chairman of the Scottish Arts Council's Visual Arts Committee addressed me with these words, 'You have brought dishonour to the meaning of art. You have brought dishonour to the meaning of art in Scotland. You have brought dishonour to the meaning of The Demarco Gallery!'

As a result, since 1980, the Scottish Arts Council, since re-imagined as Creative Scotland, has declined to offer my programme an annual grant to help pay for the basic costs of running the Demarco Festival programme.

Of course, I did not manage on my own to achieve the enormous task of bringing dishonour to the meaning of art! I was fortunate to be collaborating with Joseph Beuys during that 1980 Edinburgh Festival. In 1974, I had featured work by the convicted murderer Jimmy Boyle in my EDINBURGH ARTS Festival exhibition and I had invited Joseph Beuys to meet him in the Special Unit of Barlinnie Prison in Glasgow. They established an artistic understanding.

However, it soon became apparent that the Scottish Prison Services were uncomfortable with the publicity surrounding the remarkable success of the Special Unit in reforming and bringing out the creativity of dangerous individuals. As a sculptor, Jimmy Boyle, branded by the Scottish tabloids as 'Scotland's most dangerous man', was in the process of being transferred from the Special Unit after years of exemplary behaviour as a sculptor and writer to a so-called 'normal' prison at Saughton. The authorities did not as yet have the courage to close the Special Unit down (that took place in 1994) and they were obviously testing Boyle's behaviour.

When this was brought to the attention of Joseph Beuys, he railed against the decision by going on a much publicised hunger strike. He had already written to the Secretary of State for Scotland in support of Boyle as an artist, not as a convicted criminal.

Naturally, the much publicised intervention of a world-famous German artist caused an outrage. Nevertheless, he and Boyle survived this episode, and on Boyle's release from prison in 1981, he and his wife with financial support from Sean Connery, Billy Connolly and John Paul Getty, set up the Gateway Exchange in Edinburgh for recovering drug addicts, ex-prisoners and mental health casualties.

CHAPTER TEN

Edinburgh Arts – Summer Schools and Journeys

IT IS AS WELL I attended the 1984 Venice Biennale, because through its
section devoted to the experimental performing art I was introduced to a
whole repertoire of work: La Zattera di Babele. I knew then, as they were
working with Rudi Fuchs and Lawrence Weiner and Jannis Kounellis that it
was only a matter of time before they had to be introduced into the English-
speaking world, through the Edinburgh Festival and The Demarco Gallery.

Owen Dudley Edwards, in *City of a Thousand Worlds* (Mainstream
1991), his book on the history of the Edinburgh Festival, described the
electric atmosphere of the Italo-Scottish production:

John Bett was taking no chances with the acoustic, and his sharp, keen
voice rose high and perfectly audible on the wind. The effect was that
of fragments of the play tearing through the wind, spinning themselves
into some sort of nebular state. He had made no concessions in dress:
he confronted what was evidently a large congregation of monks in
ancient raincoat (sic), which might perfectly have done duty in a social
drama of London on the problems of an exhibitionist. The blanket-clad
monks looked quiescent: after all, their relations with Macbeth had been
notoriously pacific. Were they headed by Walter Bower, the 15th-century
Abbot of Inchcolm and author of the fiercely nationalist *Scotichronicon*?
The piper gave the full generosity of his lungs to his work; more and more
of Macbeth fluttered from the air; I lay on my belly in ecstasy, with the
best view in the entire place. The Forth gently murmured its blue and white
salutation in the endless clear blue skies awaiting annexation by Richard
Demarco. God, it was Heaven!

Eventually the monks hugging their habits around them showed signs of
being directed back into their fastness, and I hurried down to join them for
Vespers. Now we were inside the stone remains, and by hiding in clefts in
the walls as the monks made their procession here and there, it was possible
to test the boom of the lines in their stone echoes, and imagine the remoter
replies from the surf. And then we were thrust down into the bowels of the
earth into a long low chamber where Carla Tatò, in white, bloodstained

86

with a blond head, and Juliet Cadzow, in funereal dark matching her raven hair dominated from a long table, Tato perpetually smashing a stone on the table top crying great raucous gusts of passion in Italian, while Cadzow, speaking from the depths of her vocal register made a heart of darkness of Lady Macbeth's several most significant speeches. We were confronted by evil and madness and deadly resolution: ambition and diplomacy and deceit, and the implacable resolution to violate even the aged sanctity of protection for a guest.

EDINBURGH ARTS came into being as The Demarco Gallery's experimental summer school in 1972. As it focused on ALL the arts and it was based in Edinburgh, the title EDINBURGH ARTS described its location and purpose. Under the aegis of Edinburgh University, EDINBURGH ARTS was capable of giving up to six academic credits to the American University graduates who represented the majority of the student body in the early 1970s.

The concept brought together a balanced mixture of artists and scientists working together among its faculty and students – particularly effectively in the case of Joseph Beuys, Buckminster Fuller, Paolo Soleri, Magdalena Abakanowicz, Hugh MacDiarmid, Lord Ritchie Calder, Patrick Reyntiens, George Melly, Roland Penrose and Tadeusz Kantor.

In the spirit of a Europe freed from the Berlin Wall, the work of EDINBURGH ARTS was expanded and brought thoroughly up-to-date in the concept of Kingston University's School of European Cultural Studies, operating in collaboration with the Demarco East Europe Art Foundation.

To this end, EDINBURGH ARTS expeditions took into account the need to travel effectively by sea, as well as by land, which led to a voyage of exploration in the spirit of Charles Darwin on HMS *Beagle*. Using a replica of *The Beagle*, a circumnavigation of the coastline of Britain was made possible and indeed this included the English and French Channel Islands, and the coastline of Ireland, Normandy and Brittany, to investigate the age-old seaways which linked all of the British Isles with France. Thankfully, the replica of *The Beagle*, called *The Marques*, was captained by two sailor-artists, Mark Litchfield and Robin Cecil-Wright who could see the value of a voyage dedicated to the discovery of Britain's cultural heritage with a distinctive maritime dimension.

EDINBURGH ARTS existed to provide evidence of the truth in Joseph Beuys' theories. He urged all his Free International University students to be prepared to work with the entire history of ideas. They were obliged to incorporate not only all the arts, but also all aspects of science, politics, philosophy, theology and economics.

From this Beuysian viewpoint, theories of Renaissance art are inextricably linked with those defining aspects of contemporary thinking to refute the heresy at the heart of Postmodernism. Inevitably, an EDINBURGH ARTS journey had to be made to Kassel, as the location of dOCUMENTA 8.

In the year 1983, they experienced a most life-enhancing artwork, *The 7000 Oaks* sculpture of Joseph Beuys. It is to be found to this day not within the gallery spaces, but in the very streets and parks and public places of Kassel itself. It consists of 7000 young oak trees, planted alongside a basaltic stone.

This heroic work will take 300 years to reach maturity. Through it, Beuys was asking succeeding generations to reconsider the importance of the oak as a sacred tree of Celtic civilisation, and the significance to the Celts of the number seven. In this work, he shows his preparedness to work with the forces of nature, with the cycle of growth and decay. It demonstrated his ability to bring the best efforts of the environment into the realm of art.

An EDINBURGH ARTS journey took place in December 1991, during the Winter Equinox, and explored the ways in which artists and students in Britain could identify the age-old roots into what must be seen as the heart of the New Europe, that region where not long ago, the Austro-Hungarian Empire reigned supreme. At its heart lies the city of Budapest, within easy distance of Vienna, Bratislava, Prague, Sarajevo, Ljubljana, Belgrade, Timisoara, Krakow, Trieste, Venice, Graz and Zurich and not that far from Sofia and Bucharest.

All of these cities belong to that part of Europe in which the political strategy devised by Gianni De Michelis, and known as PENTAGONALE, can offer some degree of support to those countries still operating with soft currency restrictions.

This EDINBURGH ARTS journey involved 12 participants. Half were representatives of Kingston Polytechnic School of Art. For this reason, it was planned as a journey from Kingston, and the headquarters of the Thames, through the Channel Crossing between the Kent coast and the Pas-de-Calais area around Lille. It continued overland through Belgium, the Netherlands, Luxembourg, Germany, Switzerland, the Valley of the Po, towards the Veneto and the frontiers between Italy and Austria and Slovenia. In this way, it concentrated upon the artists and architects who long ago built and decorated the 8th-century Tempietto of Civedale, close to the border city of Gorizia, and compared them with those 20th-century artists from this borderland, and serious collectors of the avant-garde such as Egidio Marzona who has chosen to live in an Alpine villa near to the Italian-Austrian border town of Tolmezzo. Fifty miles to the south there is Gabriella Cardazzo's country house and its manifestation of contemporary art.

The Italians fought the Austrians around the Castle of Gorizia in World War I. Now near to that castle can be found the largest Autoport in Europe, the crossroads where East meets West, and North meets South for all the lorry drivers of Europe to contemplate how their journeys could extend beyond Istanbul into Asia and the Arab World.

From Gorizia, the EDINBURGH ARTS expedition turned back towards the Channel, towards the Royal Chapel of Charlemagne at Aachen. There the glory of Carolingian art would be linked to the unknown jewellers, sculptors and painters of the Longobards, whose artefacts are displayed in the Civedale Museum. It is notable that juxtaposed with Charlemagne's Chapel in the Church of St Fillan, the Scottish Celtic missionary who began his journey to Germany from Pittenweem, one of the ports of the East Neuk of Fife.

The return journey had to be made via Colmar as a place of medieval religious pilgrimage, renowned for the Grünewald's Isenheim Altarpiece. The extremes of the most tender emotions contrasted with the full horrors of crucifixion are expressed to unimaginable limits in the Birth, Death and Resurrection of Christ.

Nowadays, it is within four hours driving distance from Aachen, and 15 minutes from Charlemagne's Royal Chapel is to be found a 20th century place of pilgrimage in the form of the Abbey of St Benedictusberg. Uncompromisingly of our time, it is built with modern materials, with concrete and plate glass, and the simple use of wood. It stands as an Abbey Church, the masterwork of arguably the most significant architect of the late 20th century, Dom Hans van der Laan.

As a Benedictine monk, he organised his life so that he could devote himself to prayer and his architectural philosophy. This lifestyle led inevitably to his rediscovering, in three-dimensional terms, the laws governing the Golden Mean. His hard-won knowledge of these laws has produced an architecture which refutes the heresy at the heart of all those Postmodernist buildings which now desecrate most Western European cities.

Blackfriars Street

In 1985, The Demarco Gallery moved to Blackfriars Street which became the location of many an inspirational production. Chief among these must be counted Mladen Materić's masterpiece *Tattoo Theatre* from Sarajevo – a profound full-blown play without words, made possible only by the most generous support of Dione Patullo, an established Edinburgh journalist. Her untimely death in 1989 left The Demarco Gallery without the support of one of its most adventurous and committed patrons. The fact that her son, Tom Henderson, had been tragically killed in the previous year made her death a double blow, as his commitment working for The Demarco Gallery was always invaluable in relation to The Obala Theatre.

This magical production of the 1987 Edinburgh Festival not only gained a Fringe First Award but as a result was supported by Pierre Audi and moved to his Almeida Theatre in London – and from there was launched on a world tour. It is still impossible for me to imagine that The Obala Theatre no longer exists in Sarajevo. In the early 1980s it represented all the energies and life-enhancing ambience of the Traverse Theatre in the 1960s.

The Demarco Gallery had last made use of Edinburgh College of Art in 1984 as part of its DEMARCATION and ANZART programmes involving both Australian and New Zealand artists. Two remarkable performance artists made the imprint, Lyndall Jones from Australia and John Cousins from New Zealand. Both brought new dimensions to the meaning of performance art. Controversy was certainly caused by John Cousins, performing in the Edinburgh College of Art Sculpture Court in the early hours of the morning, with a piece which involved the exhalation and ejection of air and water from his naked body to create music in harmony with his heartbeat.

He defined this as a concert. Any description defies the words I would like to allocate to him in this history. Similarly, Alastair MacLennan's 48-hour Vigil in a downstairs Life Room brought to bear his considerable powers of attention on the Protestant-Catholic divide in Belfast with yet another action possessed of similar spiritual energy and powers of physical endurance.

The three artists and musicians who constituted New Zealand's contemporary music group *From Scratch* gave much food for thought to anyone concerned with the nature of popular music originating in ancient time-honoured primitive music-making techniques. *From Scratch* gave Edinburgh the timeless sound of Polynesia, pre-dating any concepts of Western Europe. Their instruments were sculptural in form and presented a totally satisfying sculptural experience when they were left as objects in the centre of the Edinburgh College of Art Sculpture Court after the performance was finished and the musicians had departed.

I was reminded of the first classic performances of avant-garde music which took place in the ideal setting of Edinburgh Art College in 1970 – particularly Joseph Beuys performing with the Danish composer-musician Henning Christiansen, the 48-hour-long *Celtic (Kinloch Rannoch) Scottish Symphony*.

Then there was the Günther Uecker–Friedhelm Dohl concert *Sound-Scene* incorporating the three-week-long sound of an opening and closing banging door. All this in 1970 when Harrison Birthwhistle was presenting his newly composed work – the result of his collaboration with Keith Critchlow and Alan Hacker. Then, of course, there was Daniel Spoerri's *Banana Trap Dinner* recalling the original outrageous actions of the Dadaists. Six years later, there was Tadeusz Kantor's masterwork *Dead Class* before it transferred to London's Riverside Studios.

The top floor of The Demarco Gallery's Blackfriars Street premises provided the reality of the ideal indoor theatre space, which I personally envisaged, not only for the original Traverse, but also for the visual artists who would wish to make sculptural site-specific installations such as the Slovenian Group Irwin and their Neue Slowenische Kunst.

I will always regret that both Tadeusz Kantor and Joseph Beuys, who planned to use it, did not live long enough to do so. It nevertheless was the setting for some memorable productions, immensely varied in style and subject matter, incorporating every aspect of the performing arts from the modern dance of Rosemary Butcher, to the sculptural setting of a production inspired by *The Labours of Sisyphus* by Richard Crane and Faynia Williams' *Rolling The Stone* (with the whole acting area dominated by an enormous net).

Also making use of The Demarco Gallery's theatre space was Oakham School, with a world premiere of an ambitious musical entitled *Nero-The Musical*! With compelling references to Ceauşescu's Romania. I remember this as complementary to the wizardry of Fay Presto's *Hi Jinx and Lo Tricks* – complete with Jazz music and trapeze artists.

There was also the hymn of praise to James Whistler's life and times enacted with rare refinement by Hurd Hatfield (of *Picture of Dorian Gray* fame); Arts Threshold presented *The Guise*, a play about the banning of theatre in Cromwell's England. This later was presented by The Demarco Gallery in association with the Bulandra Theatre of Bucharest on a tour of Romania. Samuel Beckett's Company was directed by Tim Pigott-Smith, *Magical Thinking* by New York's Wooster Group Associates, *Mein America* by Matthew Weiss – and James O'Brien who wrote, directed and acted in his play *The Pub Bombers*, a *cri de cœur* for The Birmingham Six.

As part of The Demarco Gallery's 1988 Edinburgh Festival Conference celebrating the life of Hugh MacDiarmid, there was a virtuoso violin recital by Leonard Friedman playing a masterwork by Scotland's controversial and indefatigable composer Ronald Stevenson, entitled *The Dodecaphonic Bonfire*, and Tom Fleming's classic rendition of Hugh McDiarmid's epic poem *A Drunk Man Looks at the Thistle*.

Among the other highlights I recall from 1990 must be included Lublin's Scene 6 Theatre with *Springtide of Nations* directed by Henryk Kowalczyk. From Hungary came Márton Tasnádi's hauntingly beautiful version of *Bluebeard's Castle* as well as the ultimate expression or performance art wedded to classical ballet – György Árvai's and Yvette Bozsik's *Collective of Natural Disasters* with their productions of The *Originator* and *The Yesterday of Victory*. These revealed Yvette Bozsik as an actress and a dancer capable of wedding a rigorous self-discipline with deeply felt passion.

In 1991, The English Theatre's proper response to this was best expressed in the Talking Tongues production of *Slight Possession*, written and directed by Cambridge undergraduates David Farr, in collaboration with his producer Rose Garnett, and two dynamic actresses – Sasha Hails and Rachel Weisz. This gave new meaning to the way in which text could be integrated with movement and silence to create theatre near to the choreography of the most experimental modern dance.

There was the ultimate definition of 'performance art' as I prefer to think of it with a sense of humour, as expressed by Bobby Baker, who, with a lightness of touch, and a unique sense of the ridiculous revealed high comedy in the everyday life of an average housewife. In her hands, the buying and preparing of food becomes the very stuff and substance of profoundly moving visual imagery. What a pity Tadeusz Kantor and Joseph Beuys never saw her perform!

In contrast Rochester, that most outrageous and talented self-destructive Restoration poet, was brought compellingly to life in a heroic two-hour solo performance by Doyne Byrd in the best classical tradition of the English acting.

Not all of my productions took place during the Edinburgh Festival. In the winter of 1988 there was a memorable rehearsal performance entitled *Anatomy I – Geography of Portrayed Language* by the Scottish section of Teatra-Scuola. This was dance theatre and the act of painting on canvas involving students from Edinburgh University and Art School, supported by the Italian Cultural Institute of Scotland.

At the 1989 Edinburgh Festival, on the 50th anniversary of the outbreak of World War II, the late Elena Gaputytė, the Lithuanian sculptor, presented a haunting monumental candle-lit memorial to the 56 million who died in the war. This spiritually charged performance served to remind the audience that The Demarco Gallery Theatre was originally designed for prayer as a church. The Lothe Lachmann Video Theatre from Warsaw presented Jolanta Lothe as an actress completely at one with the most advanced and creative uses of video-based performance art in collaboration with Peter

Lachmann. Their high-tech performance was contrasted by the classical Music Hall, astonishing acting and singing of Elizabeth Mansfield as Marie Lloyd. This was also the year Angus Reid deservedly won a Fringe First with his re-enactment of the life of Keith Douglas, the outstanding soldier-poet of World War II.

It was inevitable that certain productions required space beyond the four walls of The Demarco Gallery. The Old Grassmarket Mission was transformed into Mladen Materić's ideal of theatre space, reminiscent of his own Theatre Obala in Sarajevo, in order for him to present not only a reply of Tattoo Theatre, but also of a British premiere of *Moonplay* which was later transferred to London's Institute of Contemporary Arts.

Dione Pattullo's single-minded determination to surmount all difficulties in presenting such a unique theatre company proved to be the crucial factor in the success of these productions, in a theatre space which was transformed into an authentic and compelling Bosnian-Herzegovinian ambience, almost unthinkable in the light of Sarajevo's subsequent suffering.

However, the most spectacular space of The Demarco Gallery's Theatre was undoubtedly that of Inchcolm Island together with the good ship *Maid of the Forth*, both providing the setting for John Bett's spectacular 1989 production of Shakespeare's *Macbeth* with Scottish actors, giving a new meaning to the play literally within the domain of the Thane of Fife and his wife. John Bett was given but 12 days to create his masterwork.

Who will ever forget the rain driving against the throne and crown of Macbeth, played *con bravura* by John Cairney as he confronted Macduff to learn that his reign of terror was at an end, as the sun set spectacularly over the Forth Bridge and the moon rose over Edinburgh Castle four miles distant across the water of the Forth?

Roy Hanlon gave a fine performance as the Porter, as did Gerda Stevenson as Lady Macbeth. Eric von Ibler, as Director of Music for the production and Chorus Master of Edinburgh's Schola Cantorum, orchestrated a musical element which evoked the authentic sounds you would expect to have heard from medieval monks at prayer in Inchcolm Abbey.

This followed the 1988 production of *La Zattera di Babele* by the Rome and Sicily based Company of Carlo Quartucci and Carla Tatò. Their production of the Scottish Play brought together the sound of both the Italian and English languages. John Bett and Juliet Cadzow made sure that the sound of English was suitably Scottish in accent. This production brought together the basic principles of classic theatre and performance art.

It began at The Demarco Gallery, continued by bus journey and sea voyage to end at Inchcolm, a production which hit an operatic high note with the recorded sound of Verdi's *Macbeth* and linked not only the official Edinburgh Festival with the Fringe, but also every imaginable use of contemporary dance, music, acting, performance art and even sculpture of the highest quality associated with Jannis Kounellis and Giulio Paolini, two of the Italian avant-garde artists prepared to work with La Zattera di Babele through Rudi Fuchs, director of the now legendary dOCUMENTA 7, in itself questioning the normal definitions implied by the words 'Gallery' or 'Theatre'.

The Italo-Scottish production was enlarged upon when it was presented literally above cloud-level in the precipitous mountain-top Sicilian town of Erice, in a world seemingly inhabited by Greek and Roman deities.

CHAPTER ELEVEN

PENTAGONALE

IN ITS 25TH anniversary year, The Demarco Gallery focused all its energies on the concept of PENTAGONALE – originating in the political strategies of Italy's Minister of Foreign Affairs, Gianni De Michelis. It was his political acumen and his support of the European Community which brought PENTAGONALE into being as a political, economic, scientific and cultural Pan-European community. It was designed to bring Europe closer to Austria, Hungary, and the former states of Czechoslovakia and Yugoslavia.

Poland joined to make it PENTAGONALE PLUS, with Romania and Bulgaria still waiting patiently to follow Poland's example. The 1991 Demarco Gallery's exhibition and theatre programme was therefore possessed of a very distinct Italian, Austrian, Hungarian, Czechoslovak, Polish, Yugoslav, Romanian and Bulgarian mixture suggesting that The Demarco Gallery's future lay very much in what could be seen as Europe's new heartland.

The Italian contribution to the PENTAGONALE PLUS programme questioned the very idea that a theatrical performance needs to be presented in a clearly designated theatre space. The Laboratorio Teatro Settimo from Turin, consisting of four actors, devised their work entitled *Stabat Mater* so that it had to be performed in the domestic setting of a house or flat. Their performances ended with the performers preparing coffee for the audience.

I was indeed indebted to Nina Mehta for persuading them to perform as part of The Demarco Gallery's commitment to the concept of PENTAGONALE. She recognised them as being representative of that creative spirit which so successfully animates those Italian artists with whom she had been in fruitful dialogue in Italy over a period of seven months in 1990 – from the contemporaries of 1950's avant-garde like the 73-year-old Mimmo Rotella, to recent art school graduates such as 23-year-old Francesco Chiais, and the directors and actors of Milan's Out Off Theatre.

In writing this I recall that I was indebted to James O'Brien and his brother Daniel, who together masterminded a truly international and celebratory 1992 programme, which strongly suggested that the words of Joseph Beuys were as relevant then as they are now: 'New Beginnings Are In The Offing …'

The history of The Demarco Gallery's commitment to the performing arts in the form of theatre, music and dance, and performance art, could not have been realised without a most extraordinary annual occurrence of what I must call miraculous situations and events. This has always involved an almost countless number of friends, supporters and patrons prepared to work well beyond any normal and imaginable points of commitment.

I am not able to name everyone but as I write I am thinking of Christine Wiggins, The Demarco Gallery's first ever administrator, whose husband David was to become a leading figure in the formative years of Edinburgh's Bernicia Ensemble which helped the Gallery establish its reputation as a setting for classical music.

I cannot forget Jennifer Gough-Cooper, so clearly identified with every aspect of The Demarco Gallery's now legendary 1970 Official Edinburgh Festival exhibition programme of the German avant-garde – Strategy: Get Arts, and the Harrison Birtwistle, Joseph Beuys, Günther Uecker, Friedhelm Döhl concerts involving unimaginable new music. She received much-needed support from her mother Vivien, and brother Henry.

None of the German artists will ever be able to forget either the unstinting support given by Sandy Nairne, Sally Holman, Leslie Benyon and Hamish Pringle, in helping to mastermind what turned out to be a Festival within a Festival.

Tadeusz Kantor's Cricot 2 Theatre productions in 1972 of *The Waterhen* and in 1973, *Lovelies and Dowdies,* could certainly not have taken place without Sandy Nairne and Sally Holman and their preparatory work with Kantor in Cracow, and there is no doubt that the Cricot 2 Theatre's 1980 production of *The Dead Class* could not have happened without David Gothard and Mathilda O'Brien.

I know it was Nancy Meckler and her 1970 Freehold Theatre production of *Antigone* which gave me no choice but to commit The Demarco Galley to the 1970s spirit of avant-gardism in Britain. During the period when The Demarco Gallery moved from Melville Crescent towards temporary theatre spaces, and eventually to Monteith House, I was entirely indebted to the support of Anne Goring, Clare Street, Louisa Bell, Jean Sanshagrin, Julian Bannerman, Helene Verine, Murdoch Lothian, Annie Bewicke-Copley, Charlotte Doyle, and Colin Lindsay-MacDougall.

Certainly The Demarco Gallery's Summer School programme of performances and exhibitions could not have occurred without Charles Stephens, Adelaide Shawnee Harris, Mark Francis, Johnny Goring, Chris Aggs, Helen Douglas and David Jansheski and Zibby Campbell also contributed many creative ideas to the Gallery's Theatre Festival at Heriot's School in 1986.

1963. *Lens – A Youthful Focus on the Edinburgh Festival.* (Roddy Martine [RM] Collection)

1963. The editorial team of *Lens Magazine 1963.* Mary Macphail, Lorna Simpson, Catherine Cuinet, Karen Taylor, Roddy Martine, Nick Oppenheim, John Crerar, Bill Sutherland, Rosemary Parol and Helena Gieczwska. (RM Collection)

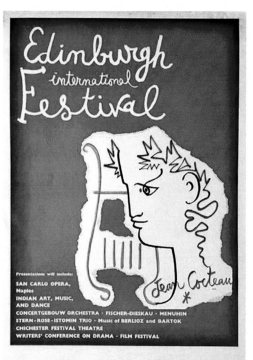

1963. Jean Cocteau's Edinburgh International Festival poster. (RM Collection)

1963. David Frost having breakfast in the George Hotel. (RM Collection)

1964. Edinburgh Traverse Festival Catalogue. (Richard Demarco Archive [RDA])

1964. Allan Harrison, Northumbrian Art Collector. Traverse Gallery Festival Exhibition. (Richard Demarco [RD])

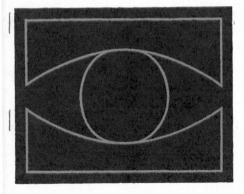

THE RICHARD DEMARCO GALLERY
CHRISTMAS EXHIBITION / DEC 1966

1966. Catalogue, Traverse Gallery Christmas
Exhibition. (RDA; DDA)

1964. Mark Boyle, Traverse Gallery Festival
Exhibition. (RDA; Demarco Digital Archive [DDA])

1967. Emilio Coia and Richard Demarco on the steps of The Demarco Gallery at 8 Melville Crescent.
(RDA; DDA)

1968. Richard Demarco and Jim Haynes. Their lifelong friendship resulted in the birth of the Traverse Theatre Club. (RDA; DDA)

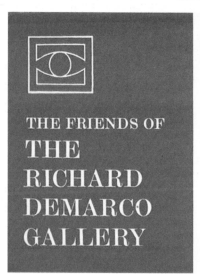

YOU ARE INVITED TO A DISCUSSION ON

THE FRIENDS OF
THE
RICHARD
DEMARCO
GALLERY

'Is Scottish Painting out on a Limb?'

PANEL: JAMES CUMMING   WILLIAM GEAR
WILLIAM JOHNSTONE   JOHN KNOX
CHAIRMAN: DOUGLAS HALL

ON WEDNESDAY, 20 MARCH AT 8.00 P.M.
AT THE GALLERY, 8 MELVILLE CRESCENT
COFFEE WILL BE SERVED AFTER THE MEETING

1968. *Is Scottish Painting out on a Limb?* Invitation card for discussion event at Richard Demarco Gallery. Richard Demarco established the Association of Friends in 1966. (RDA; DDA)

1972. Richard Demarco and Sean (Tommy) Connery in the office of the Scottish International Education Trust at 8 Melville Crescent. (DDA)

Above: 1970. Robert Filliou.
The Vocational Game (detail). *Strategy: Get Arts.*
(RD; DDA)

Right: 1973. Private View card Pavel Ille at the
Richard Demarco Gallery.
(RDA; DDA)

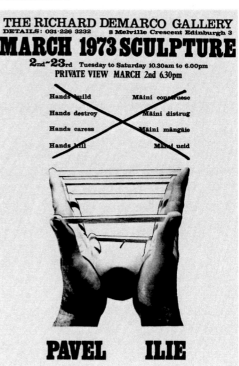

THE RICHARD DEMARCO GALLERY
DETAILS: 031·226 3232   8 Melville Crescent Edinburgh 3
MARCH 1973 SCULPTURE
2nd~23rd Tuesday to Saturday 10.30am to 6.00pm
PRIVATE VIEW MARCH 2nd 6.30pm

Hands build   Mâini construesc
Hands destroy   Mâini distrug
Hands caress   Mâini mângâie
Hands kill   Mâini ucid

PAVEL   ILIE

1973. Tadeusz Kantor's production of *Lovelies & Dowdies* at Forrest Hill Poorhouse, EDINBURGH ARTS. Maria Stangret as 'The Domestic Beast'. (In the photographs of the performance on this and facing page, Sean Connery, Tina Brown and Auberon Waugh can be seen in the audience.) (RD; DDA)

1973. Tadeusz Kantor's production of Lovelies & Dowdies at Forrest Hill Poorhouse, EDINBURGH ARTS. (RD; DDA)

1973. Tadeusz Kantor's production of Lovelies & Dowdies at Forrest Hill Poorhouse, EDINBURGH ARTS. (RD; DDA)

1974. Joseph Beuys creating his masterpiece *Three Pots for the Poorhouse Action* in the Demarco Gallery's Forresthill Poorhouse. (RD)

1974. Front cover of the art journal *Art and artists* featuring a painting by the Romanian artist Paul Neagu. (RDA; DDA)

1976. Peter Diamand, EIF Director 1965–78, as featured on the front cover of the August edition of *Business Scotland*. (RM Collection)

1977. *Instant Sunshine* with Miles Kington. (RM Collection)

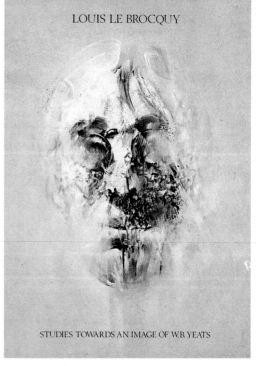

1977. Catalogue, Louis le Brocquy. Studies towards an image of WB Yeats. Demarco Gallery Festival Exhibition at Monteith House. (RDA; DDA)

1978. John Drummond, EIF Director 1977–83.
(RM Collection)

THE RICHARD DEMARCO GALLERY

EDINBURGH ARTS '79

A 7,500-mile Journey into the origins of Western culture

All enquiries and applications should be sent to:

The Administrator, Edinburgh Arts '79
The Richard Demarco Gallery Ltd.

Monteith House
61 High Street
Edinburgh EH1 1SR
Scotland
Telephone 031-557 0707

PRELIMINARY APPLICATION FORM

1 The Gallery reserves the right to refuse any application for participation without assigning any reason therefor.

2 To assist in the assessment of their applications, applicants are invited to supply details of their past and present involvement in activities relevant to the Journeys. Any such material sent must be clearly marked. Applicants who wish their material returned MUST enclose a STAMPED ADDRESSED ENVELOPE in the case of the UK. Those outside the UK should enclose a STAMPED ADDRESSED ENVELOPE and CHEQUE FOR RETURN POSTAGE to be made payable to EDINBURGH ARTS '79.

3 The sponsors and staff of Edinburgh Arts '79 do not hold themselves or their associates responsible for the loss or damage of work material sent.

4 Each successful applicant must obtain personal medical insurance for the Journey. Edinburgh Arts Europe '79 and its associates are in no way responsible for any financial outlay incurred through illness of any participant on Edinburgh Arts. A photostat copy of personal medical insurance covering the time of participation in Edinburgh Arts will be required.

5 Edinburgh Arts Europe '79 exists for artists who wish to extend their work into new areas of time and space not usually offered by a contemporary art gallery.

6 No excess art baggage — physical and mental — should be carried from the past of each participant. New dimensions should be revealed in the art of each participant. Edinburgh Arts '79 will NOT provide ideal space for those artists wishing to work only within the space of a studio over an extended period of time. Edinburgh Arts is about risk and experiment.

7 Only if a participant's past work is particularly relevant will it be possible to consider it for any of the Edinburgh Arts exhibitions which follow directly out of the Journeys.

8 Special consideration will be given to applicants who have applied to Arts Councils or Scholarship Foundations for matching grants, or grants towards the cost of participation fees or of travel of applicants towards the point where they would join the Edinburgh Arts Journeys.

9 The Visual Arts Officers of the Arts Councils of Scotland, England (including all areas recently created out of a policy of devolution, e.g. Southern Arts, Northern Arts), Northern Ireland and Eire have been notified of the fact that British and Irish applicants would be applying to them for scholarship support. Also the Visual Arts Officers of the Canada Council and Ontario Arts Council and the British Council (for Yugoslav, Polish, German, French, Italian, Maltese and Hungarian applicants).

The Barque MARQUES during her eleven-month circumnavigation of South America as HMS BEAGLE for the BBC film "The Voyage of Charles Darwin", 1977–78.
The EDINBURGH ARTS Journey to the Mediterranean from 23rd June to 30th July will be made on board the MARQUES.

jimmy boyle

sculpture

MacRobert Arts Centre Gallery
University of Stirling
9-27 October 1979

Gallery open 11am-5pm (Monday to Saturday) and 2-5pm (Sunday)
Also at live theatre performances

1979. Jimmy Boyle Sculpture at MacRobert Centre.
Demarco Gallery Exhibition in collaboration with the
University of `Stirling. (RDA; DDA)

1979. Application Form, EDINBURGH ARTS.
(RDA; DDA)

1979. On board *The Marques* for EDINBURGH ARTS. The Demarco Gallery under full sail towards the Port of Leith and the Edinburgh Festival. (RDA; DDA)

1980. This is Richard Demarco calling! Arranging the 10th anniversary exhibition of *Strategy: Get Arts*. (RM Collection)

1980. Sheila Colvin, Deputy EIF Associate Director 1978–89 under the Directorship of John Drummond and Frank Dunlop. (RM Collection)

1980. The Furbelow Family with Alice Beberman, a Demarco Gallery Edinburgh arts student.
(RM Collection)

1980. Andrew Brown and Elizabeth Smart.
(RM Collection)

1981. Emilio Coia and Yehudi Menuhin at Emilio's Edinburgh Festival Retrospective Exhibition held at the Merchant Company Hall. (RM Collection)

1982. Michael Dale, Director of Edinburgh Fringe and Andrew Cruikshank, Chair of Edinburgh Fringe taking part in the Festival Cavalcade. (RM Collection)

1982. Roddy Martine interviewing Rudolph Nureyev for *Scottish Field* at the Palais d'Orsay in Paris. Photo: Eric Thorburn. (RM Collection)

ANZART
AUSTRALIAN &
NEW ZEALAND
ARTISTS
IN EDINBURGH

A R K L E Y ★ C O U S I
N S ★ D R U M M O N D ★
F R O M S C R A T C H ★
J O N E S ★ K I L L E E
N ★ L E T H B R I D G E
★ L O W E ★ M A R R I N
O N ★ M c C A H O N ★ M
I T A ★ N I C H O L A S
★ O L S E N ★ R O O N E
Y ★ S H A R K L E W I T
T ★ T R U S T T U M ★ T
Y N D A L L ★ W E L L S

Edinburgh International Festival 1984
A new contemporary art publication from The Richard Demarco Gallery

ANZART: AUSTRALIAN & NEW ZEALAND ARTISTS IN EDINBURGH

Published by the Richard Demarco Gallery, Edinburgh, in collaboration with the Queen Elizabeth II Arts Council of New Zealand and the Visual Arts Board of the Australia Council, this 96 page colour catalogue fully documents a unique event–the first combined Australian and New Zealand exhibition of contemporary art to be seen in Britain–which was specially assembled for, and presented as part of, the 1984 Edinburgh International Festival. 'Anzart in Edinburgh' was the third 'Anzart' exhibition–the first was held in 1981 in Christchurch, New Zealand, and the second in Hobart, Tasmania, in 1983. This exhibition, which was therefore the first joint exhibition to be seen outside Australia and New Zealand, ranged from the masterly word paintings of veteran Colin McCahon to astounding performances by 'From Scratch'. Lyndal Jones and John Cousins. Painting, sculpture, music, installation, film and performance art were all represented. The catalogue contains reproductions (many in colour) of the work of each participating artist along with their individual statements and biographical details and is thus a unique record of Australian and New Zealand art as it is NOW. It also contains an introduction by Richard Demarco and essays by Denise Robinson and Wystan Curnow.

Size 270 x 210mm. 96 pages, thread sewn.
Price: £5.00 (plus post and packing).

Available now from:
The Richard Demarco Gallery
10 Jeffrey Street, Edinburgh EH1 1DT
(031-557 0707)

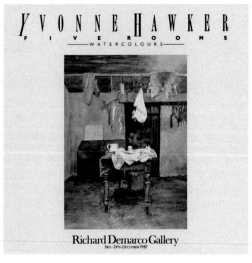

1984. ANZART – Australian and New Zealand Artists in Edinburgh in collaboration with Nick Waterloo in Australia and Ian Hunter in New Zealand. (RDA)

1987. Yvonne Hawker painted her studio in the remote landscape of Ayrshire. Watercolours Catalogue, Richard Demarco Gallery. (RDA; DDA)

1987. Demarco Gallery production of Mladen Materić's *Tattoo Theatre* transferred to the Almeida Theatre in London. (RDA)

1990. In the Demarco Gallery on Blackfriars Street, Mimmo Rotella creating an artwork later sold at Sotheby's for £8,000 in aid of The Demarco Gallery. (RDA; DDA)

1990. Fringe in the Park. (RM Collection)

1996. Roddy Martine chauffeuring the magician Fay Presto in the Edinburgh Festival Cavalcade. The Demarco Gallery presented Fay Presto in Blackfriars Church. (RM Collection)

Bridging the Gap between Edinburgh, Dundee, Scotland & the Baltic

Demarco in *Dundee*

The Edinburgh Festival at Dundee Rep, Venue 191

Tues 13 - Sat 31 August 1996

DUNDEE REP THEATRE VENUE 191 Box Office Tel: (01382) 223530

1996. *Demarco in Dundee* – Edinburgh Festival at Dundee Rep. Poster design by John Martin, founder and director of Forth Studios. (RDA)

BEYOND CONFLICT

AN EXHIBITION BY TWENTY-FOUR SCOTTISH ARTISTS
A CULTURAL DIALOGUE BETWEEN SCOTLAND AND ISLAM

Presented by
THE DEMARCO EUROPEAN ART FOUNDATION
in collaboration with
BlinkRed.com, Aid International and Apex Hotels
with financial support from
The Russell Trust
At the European Parliament in Brussels - 6,7,8 November 2002

2002. *Beyond Conflict* exhibition, resulted from a conference in Edinburgh of Members of the European Parliament. (RDA)

Sir Jonathan Mills, EIF Director (2006–14) on the rooftop of the EIF Hub.
(RM Collection)

DEMARCO'S FESTIVAL

An Exhibition in **seven** parts illustrating Richard Demarco's 60 year engagement with the Edinburgh International Festival.

1   **Artworks from the Demarco Archive** (paintings, drawings, prints & sculpture) from Demarco Gallery exhibitions & performances contributed to successive Edinburgh Festivals e.g. the legendary **'Strategy: Get Arts'** (1970) & Kantor's **'Dead Class'**, including original work by Beuys, Kantor, Abramovic, Uecker, Wewerka, Neagu, Fijalkowski, Hamilton Finlay, Moffat, Hollein, Rotella, Bitzan and Ackroyd.

2   **Photographic documentation** of every Festival from 1947 to 2006 revealed through Festival publications and material from the **Demarco Archive** & other sources.

3   **Edinburgh Festival Posters** commissioned from Forth Studios by **John Drummond**, Edinburgh Festival Director from 1979 to 1983.

4   Exhibition inspired by the **Scottish National Portrait Gallery's** collection and building connecting the Edinburgh Festival to the **Scottish Enlightenment**, with special reference to the 200 year old **Hunterian Museum** in Glasgow, and figures in the arts & sciences such as **Burns, Stevenson, Scott, Byron, Telford, Cockburn, Carlyle** and **Watt**.

5   Exhibition linking the **history** of the **Festival** and the spirit of **modernism** and the **avant-garde** with the Venice Biennale, Documenta (Kassel) and Hamilton Finlay's 'Little Sparta', in relation to Ruskin's trans-Alpine journeys.

6   Specially commissioned series of **moving image** portraits by Hamilton & Ashrowan exploring the concept of the artist's journey, as illustrated by Demarco's **'Edinburgh Arts'** expeditions to **Poland** and **Romania** from the 1960's to the present day.

7   An exhibition of designs by students of **Napier University's** School of Creative Industries and Architecture for **Jonathan Mills' Edinburgh Festival Project** to transform five of the principal Festival venues with photographic projections of images from the Festival and **Demarco** Archives.

ENTRANCE TO THE EXHIBITION IS **FREE**

PLUS: The seven parts of the Exhibition are related to a **daily programme** of **'FESTIVAL CONVERSATIONS'** in which Richard Demarco will discuss past Edinburgh Festivals with various well-known figures in the arts and sciences. Every morning during the Festival in the Antiquaries Library of the Portrait Gallery 10.30 - 12 noon. Tickets £6 from the Portrait Gallery Bookshop. See separate Poster/Leaflet for programme details.

Demarco with Joseph Beuys, Edinburgh Festival 1970 (Photo George Oliver)

DEMARCO'S FESTIVAL — LY TO 2 SEPTEMBER 2007 • SCOTTISH NATIONAL PORTRAIT GALLERY, 1 QUEEN ST DAILY 10AM-5PM (THUR TILL 7PM) • DURING EDINBURGH FESTIVAL DAILY 10AM-6PM (THUR TILL 7PM)

2006. Richard Demarco with camera, filmed by Samir Mehanović on Skateraw beach, East Lothian for his film *Richard and I.* (Samir Mehanović)

2007. Demarco's Festival programme commissioned by Jonathan Mills for his inaugural International Festival. (RDA)

2015. *Beyond Borders – International Festival of Literature and Thought.*
(Beyond Borders)

2023. Nicola Benedetti, Director Edinburgh International Festival.
(Scottish Government CC 2.0 via Wikimedia Commons)

2020. Richard Demarco planting an oak in memory of Rory McEwen at Marchmont House, Berwickshire; Hugo Burge second from right. (RM Collection)

It is indisputable that The Demarco Gallery's Theatre Programme truly matured during the 1980s. It was born in the period around 1980 to 1981 when The Demarco Gallery found itself without an annual grant from the Scottish Arts Council and could no longer present major exhibitions.

With The Demarco Gallery being tested annually well beyond normal levels of endurance, a heroic effort and commitment was required to every manifestation of the performing arts, which the Gallery considered complimentary to the most experimental aspects of its record of exhibitions. The Demarco Gallery could not have survived without, for example, the untiring efforts of Ray Anderson, Clive Rubin, Bernard McLeod, Sam Henderson, Danny Withall, Niki Braithwaite, Emily Ash, Jonathan Chapman, Jo Manby, Sarah Gudgeon, Anya Galuszka, Peter Arden and David Petherick.

Jane MacAllister's arrival in the summer of 1979 coincided exactly with the beginning of this well-nigh impossible period. She faced 12 years of unrelenting challenge, using all the resources within her artistic soul, and with great courage, conviction and imagination, and above all loyalty, defended The Demarco Gallery's philosophy against heavy odds. To define her role with any title would be woefully inadequate, particularly those currently used in art world circles such as Deputy Director, Artistic Director, Administrator or Producer. The only title I can think of would be Art Patron Extraordinary.

She personified a deep commitment to every aspect of art language without which The Demarco Gallery would not have been able to endure; and indeed without which all contemporary art manifestations become meaningless.

1990 ended with the news of Tadeusz Kantor's untimely death. His presence was sorely missed by us all but thankfully there were bittersweet memories of his Cricot 2 actors performing in the newly re-opened Empire Theatre (now The Edinburgh Festival Theatre). Their production of *Today is my Birthday* (in aid of The Demarco Gallery East European Art Foundation) was a triumph and an outstanding event even without his presence.

It was comforting to see the Cricot Company in The Demarco Gallery after their performance enjoying the extraordinary film made by Gabriella Cardazzo and Duncan Ward. The film was in every sense celebratory, revealing Kantor's capacity to express the genius of the Christo-Judaic tradition of art making which was at the heart of The Demarco Gallery's 25th Anniversary Exhibition and Conference, PENTAGONE-PLUS, and which brought Gianni De Michelis as Italy's Foreign Minister to the Edinburgh Festival and enabled him to spend a memorable day with Jack

Lang, as Minister of Culture in France on The Road to Meikle Seggie, the road which leads The Demarco Gallery inevitably into the New Europe.

In 1992, Paulina Kolczynska, Anya Kemalow and Paweł Frelik represented the Polish aspects of The Demarco Gallery's Edinburgh Festival programme. Krzysztof Borowiec and Jerzy Lużyński brought back the unforgettable Polish-Russian Grupa Chwilowa with *A Stop in the Desert*, with two of Moscow's leading actors Aleksiej Zajkev and Irina Nabatova, who had enchanted audiences the year before with arguably the most compelling piece of theatre worthy of comparison with Tadeusz Kantor's Cricot 2 Theatre.

CHAPTER TWELVE

The Edinburgh Festival is Not Interested in the Visual Arts

IN THE YEAR 1992, Brian McMaster began his 15-year directorship of the Edinburgh International Festival, thus ending the 25-year-long period when I was Director of the official Edinburgh International Festival programme for the contemporary visual arts. Brian McMaster had decided that no aspect of the visual art world would be included in the official Edinburgh International Festival programmes.

The visual arts were therefore demoted to the programme of the Edinburgh Festival Fringe. I had scrupulously avoided separating the visual arts from the performing arts in my official Festival programme. I was careful to include the world of literature so that, in the great European tradition, all the arts could be seen to be at one with the history of ideas, including all aspects of scientific endeavours. In 1992, I was therefore fully prepared to emphasise the importance of literature in my Festival programme, despite the fact that it was for the first time now consigned to the Fringe. I was convinced that, in my collaborations with artists such as Joseph Beuys, Tadeusz Kantor and Paul Neagu, they had great respect for the art of that supreme 20th-century writer of the calibre of James Joyce, who was, of course, Samuel Beckett.

I was therefore, pleased, when John Calder, as a true friend and important publisher of Samuel Beckett, was pleased to be part of the Demarco Festival publication. This related to the Demarco programme at Blackfriars Church. By 1992, I was involved with the academic life of Kingston University and therefore I was in a position to invite John Calder to deliver a two-day master class as a follow-up to his involvement in my 1992 Festival programme. The text of John Calder's essay was in defence of the truth embedded in the life and art of Samuel Beckett, and it read as follows:

> If any modern writer might have expected a lifetime of neglect, it is Samuel
> Beckett, whose outlook and aesthetic have always gone both against
> fashion and the optimistic mores that every state tries to encourage in its
> citizens. But such is the power of his work that he has achieved a form of
> acceptability outside fashion, while those who have learned most from him,
> Pinter and Stoppard in particular, have become high fashion. Before the

war, in a letter to a friend, he had already declared, '... my own language appears to me like a veil that must be torn apart in order to get at the things (or Nothingness) behind it... To bore one hole after another in it, until what works behind it – be it something or nothing – begins to seep through. I cannot imagine a higher goal for a writer today.'

Elsewhere he has expressed his despair of achieving a literature not independent of words which tend to obscure meaning, and he once suggested that the purpose of art might be to portray failure, saying of the artist that 'failure is his world and to shrink from it desertion, art and craft, good housekeeping, living.' Yet Beckett has become accepted, in literary, dramatic and academic circles, as the most significant living writer in the sense that Dante, Cervantes, Shakespeare and Goethe were in their own time. Equally significant, although known only to an educated few, Beckett has given the 20th century its own mythology. If our present age is tragic, we should not forget that out of tragedy the greatest art often emerges.

Born in Foxrock, near Dublin, in 1906, Samuel Beckett had little success with his pre-war writing, today considered his early period, comic depictions of philosophical young men out of step with their time and world, self-mocking and replete with uncomfortable home truths. During the war, he joined the French resistance and when his group was uncovered by the Gestapo, went into hiding in the Vaucluse until the liberation.

Since then he has written in both French and English, translating himself. His wartime experiences and observations of human behaviour at a time of upheaval are a principal source of the novels and plays that subsequently made him famous. In particular, *Waiting for Godot*, the most revolutionary and successful of all plays written since 1945. In spite of the power and critical success of the dramatic works that followed Godot, and the compressed perfection of the plays written during the last 20 years, it is with his first performed play, a depiction of two tramps killing time while waiting to be given a job, that he emerged as one of the greatest dramatic poets since Shakespeare, and conquered the stages of the world. The 20th century and its anxieties are beautifully encapsulated in the situation, speculations, characterisations and language of Godot in both naturalistic and metaphorical terms. The novels that he wrote at the same time, *Molloy, Malone Dies*, and *The Unnamable*, although less popular, accomplished a similar revolution in the art of fiction. This period, from about 1947 to roughly 1970, is considered his middle period.

What Beckett has done is to reject the conventional hero with whom the reader tends to identify, in order to create a new anti-hero, closer to what we really are, rather than as we like to see ourselves. Most post-war writing is either about middle-class culture, with its inbuilt values, concern with situation and emotion, and ability to flatter to reader by helping him or her to identify with a character that he or she would like to be, or else it is about working-class culture with its class-awareness. Political commitment and envious anger, the latter manoeuvred as a weapon against the establishment of the moment.

The great polemical art movements of Europe, Impressionism, Expressionism and Surrealism, have only really surfaced in Britain through James Joyce, and in America through William Burroughs, whereas in Europe art literature based on a political or philosophical premise is still thought of as a branch of painting.

Beckett had avoided the pitfalls of other writers in that his characters are not symbols of a social class or a philosophy, nor are they wish-fulfilments to flatter the audience. Whether one can identify with a Beckett character depends very much on the individual. Beckett's characters are mostly tramps, drop-outs or work-shy loafers, interested principally in their thoughts. They could come from any class or none. Their thoughts are interesting because they are uninhibited and therefore honest, either understanding their own predicament, or failing to do so in a way that enables the audience or reader to see what it is that the mind is hiding from itself.

Citizen of Europe

When I was 52, Elizabeth Lyon interviewed me for *Artwork*, and observed,

It's been suggested that the reason Buckminster Fuller never got a Nobel Prize is that there is no category broad enough to reward a multi-faceted genius. The prizes are for people who make a great contribution in small, well-defined cases. And anyway, these rare people with many talents are somewhat suspect in a modern world – like witches!

The same could be said for Richard Demarco who also suffers from being impossible to pin down. In his world, where the artists and the arts administrators often take opposing sides, he has flourished with both feet in both camps at the same time. But at the same time he has discovered that such success couldn't be universally popular.

1992 was the year in which I found myself, to my astonishment, the recipient of the Award of the British Centre of the International Theatre Institute. The award was celebrated at a delightful luncheon at the Garrick Club in London, and to my delight was presented by Richard Eyre, not just as Director of the National Theatre, but as a veteran of the Edinburgh Festival from his days at Edinburgh's Lyceum Theatre. We were able to reminisce about Tadeusz Kantor's first ever production in the world of English-speaking theatre at the Poorhouse, Forrest Hill, when Richard, as *The Scotsman*'s theatre critic, was the first to write in unstinted praise of Kantor's genius.

Little did either of us know that on that same day of celebration, 27 April, International Theatre Day, the Polish Centre of the International Theatre Institute had also decided to give its award to what I must consider to be all those dedicated souls who have put their considerable efforts into helping me transform The Demarco Gallery at the Edinburgh Festival into a stage and testing-ground for international theatre.

Our programme was expressed with emphasis on a distinct Eastern European tradition inspired by the world of Stanisław Witkiewicz who committed himself to art philosophy between the two world wars. The Polish International Theatre Prize was therefore aptly named the Witkiewicz Prize.

The Polish Award enabled me to spend seven days in Poland searching out new aspects of Polish theatre which augured well for The Demarco Gallery's future Edinburgh Festival productions. I was able to observe the Poznan Dance Theatre in performance on the largest stage in Europe, in Warsaw's Opera House. I witnessed an extraordinary evocation of the world of James Joyce's Dublin performed by the company of actors directed by Henryk Baranowski. I focused on Molly Bloom's soliloquy. The play is entitled *Yes, I Will, Yes! Molly Bloom* and was played by Monika Niemczyk, an actress of outstanding ability, who managed to convey the unutterably Irish-ness of Molly's spirit, not only in her physical appearance, but in the very sound and rhythm of her voice, so that her Polish language embodied the quintessential music of Joyce's words.

Janusz Wiśniewski as director of his own eponymous theatre company enabled me to see the final dress rehearsal of his latest work which when translated is entitled *Wonderful Life*. It was full of ironic images of the ongoing European turmoil. It was Janusz Wiśniewski who presented me with the Witkiewicz Prize in the Ateneum Theatre which was also the office of the Polish Centre of the International Theatre Institute. As an artist, as well as a man of theatre, Janusz had actually designed the award in the form of one of his paintings.

The Director of the Institute, Janusz Warminski spoke of his happy memories of the 1963 Edinburgh Writers' Conference to the 60 representatives of the Polish theatre world who attended the ceremony and reminded me that among the Polish delegates was Zbigniew Cybulski, the Polish film actor and star of *Ashes and Diamonds*. He refreshed my own memories of the Polish 'James Dean' who seemed always to wear dark sunglasses throughout his stay in Edinburgh.

At a special ceremony held at the European Parliament Office in Brussels on Monday 19 August 2013, I was presented with the European Citizen Medal by the President of the European Parliament Martin Schulz. It is a day I will remember forever. I was the only United Kingdom citizen and arts person to receive this great and unexpected honour.

Awards are awards and I am humbly and immensely grateful for the recognition they bring, but in so many ways this European Citizen Award is representative of all the values that I have pursued throughout my life.

Let me just say that there is no Polish art. There is no Scottish art. There is no English art. There is no German or French art. There is no Italian art. There is no American or Chinese or Japanese art. There is only Art. The culture that binds all of us together in totality as Europeans belongs to the world.

New Horizons – Cultural and Educational

New systems have to be created in politics and economics, and certainly in whatever is meant by Culture and Education in all of their many manifestations. Artists, academics and students should be prepared to receive the challenges of a Europe returned to what must be regarded as the natural order once defined by the Renaissance and by the noble concept of Christendom. Europe will have to be taken seriously if it accepts the challenge, and even more seriously if it fails to do so.

These young Europeans who will inherit the systems of higher education offered by the dawning of the new millennium will require much more than what universities are presently prepared to offer. I can imagine most will be found wanting if they cannot provide a true 'New European' dimension. The days of 'bi' and 'tri'-lingual educational systems have arrived, certainly in those European countries which consider, for good or ill, that English is still the new 'Lingua Franca'.

I was a delegate to an international conference in Utrecht, in which the problems facing the youth of Europe were considered. I was the Co-Chairman, together with Adam Krzemiński, the Polish journalist of the working group on 'Culture' in relation to this conference organised by the Dutch Ministry of Welfare, Health and Cultural Affairs, the Council of Europe and the European Economic Commission.

The conference was entitled *Youth Mobility and Youth Policy in a New Europe*. The paper produced by this workshop is altogether relevant to all who consider Education and Culture to be two sides of the same coin in any concept of a New Europe. For this reason I wished everyone who experienced the exhibition PENTAGONALE PLUS to consider the following points which were stated in the report of the Working Group on Culture submitted to all the conference delegates.

What is Culture – particularly Youth Culture?

The group agreed with the definition provided by Janez Skullj of the Slovenian Youth Council: 'Culture means the way of our lives: what we eat, what we wear, our religions, languages, the media we listen to, look at and experience. It is the qualities of our life.'

Is there a distinction between Culture and Education?

No. The consensus of the group felt that Culture and Education were indistinguishable, and that both related to the imparting of values to succeeding generations.

Can such education happen within existing structures?

Peter Lauritzen, representing the European Youth Centre of the Council of Europe, reminded us that such a conclusion was not new: five years earlier a meeting of Education Ministers at the Council had agreed that 'schools do not prepare youth at all for life in Europe...'

Manuela de Bois-Raymond, Professor of Youth Sociology at the University of Leiden, forcibly reiterated the point that educational institutions were, by-and-large, incapable of even addressing this issue, and she stated that Youth Mobility must be connected to concepts of culture to give it meaning and that the educational system must be mobilised to confront this challenge.

Despite the enormous difficulties inherent in the challenge presented to all of us as New Europeans, and the complexities being revealed with the collapse of the old order, there is evidence that new systems are already coming into being to accept the challenge. One of these must surely be the European Youth Parliament, a charity which continues to encompass 40 European countries regardless of Brexit. It provides a forum which allows the energy and idealism of young people in Europe to be expressed in such a way that it can have a direct influence on the elected representatives of the European Community.

The founder of this Youth Parliament, Bettina Carr-Allinson was planning a meeting of over 500 delegates to attend all the sessions of the Parliament which today has its headquarters in Berlin.

The meeting took place in Strasbourg that September in collaboration with The Demarco Gallery East Europe Art Foundation, and the accompanying exhibition featured images of the New Europe as seen through not only the youth of EEC countries but all those countries prepared and ready to form a concept of Europe never before realised in Strasbourg.

This exhibition led to the publication of a suite of prints with 24 images. Each image expressed the European cultural identity of their country, seen through the eyes of the students as well as their ideas of the New Europe. Those judged to be most worthy received a scholarship which enabled them to use the facilities for printmaking available at both Aberdeen's Peacock Printmakers, and Kingston University's Printmaking department. Thus these institutions were able to welcome a family of young international artists working together for the first time.

My personal experience of the 'lockdown' in response to the Coronavirus pandemic of 2020 had caused me to discover innumerable pieces of paper hidden until now in that part of the Demarco Archive existing in the narrow confines of my domestic space within the limitations of my Edinburgh home.

My attention today is drawn to the fine details constituting this small part of what I must regard as a large-scale work. I am, therefore, dependent on what I could define as 'chance', certainly not by design, on discovering the core of this *Gesamtkunstwerk*.

These pieces of paper take the form of diaries, basic correspondence, essays, newspaper cuttings, artists' statements and mundane administrative paraphernalia: all related to a large library of exhibition catalogues, theatre programmes, novels, histories, dictionaries, etc. I am in a state, therefore, of bewilderment, conscious that this year is testing humanity on a global scale, and particularly the so-called 'world of art' now that it is equated with sport, all manner of leisure activities and the world of self-aggrandisement.

I have awakened to this day of bright sunshine in Edinburgh, having to take seriously into account a vivid dream in which I was giving a lecture to a university audience on the value of the Demarco Archive as a unique academic resource.

Last night, before experiencing the dream world, I found by chance ideal bedtime reading material in the form of the Edinburgh University publication of Professor George Steiner's lecture celebrating the 50th anniversary of the Edinburgh Festival. It was entitled *The Festival Overture*. In his opening paragraph, George Steiner writes:

Whatever its joys, a festival, because it sets aside normal time, because it assembles human beings in a unison of feeling, will compact a touch of morality – 'Come away, come away Death' sings Feste to Orsino in Shakespeare's *Twelfth Night* in a line whose magical duplicity enacts, beyond paraphrase or logical justification, the secret sadness, the tristitia which gives to a true Festival its joyous gravity.

I read this in relation to the insightful book written by Matei Stircea-Craciun, the Romanian art historian, on the art of Paul Neagu. He writes about the importance of Paul Neagu's sculptures expressed in the form of hyphens. He writes that Paul Neagu's hyphen sculptures expressed in the form of hearts and skulls define the point where mythology meets the möbius strip in a streamlined asymmetrical work which is as mystical as it is aerodynamic.

Despite this fact, if not because of its relation to earliest modernist sculpture, Donald Kuspit, the celebrated American art critic, calls Neagu's hyphen sculptures at once 'pre-historic and post-historic – or to put it another way, Neagu is an artist who sees the skull beneath the skin and has found a hyphen in and beyond it.'

On another piece of paper there is a particularly significant quote in the form of a manifesto. I must consider it when I imagine the possibility of the Edinburgh Festival's future. This year (2020), for the first time in over 70 years, there will be no Edinburgh Festival. The question I must now ask is, 'Can the Edinburgh Festival continue to exist with the present imbalance between the official programme and its Fringe?'

I should imagine that the present Director of the Edinburgh International Festival should take into consideration the text of this manifesto. It states unequivocally that 'Art is the name we have given to humanity's most primal response to the mysteries of existence.' It was in the face of this mystery that dance, music, poetry, painting and sculpture were born.

Thus, in the dawn of the current era, art has been under threat. In the name where it belongs on the cultural landscape, two idols stand like golden calves demanding worship. They are pornography, the use of aesthetics to manipulate through desire and propaganda, the use of aesthetics to manipulate through fear. Even when true art is made, powerful economic and political forces are there to subjugate it to these idols.

The work of art is apolitical, the artist, Oscar Wilde said, is 'free to express everything'. I personally believe that enduringly profound art aspires to the condition of prayer as expressed in the Edinburgh Festival's production of Giuseppe Verdi's *Requiem* and in the sublime vocal sound of German Lieder sung by Kathleen Ferrier under the baton of Bruno Walter conducting the Vienna Philharmonic Orchestra and the acting of Richard Burton and Claire Bloom in their Shakespearian roles as Hamlet and Ophelia. I belong to a generation sadly dwindling fast which can remember the first Edinburgh Festival in 1947. John Falconer, as the Edinburgh Festival's patron, wrote an introduction in the official programme that this historic event is about 'the flourishing of the human spirit' and 'it is in no way a commercial venture.'

Can these words define the next Edinburgh Festival? Can future Edinburgh Festivals take seriously the significance of Paul Neagu's hyphen sculptures?

The Edinburgh Festival was born because Rudolf Bing, as its founding director together with a few friends, firmly believed that the language of the arts could effectively heal the wounds inflicted by World War II. Can the current Director of the Edinburgh International Festival find friends to help define the future of the Edinburgh Festival so that it can be seen to heal the pain and suffering caused by the Coronavirus pandemic?

There is undoubtedly a challenge to re-charge the Edinburgh International Festival with the spirit of friendship in the inescapable truth that art is a word re-defining the nature and purpose of Britain's National Health Service. The same sentiment might also be concluded in regard to Vladimir Putin's unforgivable Special Military Operation in Ukraine.

Where Do We Go From Here?

The Edinburgh International Festival must attract the burgeoning global world of the visual arts. This would be my response to Nicola Benedetti's leading question – 'Where do we go from here?' I have always imagined that the Edinburgh Festival could compete with the two festivals which take seriously the growing global world of the visual arts.

This has caused the Venice Biennale and the City of Kassel's dOCUMENTA exhibitions to attract a distinctly multilingual audience. This global audience should swell the ranks of Edinburgh Festival-goers. Unfortunately, the Edinburgh Festival has not attracted this global audience, certainly since the '90s and the first decades of the Third Millennium. In these decades, the nature of the art world has changed permanently and now it is difficult to find a demarcation line separating the visual from the performing arts. Since the decline of the '90s, I have endeavoured to entwine the visual and performing arts in all my Edinburgh Festival programmes with those I have presented during the Venice Biennale.

Thankfully, I have been able to collaborate with Sonia Rolak, a Polish artist who has settled in Venice. Her Studio and Art Gallery are on the Venetian island of the Giudecca. A combination of both her studio and gallery has enabled me to present aspects of the Demarco Archive during the Venice Biennale. I have also invited Sonia Rolak to hold an exhibition during my Edinburgh Festival programmes.

PART TWO

RODDY MARTINE'S EDINBURGH FESTIVAL

CHAPTER ONE

A Winner on All Fronts

UNLIKE RICHARD DEMARCO, I cannot offer a personal memory of the first Edinburgh Festival which sprang into life in the autumn of 1947. While Richard was already 17, I was eight months old. He was there. I was on the island of Borneo in South East Asia (with my parents, of course).

It was 50 years later, while researching a history of the Edinburgh Military Tattoo with its origins in a small army parade in Princes Street Gardens, that I became acutely aware of the miracle that was the creation of the greatest international celebration of music, dance, theatre, opera and the visual arts the world has ever known.

And I would like to imagine that at least a handful of Edinburgh's city fathers must have known what they were letting themselves in for when they gave John Falconer, the city's Lord Provost, the green light to go-ahead to hold a three-week festival in the soot-blackened old capital of Scotland primarily to heal the scars of a bitter, brutal and devastating war the likes of which no-one had ever before known.

Consider if you will what Britain, indeed Scotland, must have been like in 1947. Sombre, drab and impoverished, with battalions of world-weary troops returning to a homeland barely able to feed them. Then try to grasp what a courageous, utterly insane concept it must have seemed for somebody to throw a party.

But the proposition was far from straightforward or, if anything, expected, since the instigator, the Vienna-born Rudolf Bing, who had come to England in 1934 to ally his genius with Glyndebourne, had set his sights on Oxford. For a number of reasons, it was rapidly concluded that this was not going to happen and it was the Edinburgh-born Henry Harvey Wood, who had been seconded to the British Council, who came up with the brainwave of his birthplace. The fact that the British Council was permitted to enable grant funding in Scotland but not in England, was considered also to be a plus. The story is comprehensively documented in David Pollock's *Edinburgh's Festivals: A Biography*.

Those concerned unanimously rose to the occasion but I surmise that a special applause deserves to be directed towards the Countess of Rosebery, a committee member, whose husband, the recently appointed founding Chairman of the Scottish Tourist Board, and who resided on the Dalmeny estate on the shores of the Firth of Forth, unexpectedly came up with the necessary funds to finance the required feasibility study. It is such a good story. The Rosebery's racehorse Ocean Swell had won the Derby at Newmarket in 1944. It was therefore a racehorse that seeded the Edinburgh Festival and methinks he deserves a statue.

In the event, Rudolf Bing became the first Director of the Edinburgh Festival, conceived to 'provide a platform for the flowering of the human spirit', and he pulled out his trump card. This was his lifelong friendship with Bruno Walter, the renowned conductor of the Vienna Philharmonic Orchestra. As Jews, both of them had survived the horrors of Nazi persecution. Europe was at peace again, at last, and the Edinburgh Festival was their tribute to that peace.

Lens – A Youthful Focus on the Edinburgh Festival

It was July 1963. I was a schoolboy at Edinburgh Academy and I had achieved the great age of 16 when I noticed something rather important and excessive was going on during the summer holidays in the dull old soot-coated (as it was then) city that surrounded me.

Something called the Traverse Theatre dedicated to the avant-garde had opened its doors in a former doss house down a seedy vennel off the Lawnmarket. The parents of a friend took me to investigate. I told my own parents we were going to a musical at the Lyceum Theatre. We saw Lotte Lenya instead.

The Usher Hall was bursting with international orchestras. There was European opera and ballet at the King's Theatre. Suspiciously highbrow, maybe, but I started to hear foreign voices in the streets. For all of three weeks there was canon fire on the esplanade of Edinburgh Castle. Miss Jean Brodie's city of Hume and Boswell was returning to its international Enlightenment roots. No petty provincials here.

For a teenager stifled by rugby, boring mathematics and scholastic pressure to conform, it was all wildly exciting AND dangerous. The Festival programme featured the drawing of a harp and the head of a male wearing a wreath of leaves by the French surrealist Jean Cocteau. Not that I'd ever heard of him but I loved the image.

Such a Presbyterian flirtation with decadence. I wondered what my long ago relative, the reformer John Knox, would have made of it all? Travelled and worldly before the Victorian Kirk required a bogeyman for its prejudices, I like to think he would have applauded. Maybe not. But I did.

Spurred on by my art teacher John Firth, my curiosity was aroused. I was by then the precocious editor of a duplicated and stapled school magazine and with my budding classmates (all mid-teens), we unanimously resolved to produce a weekly Festival magazine. We placed a small article in the now long-defunct *Edinburgh Evening Dispatch* and recruited several girls to the cause.

With an astonishing sense of entitlement, we actually believed the great Festival-going public would be interested in what we had to say for 6d a copy. Much to our astonishment, it appeared that they did.

One of our gang, John Crerar, had a father who owned Mackenzie & Storrie Ltd., a print works in Leith; another, Bill Sutherland, had a father who set us up in an empty basement office in William Street. My best friend Nick Oppenheim was a whiz kid at selling advertising. Coincidentally, his father owned the Royal Lyceum Theatre and his sister's husband who was in textiles, donated us a bolt of maroon velvet for the office curtains. We even borrowed a manual typewriter.

In those days, John Menzies in Princes Street was the primary periodical distributor in Edinburgh and, with some amusement, agreed to sell copies for us. Thus *Lens – a youthful focus on the Edinburgh Festival* came into being with blocked red, blue and orange front covers featuring Edinburgh Castle and a camera.

Next came the endorsements and we somehow persuaded the Edinburgh Festival Director Lord Harewood to write a suitably thought-provoking foreword:

Normally one can only find out what people want by choosing something, putting it on and then waiting to see if, in the first instance, they buy tickets and, in the second, if they like what they had no direct hand in choosing. Now *Lens* is to tell us what the Younger Generation wants, or at least I hope that is its constructive object. Please don't fob us off with parrot cries of 'We want something livelier'; Edinburgh isn't fundamentally interested in its Festival.

Remember, this was 60 years ago! It was a challenge. He continued:

Edinburgh is too large to know what it fundamentally thinks about anything; and the people who want something livelier (are the *Fantastic Symphony* or the *Beggar's Opera* so deadly?) really mean different.

Dankworth instead of Debussy, Bilk rather than Bach, Brubeck and not
Britten.

If you can tell us what you want, and why you want it, we shall be in
your debt. A lot of critics will be envious too.

Did any of us know what we wanted? I don't think so but we were eager to
grasp at every available opportunity and it was the Edinburgh Festival that
made it possible for 12 teenagers to put the world to rights. After all, the
Edinburgh Festival was supposedly conceived as an international melting
pot of genius and innovation and the best is always yet to come.

And besides, in his *Lens* foreword, Edinburgh's genial Lord Provost
Duncan Weatherstone observed that if a Festival is to be alive, it must make
people think and talk, and 'It is only through enlightened discussion that
the full benefit of the Festival will be achieved.'

That great Senator of the College of Justice Lord 'Jock' Cameron, a
contemporary of my father, was Chairman of the Edinburgh Academy Board
of Governors, and he was our third port of call for a foreword. 'This is the
17th Festival,' he mused. 'Each year the Festival Fringe grows wider and
more extensive in its varied enterprises. In a real sense the existence and
expansion of the Fringe is a proof of the Festival itself. It is a sign too that
this Festival has brought together many who adventure and experiment in
the extension of the frontiers of all the Arts and that it provokes that clash
of argument and debate which excites and stimulates the mind of the Artist
and Audience alike.

'With so much to see, hear and do, it is only natural and proper that the
voice of the critic should be heard and from many sources. To keep alive
such an enterprise as the Festival, it is essential to keep its youthful and
adventurous spirit.'

I wonder what Jock Cameron would have to say about the multi-cultural,
multi-sexual chaos that is stand-up in the 21st century? But back in the
1960s it was a very different world. Wherefore art thou Sir David Lyndsay,
Tyrone Guthrie and *Ane Satyre of the Thrie Estaitis?*

Signing on in the Festival Press Office at the Freemason's Hall in George
Street was an incredible bonus. Although none of us were old enough to
buy a drink at the bar, Bob Cowie, the kindly Edinburgh Festival Press
Officer, took us under his wing. The professional hacks and journalists who
frequented the bar looked on us with benign acceptance. The caricaturist
Emilio Coia, over from Glasgow to illustrate for *The Scotsman* newspaper
befriended us. In later life, he was to become one of my closest friends.

And I have happy memories of banter with the harmonica playing Larry

Adler who was promoting his book *Jokes and How to Make Them*. 'You are young people and should attack more things and not worry about the power of the censor,' he told us. 'I give you leave to say what you like about me!' It sounded as if he was inciting us to riot but we were flattered. In retrospect, I think that he thought we were the joke.

My greatest scoop that summer came about by accident at the International Drama Conference housed in the McEwen Hall. Spotting the great Laurence Olivier holding court to a group of adoring hangers-on, I timidly approached and asked for an interview. Having looked up and down this skinny, bespectacled youth, as I was in those days, he turned his back on me saying, 'I don't give interviews.' I was mortified until there was a tug at my sleeve and I heard a quiet voice saying, 'Would you like to interview me?'

It was David Frost, whose BBC television programme *That Was The Week That Was* was far more exciting for my generation than the rude old Sir Laurence. He invited me to join him for breakfast the following morning at the George Hotel where he held forth and I got my story.

'One has to have an attitude and this should come through, but not be too explicit,' he insisted. 'It's like the difference between Wesker and Pinter. Wesker you know, Pinter you don't know what to expect. You mustn't be too obvious so that people will say, "Ah, Point 7b in the Frost manifesto for a Better Britain." This is important from the point of view of it being alive. If we do something that makes viewers fear legal trouble then they're with us.'

I have to admit that an awful lot of what he said passed straight over my 16-year-old head, but I basked in his attention as he ploughed into a large kipper and washed it down with coffee. Accompanied by Mary MacPhail and Catherine Cuinet, I turned up at The Caledonian Hotel to interview Yehudi Menuhin in his bedroom and we found him standing on his head practising yoga under the watchful eye of his sister Hephzibah, the concert pianist. It was his fourth visit to the Festival since it began, remembering 1947 in particular because it was during that month that his first son was born.

The world's greatest violinist, Lord Menuhin (as he became) had strong views on innovation and modern music but did not consider jazz to be modern as it had been around for such a long time.

'At its best it is very exciting with the incredibly clever jazz players who can improvise very clearly and have complete command of their instrument,' he told us.

'For instance, Johnnie Dankworth and several others. They are remarkable and at that level I do enjoy it but at the ordinary level I find it rather monotonous. I am not too partial to what I have so far heard of electronic music; although I do recognise that perhaps it has a place in the future, much like abstract art. It is very interesting but it will take some greater composer than we have had so far to compose something convincing by electronic means.'

To prove his point, he and Hephzibah were appearing together at the Usher Hall, coupling the sonority of the violin with the discrete playing of piano. They were joined by Gervase de Peyer on clarinet. The 'sonata in G' by Beethoven was in complete contrast to the other works but showed that the Maestro could equally well play music by modern composers as finely as the old masters. This was high art at its peak and has rarely been matched since.

I owe a lot to my friendship with Nick Oppenheim, not least for the Festival of the following year when he acquired tickets for the front row of the stalls at the Royal Lyceum Theatre to see Marlene Dietrich in concert with Burt Bacharach and arranged for us both to meet her backstage.

By now we were both aged 17, Nick six months younger. Marlene was 63. Yet almost 60 years later I am convinced it was the most dazzling performance I have ever seen. Post-war babies as Nick and I were, when Marlene stepped into the spotlight in that sparkling diaphanous gown, so tight it gave her almost no room for manoeuvre, and when she began to sing in that deep guttural voice – *Sag mir wo die Blumen sind wo sind sie geblieben?* – there were those beside us in the audience who wept out loud with emotion.

Backstage she signed my programme with an unintelligible squiggle and when Nick asked if she had recorded a particular song, she asked for his address. The following week he received a package of records with a handwritten letter. Now that is stardust for you.

So those were my Edinburgh Festivals of 1963 and 1964, three weeks in autumn that were to transport me into a world of maturity and a career in journalism.

Of course, the Edinburgh Festival of those days was a much more accessible village despite Lord Harewood's assertion that Edinburgh was too big to know what it wanted. The ground rules were well enough understood. Everything about it was containable.

The Fringe was the seed bed for talent and ran happily in step with its established elders and betters. Both knew their place. But then something equally remarkable was about to take place in the New Town of the city I knew and loved. Richard Demarco had been a co-founder of the Traverse Theatre from which he had energetically promoted the visual arts. In 1966, he opened the doors of a magnificent Georgian townhouse with two floors of exhibition space. As I was on the point of leaving school and starting a job with a publishing company around the corner in Atholl Crescent, The Demarco Gallery in Melville Crescent became the next best thing to my spiritual home.

Several of my friends signed on for temporary jobs and Sarah Walker Munro, who was to marry my cousin Melville Jameson, ran the brasserie restaurant in the basement. Fleur Cowles, David Hockney and Jon Schueler were among those who exhibited their paintings. I bought my first Richard Demarco watercolour, *The Road to Lochgelly*, part of The Road to Meikle Seggie series, and paid for it in five instalments!

In the years that followed, my involvement with the Edinburgh Festival waxed and waned but never entirely lapsed in importance to me. How could it? I have now lived in Edinburgh for over 60 years.

As Editor of *Scottish Field* magazine from 1977 to 1985, the Festival occupied an important place in my annual calendar. Although for the most part working out of Glasgow during the late 1970s and 1980s, I was invited to become a Trustee of the Edinburgh Festival Society. This was exhilarating for me until a rather sanctimonious incoming Labour administration decreed us elitist and appointed their own nominees.

The less said about that the better.

As a columnist with five national newspapers and four Scottish lifestyle magazines during the 1970s, 1980s and 1990s, the Edinburgh International Festival has for me been manna from heaven. I was at the Young Vic's performance of Andrew Lloyd Webber and Tim Rice's *Joseph and the Amazing Technicolour Dreamcoat* in 1972. I witnessed Tadeusz Kantor's Crico 2 Theatre production of *The Dead Class* at Edinburgh College of Arts. I was on Inchcolm Island and on the promontory of Ravenscraig Castle for Richard Demarco's productions of the Scottish Play. I took my mother to see and hear the breathtakingly beautiful Princess Grace of Monaco reading poetry at Cecilia's Hall in 1976. In 1980, I befriended the poet George Barker and writer Elizabeth Smart at the writers' event in the Assembly Rooms where I also met Gore Vidal.

In 1991, I flew to Paris to interview Rudolph Nureyev prior to his bringing the Paris Opera Ballet to the Playhouse Theatre and I took my mother to see him dance kilted as James in *La Sylphide*. I was witness to the extraordinarily indulgent punk circus Archaos on Leith Links and in the audience for John McGrath's amazing production of *A Satire of the Three Estates* in 1996. I encountered Charles Aznavour shopping in Jenners, the department store on Princes Street; saw Burt Lancaster on a bus, and threw parties for Quentin

Crisp, Peter Firth performing in *The Warp*, Fascinating Aïda, Kit & The Widow and Anton Krashny. I saw Pina Bausch's *The Man I Love* at the Playhouse and Ute Lemper with the Scottish Chamber Orchestra in the Usher Hall. I was at the breathtaking Wagner's *Ring Cycle* performed by Scottish Opera at the Festival Theatre. For several years I was a judge at the Fringe Cavalcade on Princes Street. I wrote the official history of the Royal Edinburgh Military Tattoo and launched four of my books at the Edinburgh Book Festival.

In 2019, I found myself on Christopher Biggins' lunch time sofa with an 80-year-old Ian McKellen who was otherwise performing his best loved roles in the Assembly Hall.

But enough of this boasting and name dropping. Without the Edinburgh Festival in my life I would never have met or engaged with such a multitude of brilliance and talent and been enriched both culturally and in the friendships that have surrounded me throughout my existence. Thank you John Falconer and Rudolf Bing, whom I did not know, and those who I did such as my school art master John Firth, Emilio Coia, Jim Haynes and Richard Demarco and all of those who have unintentionally contributed towards making me who and what I am.

CHAPTER TWO

Paying the Piper

CHANGE IS NOT only healthy but inevitable. Yet there are always important lessons to be learned from the past. When re-structuring the future, there is a lot to be gained from recognising the staples of what has gone before.

Every generation looks for a new broom to sweep away the dross. In the context of the Edinburgh Festival's relationship with its political sponsors, it is perhaps reassuring, if a trifle frustrating, to know that nothing in this world is entirely new, merely branded progressive, when it works. The trouble comes when you have to pay the bills.

In 1976, Peter Diamand stepped up to become Director of the Edinburgh International Festival of Music and Drama, operating for much of the year out of a Festival Society office in St James Street, London. That would not happen now. Austrian by birth, Diamand was brought up in Berlin but became Dutch. He had started his law studies but with the rise of the Nazis, his family fled to Holland where he became a friend of the pianist Artur Schnabel, who offered him a job. When the German soldiers invaded Holland and came to arrest him, he went into hiding to contemplate his future. Out of harm's way, he dreamed of a Holland Festival. In 1945, he joined Netherlands Opera. Four years later he became Director of the Holland Festival.

However, when he followed Lord Harewood to become Director of the Edinburgh Festival in 1965, he reflected that he had probably not thought, as he did often when in situ, that the job was as much about saving money as with planning programmes.

In an interview with Doreen Taylor, one of *Business Scotland*'s most prolific star writers, in 1976, he joked that he saw himself as an unskilled labourer. 'I console myself with the thought that as an unskilled labourer I might have had a worse occupation,' he told her.

Of course, the reality was that by then his contacts, knowledge and sheer influence in the global music world gave Edinburgh a standard of Festival far beyond the amount the District Council was willing to contribute. He had but to pick up a phone to summon the likes of Maria Callas; Gian Carlo Menotti, who lived locally at Gifford; Claudio Abbado and Rex Harrison, and they would arrive. It is fascinating to note that at the time, while Berlin Opera was subsided to the extent of £4 million a year, the Edinburgh Festival budget in 1976 was a modest £800,000.

'You don't need to be a prophet to say that unless the Edinburgh Festival gets more money, we shall have to reduce quantity, quality, or both,' he warned. Remember that this was 1976.

Stardust

It was a case of Hollywood meets European Royalty with all the glamour that this entailed when Her Serene Highness Princess Grace of Monaco chose the Edinburgh Festival to make her stage comeback in 1976. The former Grace Kelly of Philadelphia made a sensational return to the entertainment world appearing at St Cecilia's Hall with a poetry recital entitled The American Heritage arranged as a tribute to the United States Bicentennial.

Starting with the works of Anne Bradstreet, one of America's first poets and a Quaker immigrant born in England in 1612, the readings ranged through the 19th-century classics of American literature to such 20th-century figures as Carl Sandburg, Ogden Nash, TS Eliot and Robert Frost.

I was at the Press Conference in the Assembly Rooms in George Street and I was seated in the third row at St Cecilia's Hall. I was mesmerised by the flawless beauty and elegance of Princess Grace. It was pure stardust.

Her fellow performers were Richard Kiley, the American actor, and Richard Pasco, the English stage and screen actor. Both were appropriately articulate and confident. Their deliveries were flawless and let's face it, you can never go wrong with Robert Frost.

This was one of four performances which emphasised the sort of master stroke Peter Diamand was capable of pulling off. Grace Kelly's last film before her 'Wedding of the Century' to Prince Rainier of Monaco, had been *High Society* in 1956. In addition to the readings at St Cecilia's Hall, there was a glitzy televised gala held at the Signet Library where Her Serene Highness was introduced by the actor Tom Fleming, and serenaded by the Scottish Baroque Ensemble, Welsh harpist Osian Ellis and Austrian pianist Paul Hamburger.

Although the theatre critic of *The New York Times* was want to snidely comment she was out of practice and made a side swipe at America's progress from the early 'colonial' days, Princess Grace could have been reading the telephone directory and the audience would still have adored her.

A New Dynamic

When a newspaper reporter in 1978 complained that the incoming artistic Director of the Edinburgh International Festival talked so fast his shorthand could not keep up with him, his comment was justified. For his tenure of five years, John Drummond proved himself to be a whirlwind of energy, enthusiasm, intelligence and sensitivity towards all forms of art believing them all to be essential ingredients of the largest cultural Festival in the world.

When I interviewed him for *Scottish Field* in 1979, it soon became apparent that for 11 months of the year, his job involved continuous travel, theatre attendance at every stop, instant decisions, diplomacy, political sensitivity and salesmanship. I asked him where he lived, and he replied, 'London airport.'

Despite this, it was immediately apparent that he had hit the ground running. For his first Festival, he chose an old friend to set the theme – Serge Diaghilev, the charismatic Russian-born impresario who so profoundly influenced the culture of the West in the early part of the 20th century. It was pertinent that the 1979 Festival should coincide with the 50th anniversary of Diaghilev's death.

'It was too good an opportunity to be missed,' said Drummond. 'Diaghilev was the first person to demonstrate the links between all the arts, and there are huge lessons to be learned from this. Arts don't live in separate boxes; they should be mixed up. That is the function of a great festival.

'When Diaghilev commissioned a ballet he brought together the best musicians, choreographers, artists, writers, and dancers. The results were beautiful to look at. There are no barriers between the various disciplines.'

The Diaghilev theme therefore ran throughout the three weeks of the 1979 Festival. At Edinburgh College of Art there was an exhibition of dance costumes, many designed for the Ballets Russes. The writer and designer Richard Buckle, the dancer and choreographer Anton Dolin, and the critic Noel Goodwin lectured on Diaghilev's legacy at St Cecilia's Hall. A huge tent was erected on the Meadows to accommodate Sadler's Wells and the National Ballet of Cuba. That year there was a special emphasis on the composers Diaghilev admired.

John had a wealth of experience in mixing the arts. Born in London of Scottish parentage, he took first class honours at Cambridge and had thereafter worked for 19 years for the BBC. Perhaps it was this that convinced him he needed to win local approval since under his predecessor local talent had been largely relegated to the Fringe. He was also immensely fortunate to be supported by the remarkable Sheila Colvin who had been administrator of the Traverse Theatre before becoming Deputy Director of the Edinburgh International Festival before moving on to become Director of the Aldeburgh Festival.

Drummond brought The Demarco Gallery, the Traverse Theatre and Glasgow Citizen's Theatre into the official programme, commissioning new Scottish plays and involving Scottish Opera, The Scottish Chamber Orchestra and the Scottish Baroque Ensemble. There was a definite feeling that the Edinburgh Festival was moving closer to the people of Scotland.

'The important thing is to show that the Festival is not stuffy,' he told me. He had just returned from Holland and had noticed a staggering difference between average audiences there and in Edinburgh. There the average age group had been much younger and less traditional.

In keeping with tradition, however, John Drummond was determined to retain a wide international representation. The Boston Symphony, Halle and the Polish Chamber orchestras were in evidence, in addition to the Netherlands Wind Ensemble, Stuttgart Piano Trio and Schultz Choir with the London Baroque Players. The Merce Cunningham Ensemble, considered America's most influential dance company presented four days of events and workshops.

Bristol Old Vic presented two plays about the effects of war, and the Rustaveli Company (USSR), the Paris-based Argentinian Group TSE brought an adaptation of Balzac's satire on London Society. There were lectures from Joan Bakewell on the Brontës, and from Norman MacCaig, Dannie Abse, Judy Dench, and Owen Dudley Edwards opining on the Scottish poet Hugh MacDiarmid.

To celebrate the 25th anniversary of Edinburgh's twinning with the City of Munich, there were exhibitions of drawings and paintings by Kandinsky at the Scottish National Gallery of Modern Art there were life size nude statues in bronze and stone, the work of Wilhelm Lehmbruck (1881–1919) which caused a titter of excitement among Edinburgh's gin and bridge set.

Added to which, Richard Demarco had by then bonded with the Polish Ministry of Culture, the Scottish Arts Council, and Glasgow's Third Eye Gallery for exhibitions by two major 20th-century Polish artists, Stażewski and Witkiewicz.

The USA and Asia were yet to arrive but to my mind you could not get a much more domestic and international mix than that to set the future course the Festival Director had in mind.

Ane Satyre of Edinburgh District Council

The Leeds-born theatre impresario Frank Dunlop succeeded John Drummond as Director of the Edinburgh International Festival in 1984 and remained in place for eight years, increasingly at odds with Edinburgh District Council whose administration relentlessly wanted in on the act, charging the Festival with 'ingrained elitism' without looking in the mirror at themselves. It was the same problem that the Edinburgh Festival Council which I had belonged to in the 1970s had faced, and the same discomfort that John Drummond had had to put up with.

He who pays the piper, etc. Dunlop had inherited a deficit of £175,000 in 1984 and admitted he would not have taken on the job had he known about this in advance. However, he persevered with his enormous flair for theatricality and made enormous improvements to Scottish drama in his programme by notably yet again reviving Sir David Lyndsay of the Mount's *Ane Satyre of the Thrie Estaitis* along with Sydney Goodsir Smith's *The Wallace*, and James Bridie's *Holy Isle*. He also personally directed Friedrich Schiller's *Maria Stuart* and dramatised Robert Louis Stevenson's *Treasure Island* to considerable popular acclaim.

I was at all of these unforgettable *coups de théâtre*. Frank's departure from the Festival in 1991 meant that for the following 15 years creative budgets were curtailed to the point of strangulation while stand-up comedy on the Fringe increased to bursting point. Overnight, everybody was a comedian.

CHAPTER THREE

The Spirit of Anton Krashny –
The Festival Spoof That Took on a Life of its Own

FOR THE 1974 Edinburgh Festival, the much acclaimed Scottish Television coverage was produced by the boisterous Clarke Tait and presented by Joan Bakewell. In a Scottish Field Festival Supplement some years later, Joan recalled the night the Edinburgh Festival's greatest spoof was born. 'Every festival has its parasites and sure enough, one of them lodged in our research team, contributing little but swooping in daily to cadge free seats for concerts and shows,' she wrote.

As soon as the filming was over, Joan threw a party in her rented flat and who should swan in but the bespectacled geek himself, spouting arty jargon about all the amazing concerts and plays he had seen. Clarke and Joan, on their knees with tiredness, rose to the occasion.

'Tell me,' Clarke asked mischievously. 'What did you think of the Krashny exhibition?'

'Krashny?'

Alarm registered behind the glasses. The hook was in. Clarke played the line. 'You must know Krashny, for God's sake. Anton Krashny. His exhibition is the talk of the festival. Don't tell me you haven't heard about him?'

'Oh, Krashny, of course.' Clarke's victim blinked nervously. 'Yes... Krashny... well... actually... in my view...' The opinions poured forth and a legend was spawned. It took a few years to catch on but inspired by Richard Demarco who had imported Tadeusz Kantor's experimental Cricot 2 Theatre group to the Festival, it was decided to hold an official Anton Krashny Dinner in honour of the fictitious great man. Of course, it was all a bit of a media love-in with Joan and Clarke appointed Presidents for Life; former children's television presenter Douglas Rae, Chairman; Alastair Riley as Chief Ranter, and myself as Keeper of the Archive.

Needless to say, Krashny, uncompromisingly recognised as the world's greatest surrealist miniaturist painter, performance artist and thinker, always failed to turn up in person. Those who did turn up for that first Anton Krashny Dinner which took place in the Edinburgh Wine Bar in Hanover

Street were a suitably eclectic bunch. They included Clarke's wife Lyndsay; STV's Michael Grieve, son of the poet Hugh MacDiarmid; the broadcasters Gordon Honeycombe and Fran Morrison; Alice Beberman, who had recently been refused permission by Edinburgh Council to exhibit a giant, crocheted nipple on Arthur's Seat; Richard Demarco, naturally; the caricaturist Emilio Coia, naturally; the singer Woodstock Taylor, and cinema critic Nicholas Wapshott with Louise Nicolson, whom he would later marry.

It was Douglas Rae who came up with the rituals. Commencing with the Piping of the Scrotum, a symbolic platter of tripe on a silver plate was ceremonially paraded into wherever the event was to take place. There followed speeches from the floor, literally, in some cases. Riley's Rant addressed a topical topic, and the much cherished Krashny Awards took the form of a collection of World War II gas masks.

A second Krashny Dinner was held at the Edinburgh Wine Bar in 1979 with Nick Wapshott and Rory Knight Bruce, still at Edinburgh University, jointly carrying the scrotum. Among the guests that year were 'Professor of Pop' Paul Gambaccini; Dr Allan Maryon-Davis of the singing group 'Instant Sunshine'; the redoubtable Lionel Daiches QC and his close companion Sheriff Isobel Poole.

The Krashny Dinner was now firmly established as an exclusive feature of the last week of the Edinburgh Festival. In 1980, a small exhibition of Krashny's life and work was on view at the Engine Room restaurant. Items on display included Krashny's sandal worn during his infamous trek across the Sahara, a photograph of Krashny on horseback in Azerbaijan, some cigarette stubs left over from his time with the Bloomsbury Group at Charleston, and his quill pen and ink portrait by Emilio Coia,

As the Krashny mythology mushroomed, a spoof television documentary captured the man himself cloaked and dodging around the corners of Glasgow's Sauchiehall Street. Over the following summer, the UK media was filled with reports of unrest at Poland's Gdańsk shipyard coupled with the emergence of the Polish resistance leader Lech Wałęsa. Of course, this had absolutely nothing to do with the Krashny Dinner, but it led to significant repercussions on what happened next.

Andrew Brown had offered the use of The 369 Gallery for the dinner, and we jumped at the opportunity. For the first time Douglas and Diana Sutherland and Elizabeth Smart attended. None of us had any forewarning that we were about to become headline news.

It all began so innocently with a brief encounter between journalist Ian Buchan of Glasgow's *Evening Times*, and Nick Wapshott and Douglas Rae in Edinburgh's Assembly Rooms. Buchan was scouting for diary stories.

'Have you heard that Krashny has escaped from house arrest in Krakow?' announced Douglas. 'He's flying into Scone aerodrome in a light plane. We're holding a dinner for him tomorrow night.'

It was just too big a story for Buchan to ignore. Checking his sources, as every professional must, he contacted the Edinburgh Festival Press Office. Unfortunately, he spoke to Rebecca Irvine who just happened to be staying with me that year.

Thinking Ian was in on the joke, she confided in her best Oxford vowels, 'He's my father. Thank God he's got away. I was beginning to think I might never see him again!'

Rebecca rambled on about her father and mother having been crofters on Islay, where she was born. She was aware that she had another family in Poland, a sister older than her and triplets younger than her. Pure invention, of course. Rebecca's imagination ran riot. Everything was noted down by Buchan.

My involvement began when Ian telephoned me to discuss the guest list. When he asked me to confirm Krashny's arrival, I too assumed he was in on the joke and told him that John Drummond, Richard Demarco, Douglas Sutherland and Elizabeth Smart would be among the guests. I thought little of this until the following morning when I was contacted at my office around noon by the *Daily Express*. Could I comment on the front page headlines of *The Evening Times*?

I had not the remotest idea what the caller was talking about and immediately rushed to the nearest kiosk in Glasgow's Central Station where I was confronted by a banner headline: 'EXCLUSIVE: Top Pole flees to Safety'.

No mention was made of either Nick nor Dougal Rae, but on the front page of *The Evening Times* Friday August 22 1980, it read: 'Roddy Martine, editor of *Scottish Field*, said "We were hoping that we'd get Krashny out of Poland secretly – but this might work out for the best if he is determined not to go back!"'

I burst out laughing until the full implications of my situation dawned on me. Back at my desk, there was a queue of callers – *The Daily Telegraph*, *The Scotsman*, *The Times*, *The Daily Mail* – and urgent requests for me to call the Foreign Office and Home Office.

'But it's a hoax!' I protested.

'We don't believe you. You're covering something up!' I was told.

Similarly Clarke Tait was receiving an equally daunting number of calls at STV. At least he had been spared a mention on the front page. Aside from Rebecca, whose surname was not included, I was the only other source quoted.

My serious difficulties began that afternoon. George McKechnie, deputy editor of *The Evening Times*, on duty when the paper had gone to press, ranted at me. 'I'm going to take you to the NUJ and to the Board of SUITS! I'm going to get you sacked!' he threatened. 'This is Edinburgh journalists trying to put something over on Glasgow journalists. I'm not taking it! You're going to suffer!'

Both *Scottish Field* and *The Evening Times* were owned by SUITS so I immediately produced a report for my bemused and baffled bosses. A worrying few days followed until the blessed Joan Bakewell arranged for an article to be placed in *The Sunday Times*' Mercury column. Under the heading 'Scotland's Phantom Dissident', it reported that a sudden embarrassed silence had fallen over the Scottish media. Mercifully, the 'embarrassed silence' subsided but when he replaced Arnold Kemp as editor of *The Herald*, I discovered that George McKechnie still bore a grudge and my column in that newspaper was dropped.

Although it was generally agreed not to hold a Krashny Dinner the following year, the legend continued, even attracting a mention in the glossy *Harpers & Queen*. We later revived the dinner at the Scottish Arts Club, then at The Waterfront Wine Bar in Leith, with entertainment provided by an American brass band. Clarke died in December 1984 and somehow much of the spontaneous merriment and slapstick of Krashny died with him.

In 1988, the *Londoner's Diary* carried a paragraph about an artist called Anton Kranje, whose work was much admired by Princess Margaret. He was exhibiting at the Francis Kyle Gallery and was described as the first Australian artist to have worked directly on the Great Wall of China. He was understandably indignant when informed that he did not exist because he had been invented at the Edinburgh Festival.

In his book *City of a Thousand Worlds: Edinburgh in Festival*, Owen Dudley Edwards devoted several pages to a parody of *The Evening Times* incident, preceded by a polemic written in the style of Ernest Hemingway. For his BBC Radio Scotland show, Colin Bell persuaded Owen and I to pre-record a discussion on the importance of Krashny in popular culture. This was edited into sections and broadcast daily during the Edinburgh Festival that year. It was pure gobbledygook. Heaven knows what listeners made of it!

Thereafter, whenever I needed to contact the news desks of *The Daily Record* or *Sunday Mail*, I was invariably greeted with, 'Is this a joke?'

The legend of Anton Krashny at the Edinburgh Festival remains. There may or may not be another Krashny Dinner held during my lifetime but I am certain that in centuries to come, people will still be asking, 'Who was he?'

CHAPTER FOUR

Edinburgh's 369 Gallery and Art Movement

ON GRADUATING FROM Edinburgh College of Art in 1977, Andrew Brown, originally from sleepy Wigtownshire, followed in Richard Demarco's footsteps and rented a characterful first floor premises on the High Street of Edinburgh's Old Town and transformed it into a showcase platform to exhibit the works of his friends and contemporaries. I was Editor of *Scottish Field* that year and being always on the lookout for new talent, I commissioned Fionna Carlisle, one of the gallery's rising stars, to design a front cover for the magazine, and the arts writer Geoffrey Baskerville to write the accompanying article. As a consequence, I was invited to become a Trustee.

Chaired by Diana Milne, wife of Sandy Milne, co-director of Edinburgh's Kingston Clinic, the board of The 369 Gallery (that was its High Street address) already comprised Douglas Hall, Keeper of the Scottish National Gallery of Modern Art; the fiercely opinionated Sylvia Stevenson; Annette Hope, librarian of the Fine Art Department of Edinburgh University; the magnificent Arthur Watson of the Peacock Printmakers Workshop in Aberdeen; Lindsay Gordon of the Scottish Arts Council, and Dicky Alexander representing Edinburgh District Council.

Throughout the following decade there were memorable exhibitions from Martin Churchill, Adrian Wiszniewski, Andrew Gibbon Williams, Caroline McNairn, Pat Douthwaite, Rob McCarthy, Fiona Grant Robertson, June Redfern, Sheila Mullen, Rose Frain, Lys Hansen, Alan Watson, Margaret Hunter, Carole Gibbons, Peter Howson and Calum Colvin. In addition there was the brilliant Glasgow-based Malaysian Chinese martial arts expert Hock-Aun Teh whose sculptures were to feature at the Beijing Olympics in 2008.

As with The Demarco Gallery and Traverse Theatre in the 1960s and 1970s, The 369 Gallery from the 1980s rapidly became a social hub for locals and visitors alike. Edinburgh Festival exhibitions included the drawings of the Russian-born French artist Erte and his contemporaries who had designed for Diaghilev and drawings by the mime artist Lindsay Kemp. The majority of Scottish artists from the 1970s and 1980s were given their first opportunities to exhibit at The 369 Gallery, either in the High Street or latterly in the three floors of the Cowgate.

The 369 Gallery remained in the High Street for seven years but soon needed to expand. The High Street lease expired in 1985, and the enterprising Andrew Brown came across a derelict Georgian Warehouse under Robert Adam's South Bridge. This was an empty three-storey building in the Cowgate which had once housed J&R Allan's department store. A magnificent, breathtakingly ambitious project was launched with Scottish Arts Council and City of Edinburgh support. Spaces were transformed by architect Ron Galloway into ground and first floor galleries plus studios. Friends rallied. Their beneficence even included £30,000 from Yulla Lipchitz, New York widow of Cubist sculptor Jacques Lipchitz.

As fate would have it, adjoining spaces rapidly became occupied by The Gilded Balloon Restaurant and a large studio was adopted by Karen Koren for her first Gilded Balloon Fringe Festival Theatre. Both creations were named for the building's original incarnation The Gilded Balloon Emporium owned by one James Spitalfields, Edinburgh Draper and Silk Merchant.

In the glittering but not untroubled years between 1980 to 1990, The 369 Gallery with its largely home-grown artists reigned supreme as an art magnet for all of Scotland, and especially for those visiting Scotland's Capital. It was not at all unusual to find poets Norman MacCaig and George Mackay Brown sharing floor space with Lanark author Alasdair Gray and American comedian Ruby Wax, then enrolled at Glasgow's Academy of Music and Drama, and the actor Robbie Coltrane, who had studied at Glasgow Art School.

During the Edinburgh Festival and Fringe Festival in August, The 369 and The Gilded Balloon served both as a focal point for lovers of figurative art as well as providing a Fringe venue. In a classic understatement, the Glasgow-based art critic Clare Henry quoted Andrew Brown as saying, 'It's a matter of believing in the art you exhibit. I see myself in the tradition of the late 19th-century dealers who only promoted the work of their friends.

'It's easier to sell the paintings of dead artists. Artists who are alive often get drunk, burden you with their problems, are untidy, a pain in the neck but they are marvellous to know and to work with.'

Among The 369 Gallery's most luminous stars was Caroline McNairn who had been at Edinburgh University and Edinburgh College of Art with Andrew. She had four solo exhibitions at The 369 Gallery and acted as a lecturer and adviser. The 369 Gallery was where she met her future husband Hugh Collins, on day release from the Special Unit of Barlinnie Prison where he was encouraged by Joyce Laing and Andrew Brown. 'I was blown away,' he confessed. 'I'd never seen paintings like this in my life. I fell in love with Caroline's work.'

Born into the violent world of Glasgow 's razor gangs, drugs, and protection rackets of the 1970s, Hugh was just short of 17 when he became embroiled in a fatal knife fight in the Lunar Seven Bar in Glasgow. 'I was never a gangster, only a bampot,' he recalled sadly. His story is candidly told in the first volume of his biography *Autobiography of a Murderer*.

Although eyebrows were raised, Caroline married Hugh when he was released from Barlinnie in 1993, and it was under her guidance, building upon the creative potential unleashed to him at Barlinnie's Special Unit, that he not only metamorphosed into an accomplished sculptor but a successful writer.

Understanding that Scottish art was most admired at home only after winning accolade abroad, The 369 was the first British Gallery at the Chicago Art Fair (1982), followed by other shows in Chicago, New York and Santa Fe, and after that in France, Germany, Scandinavia, Hong Kong, Malaysia and China, plus an impressive exchange with the Soviet Union. Russian artists showed at the Edinburgh International Festival in 1988, and encouraged by John Smith, leader of the UK Labour Party, and his wife Elizabeth, Chair of the GB–USSR Friendship Society, Scottish artists travelled to Moscow in 1989, where Caroline McNairn's work was acquired by the Pushkin Museum, the first Western paintings to be included in a Soviet museum collection in the 70 years since the revolution.

Alas, the crunch came for The 369 Gallery in the early 1990s when beleaguered by financial problems and faced with the withdrawal of support from the Scottish Arts Council and Edinburgh Council, it was forced to close. The last fling was Angel Over the Ukraine, a spectacular exhibition of young Ukrainian artists organised by Andrew Brown in conjunction with the Mayor of Kiev and held in the glorious Mansfield Traquair Church during the 1993 Edinburgh Festival and opened on television by John Smith.

The building was otherwise re-allocated by property developers until 2002, when an electric fault in a rear office ignited what came to be known as the 'Cowgate Fire'. All three floors of Cowgate building were destroyed and the only part of The 369 Gallery to survive are the three windows, the Bridge of Sighs, over the Cowgate which had served as Andrew Brown's studio.

CHAPTER FIVE

What Is It About the Scottish Play?

FOR CENTURIES, OR at least going on six of them, audiences have been thrilled by the dark and dastardly deeds of a Scottish king and his ruthless wife in their doomed quest for power. 'I see the land of Macbeth, so when shall we two meet again, in thunder lighting or in rain?' wrote Joseph Beuys to Richard Demarco.

Three years after Beuys's death in Düsseldorf in 1986, Demarco chose the ruins of the medieval priory of Inchcolm Island in the middle of the Firth of Forth as backdrop for that great Shakespearian drama.

When asked by the *Scottish Daily Express* to name my three most memorable experiences of the Edinburgh Festival of 1989, I wrote: (1) Travelling to South Queensferry in the pouring rain to catch the ferry, Maid of the Forth, to see The Richard Demarco Gallery's production of *Macbeth*, directed by John Bett. (2) Boarding The Maid of the Forth at South Queensferry in the pouring rain to sail to Inchcolm Island to see Richard Demarco's production of *Macbeth*, directed by John Bett and (3) seeing Richard Demarco's production of *Macbeth* directed by John Bett on Inchcolm Island in the pouring rain. Nobody who was there will ever forget the experience.

In 1996, Richard Demarco chose the dramatic ruins of Ravenscraig Castle overlooking the North Sea and former linoleum town of Kirkcaldy in the Kingdom of Fife, for a repeat, this time staging the Belarus State Theatre directed by Valery Anisenko with an all-Belarusian cast.

Once again, those of us who huddled together on deck chairs under rugs and umbrellas on that windswept cliff top will never forget the drama of a rain drenched Lady Macbeth cavorting across the battlements, her clinging robes leaving nothing to the imagination.

In the audience were Norman and Ann Irons, Lord and Lady Provost of Edinburgh, and Timothy Clifford, Director of the National Galleries of Scotland, with his wife Jane. It was a triumph.

This was outdoor theatre at its most extreme and certainly one of the most unusual interpretations I have ever seen. Few amongst us, if any, understood the language, but that did not matter. We all knew the story anyway.

What Is It About Bow Ties?

Peter Diamand's inert shyness and suspicion of journalists was more than compensated for by the Edinburgh Festival's immaculate first Publicity Officer Ian Crawford, whom many, including myself, came to see as their first point of contact to find out what was going on. Those were the days of old-style media networking over long expense account lunches in smart restaurants and it was not without reason that after he had retired from the Festival, I recruited Ian as a wine writer for *Scottish Field* and other magazines I edited. And to write about golf, which was his other great passion. His knowledge of both was next to none. Ian had enormous style and chutzpah and when Diamand retired the rumours ran around that he was the obvious candidate to replace him. That did not happen, but when the more accessible John Drummond arrived, Ian continued to be an enormous support in helping him cope with the hostility of a not always sympathetic front line of theatre and art critics.

From Inverness, Ian began his career as a reporter with the *Edinburgh Evening Dispatch*, and was a stand-in for Banquo in an early Fringe production of *Macbeth*, making him a Festival stalwart thereafter. He was appointed to the Edinburgh International Festival in 1973 when the Festival Society ended its convenient relationship with the Scottish Tourist Board.

Bearded and often kilted, he created a flamboyant figure whom everyone recognised, so much so that he was responsible for setting up the Festival's first major sponsorship deal with BP in 1977 for *Carmen*, conducted by Claudio Abbado and starring Teresa Berganza and Plácido Domingo. Fluent in Italian and French, he had been too young to join the Royal Navy at the outbreak of war but had signed up instead with the merchant navy. His ship was torpedoed but he survived and spent ten days in a boat with other survivors. After this he took part in the allied invasion of Sicily and Yugoslavia and entered Venice on the last day of war.

Ian had been a travel editor for the *Sunday Express* and a leader writer for the *London Evening Standard*. Not a lot of those who congregated in the Edinburgh Festival Press Club knew that. Writing for *Scottish Field* in 1977, he was typically forthright in his opinions.

> Just how long this kind of miracle can be kept up is a problem which must deeply vex the mind of whoever is in charge. To maintain the present quality more money must be found, almost certainly from the private sector... there is pressure too in many places for the Director to be, if not a Scot, then at lease resident in Scotland and to close the Festival's office

in London. Emotionally and politically, this is a big question. The Festival has always had a London office since the days when the administration was in the hands of Glyndebourne, which already had a London office, and directors subsequent to Sir Rudolf Bing always had a clause in their contracts which ensured them an office in London where immediate contact could most easily be made with the world of international arts.

Enough said. Kind-hearted and genial, Ian made it to the age of 89, the year before his death attending the Opening Concert of the 2011 Edinburgh Festival at the Usher Hall.

When Ian Crawford retired, the post of Edinburgh Festival Press Officer was filled by Clive Sandground. It was an old-fashioned sophistication, but the one sartorial memory I will always have of these two remarkable men is that they regularly wore bow ties, not garish but neat, endowing both of them with an understated intellectual superiority.

Clive had been my editor-in-chief at Holmes McDougall, publisher of *Scottish Field*, and when he took me out for lunch I always knew to write off the remainder of the day. Before I knew him, he was certainly ranked as one of the most loved figures in Scottish journalism and before taking up the post of Publicity Officer for the Edinburgh International Festival, he had been editor of the *Scottish Daily Express*, then editor of *The Sunday Mail* until 1981. Three days after his resignation from *The Sunday Mail*, he was appointed Features Editor of *The Sunday Standard* a week before the first edition appeared in the newsagents. Clive certainly knew his way around the tabloids. With every job departure, until his wife put her foot down, he bought a yacht, calling them in turn *Redundancy One, Redundancy Two* and *Redundancy Three*.

Hindered by a limp, a legacy from childhood polio, Clive brought out the best in everyone who worked with him and I remember so well the joyful atmosphere among the recruits whenever I popped in to see him at the Festival Press Bureau. A good friend to me, he collapsed and died while walking in Byres Road, Glasgow in 1993.

Hallucinating on Abbey Mount

One of the more extraordinary feats of endurance I have ever experienced, actually the only one I have ever genuinely attempted, was when I dropped into the rather run-down and seedy Regent Theatre on Abbey Mount close to Holyrood Park for an astonishing 24-hour theatre marathon performance called *The Warp*. I had got to know the playwright and actor Andrew Dallmeyer and his beautiful wife Vivienne Dixon, and their house guests at their Anne Street home that year included Neil Cunningham, starring in Heathcote Williams' *The Immortalist,* under the Demarco productions banner, and Peter Firth, flushed with success from his boy performance in Peter Shaffer's *Equus*. Another regular at Anne Street was Sylvester McCoy who had starred in Dallmeyer's play *Hello Dali,* based on the life of Salvador Dalí.

All of them were taking part in one or other of the segments or cycles, with the lead actor on stage for a night and a day. You booked for as many instalments as you could stay awake for. Friends of mine even took along sleeping bags. Directed by Ken Campbell, who I had also been to see on an alternative Road Show stage dropping a ferret down his trousers, the gist of *The Warp* story followed the hallucinatory life of musician, poet and artist Neil Oram, a legend in his own London jazz cafe.

As an audience, and it was a moveable feast audience, we were encouraged to follow the action around a large number of improvised sets where the hero, the Phil Masters character as he was called, even went so far as to take a bath in front of us. The most hilarious scene was when we were all ushered out from the hall's darkened interior into the bright sunshine of Holyrood Park by dancing policemen and required to sit down and form a circle to listen to the Indian mystic Bhagwan who was suitably attired for Krishna.

It was all so very love and drugs in the hedonistic 1960s, where the play was set, and there we were sitting in the sunshine only a few yards from Holyrood Palace. I even seem to remember the Royal Standard fluttering on the rooftop. I wonder if Her Majesty noticed the rather alternative gathering assembled in her back garden?

CHAPTER SIX

Le Bourgeois Gentilhomme

RUDOLF NUREYEV IS immortalised as one of the greatest icons of the ballet world in and beyond the second half of the 20th century. In 1984, prior to his arrival in Edinburgh with the Paris Opera Ballet, of which he had become director, I flew to Paris to interview him for *Scottish Field*, accompanied by Eric Thorburn, one of Scotland's finest photographers. Having landed at Orly Airport,

Eric and I were greeted in Paris under attack from torrential rain and the traffic came to a dreary standstill. It took us two hours to reach the city centre by taxi and locate the magnificent 3,000-seater Palais de Sport where the Paris Opera Ballet was rehearsing *Le Songe d'un Nuit d'été* (*A Midsummer Night's Dream*). The day that followed was a life-enhancing experience.

Rudolf Nureyev was dressed in mottled brown leather scalloped trousers of a Cossack style fit, high-heeled boots, a brown leather Lenin cap, a knitted shirt resembling one of those hand-woven tapestry wall hangings which might not have been out of place in a Scottish contemporary art gallery, and a brown leather jacket which would not have been out of place in a Spitfire cockpit. In some ways he resembled an oversize, overheated caterpillar. He was walking with a limp acquired, he said, from the exertions of a recent tour – Berlin, Milan, Zurich – and, as he went on to explain, from dancing in high-heeled shoes.

At 46, Nureyev passed for at least ten years younger and on first sight appeared both disarming and charming, totally unspoiled by the invasive international adulation that had pursued him since his much publicised defection from Soviet Russia in 1961.

Solitary, cap forward on brow, and seated haughtily in the great auditorium, he fulfilled every sartorial expectation of the melancholy Tartar romantic – the image which had so powerfully captivated the collective imagination of the West. I reminded him that he had signed his autograph for me at a concert in Menton in 1964 and he laughed. 'You must have been quite young then – just a little boy. But you are a big boy now!'

He grinned, inferring from my dishevelled six-foot-five rain-soaked appearance that he had aged a great deal better than I.

In regard to the Edinburgh Festival, he recalled performing at the King's Theatre in 1975 and dancing with Lynn Seymore and eating grouse for the first time and staying in a hotel on a corner but he couldn't remember the name. I suggested it must have been either the Caledonian or the Balmoral, depending upon which end of Princes Street he remembered best. A reputation for 'hell raising' when off stage, and a starring role in Ken Russell's over-the-top film about his namesake Rudolph Valentino, had added lustre to a public image not exactly blind to his assertive sexuality. Of course, this encounter was before the ugly spectre of AIDS reared its deadly head.

Ever restless, Nureyev was never comfortable in one place for too long. 'I've already done my quota of 40 performances for Paris Opera and I can't just sit here and rot,' he confided. 'No, I keep moving.

'Paris is lovely and I have a beautiful apartment, but suddenly there is an itch and I have to get up and go. I spent 18 years in London but Paris next to Monte Carlo is ideal for going anywhere. Once you get on a plane it really doesn't matter where you live.' Thus spoke a lonely man.

Meanwhile, the Paris Opera Ballet offered him the strength of tradition and the opportunity not simply to continue to dance but to hand on his fabled choreography skills to successive generations.

The prima ballerina Margot Fonteyn remarked on these skills in her autobiography. 'I learned a great deal from him simply from watching him in class. Never had I seen each step practised with such exactitude and thoroughness. It was paradoxical that this young boy everyone thought was so wild and spontaneous in his dancing cared so desperately about technique whereas I, the cool English ballerina was so much more interested in the emotional aspect of the performance.'

Comedia Dell 'Arte was the Paris Opera Ballet's production that year at the Playhouse Theatre, sponsored by the Bank of Scotland. It encompassed three set pieces – *Harlequin, Magician of Love* (Choreography Ivo Cramér; Music Édouard du Puy); *Carnival* by Fokine and Bakst (Music: Schumann) and *Le Bourgeois Gentilhomme* (choreography by George Balanchine; music by Strauss). Nureyev danced in the former and latter, and *Carnival* starred the Paris Opera's exceptional star Patrick Dupond.

Watching the cast rehearse on stage in the Palais de Sport, which incidentally was where Nureyev had defected from the Kirov Ballet, and sitting beside him in the stalls as he shouted out his directions, was to prove an unforgettable experience for me, but when it came to the rehearsals at the Playhouse Theatre in Edinburgh a few weeks later, his mood took a turn for the worse.

For over 50 years, Emilio Coia, doyenne of the Glasgow Arts Club, was the house caricaturist for *The Scotsman*, annually holding court at the Scottish Arts Club in Edinburgh's Rutland Square. My first encounter with him had been in 1963 when he dominated the media pack at the Edinburgh Festival Press Club when it was housed in the Freemasons Hall in George Street. A distinguished, lovable and cheeky personality, Emilio had wasted no time in latching on to my group of budding teenage *Lens* reporters, always informing me that one day he would draw my portrait – with a long black beard! It was Emilio's way of saying not to get too pleased with oneself. I am happy to say that a decade or so later he became one of my most valued friends.

At every Edinburgh Festival, until his death in 1997, quirky yet stylish black and white Coia drawings brightened up the arts pages of the *The Scotsman* daily, capturing a global canvas of famous faces and foible with his acerbic pen and ink sketches. Emilio did eventually do a drawing of me for his retrospective exhibition held at the Merchant Company headquarters in Hanover Street in 1981, but he drew the long black beard on my head. I had a lot of black hair on my head in those days!

As was his practice, Emilio had gone along to the Playhouse rehearsal in 1984 and he had installed himself in the wings of the stage. The problem was that nobody had notified Nureyev that a stranger was lurking in the shadows. No doubt stressed from his exertions, when he spotted Emilio he strode up to him demanding to know who he was and what he was doing.

Emilio attempted to explain but made the mistake of handing over some of his drawings which the petulant Nureyev proceeded to rip into pieces and throw into the air before turning on his heels to stride haughtily off stage.

Humiliatingly chastised, Emilio was mortified but he got his revenge the following morning when the episode made headlines in *The Scotsman*. With the Paris Opera Ballet scheduled to return the following year, I attempted to mediate by suggesting to Nureyev's assistant, the very patient Madam Marie Suzanne Subit, blonde and chic, that Emilio might go to Paris to illustrate a feature article for the forthcoming 1985 Festival performance. My suggestion was politely declined. I thought this a shame.

However, Nureyev did return to Edinburgh the following year to perform in a kilt as James in *La Sylphide* at the Playhouse Theatre. Although still beyond equal, his appearance, his physical prowess and beauty was deteriorating fast. He died in France eight years later.

CHAPTER SEVEN

Déjeuner sur l'herbe

ALICE BEBERMAN, A Liza Minelli lookalike from Champagne, Illinois, first met Richard Demarco in London in 1972, during his first EDINBURGH ARTS programme. She was spending the summer with her college friend Carol Swift in Bristol, and says she took her toothbrush and hopped on a bus to become what most likely could only be described as the first EDINBURGH ARTS 'hanger-on'.

While on a lecture tour of the USA, Richard later stayed with Carol and Alice in their student apartment at Illinois Wesleyan University in Bloomington, Illinois, and he invited Alice to show her work at The Demarco Gallery in Edinburgh's Melville Crescent in February 1974. He also convinced her to participate in his forthcoming EDINBURGH ARTS journey that summer where, she says, she spent the entire journey crocheting with a giant hook and balls of wool, a breast to cover the top of Arthur's Seat in Holyrood Park as part of the Demarco Festival Arts Exhibition.

Alice's installation was intended as a thank you to Mother Nature. At that time, sheep grazed in Holyrood Park and Alice's concept was that the wool harvested from these sheep be recycled back into the grass-covered hill in the form of a breast sheep mountain. Covering the Edinburgh Festival for the BBC that year was Esther Rantzen who sent a film crew to accompany Alice to the top of Arthur's Seat where she fitted a giant red nipple to the triangulation point from which the breast sloped downwards. The same programme also featured several other artists from the Demarco stable who were exhibiting works in a High Street space they had transformed into a brilliant white exhibition hall with paint supplied by Vymura and whose representative taught them how to properly hold their brushes. While they painted the walls, they chanted, 'White White White! White With Vymura!'

At this exhibition, Alice contributed a smaller breast landscape of undulating hills made up from crocheted paps with the label underneath reading, 'Please touch but do not fondle.'

Alice says the inspiration for her breast landscapes came from being part of the EDINBURGH ARTS journey through the landscape of Scotland and seeing the Paps of Fife. She later gifted a small breast landscape cushion to the film star Cary Grant whom she had befriended whilst living in Bristol.

However, it was not lost on the media that the artist creating BREAST art was coming from BRISTOL. Ha ha!

All of the artists involved with Richard Demarco in 1979 assembled in his New Town flat to watch Esther's broadcast on Modern Art at the Edinburgh Fringe, and were joined there by Joan Bakewell, who was that year covering the Festival for STV. Esther's coverage was scathing, completely missing the point of the outrageous sense of humour involved, but Joan tactfully explained, that in fairness to Esther, the real power behind any editorial role in the media lies with the personal prejudices of the producer. As true then as it is now.

Alice's next creations were four hand-crocheted anatomically correct body suits which she christened The Furbelows. In May 1979, The Furbelows took part in an art show at the Open Eye Gallery in Liverpool and on a walkabout in a shopping centre were arrested for obscenity. The unfortunate boys and girls who had been wearing the costumes were awaiting trial when undeterred, Alice approached Andrew Brown at The 369 Gallery, the artist Fionna Carlisle, Fionna's then husband Alpin Smart, and a Northumbrian boy called Radcliffe Royds to put on the costumes and become Furbelows for that year's Edinburgh Jazz Parade along Princes Street. Mike Hart, who oversaw the Jazz Parade, told me that he thought the whole episode was hysterically funny.

The parade route was along Princes Street where waves of laughter followed the spectacle. Almost as soon as they appeared in the Grassmarket dancing to a jazz quartet on the back of a lorry as The Furbelow Four, they were arrested by a magenta-faced police sergeant who crossly marched them off to police headquarters in the High Street. He became even more apoplectic on discovering that Andrew was wearing a girl costume.

I was summoned to bail them out but mercifully my arrival coincided with that of a brace of lady constables who simply fell about laughing. A Chief Inspector came to find out what all the noise was about and The Furbelows were promptly sent home.

From then on The Furbelows became a 369 Gallery's 1979 Fringe attraction, re-enacting a series of tableaux depicting famous old masterworks of art – Manet's *Déjeuner sur l'herbe*; Botticelli's *The Birth of Venus*, Rubens' *The Three Graces* and Goya's *Nude Maja*.

In swinging London, the impresario Sam Chesterton persuaded Alice to bring them along to a magazine launch party at the Embassy Nightclub. The group embarked on a Cotter's Bus with the costumes stored below with their luggage. Alice told the models that if the costumes were stolen before they got to the gig, they would just have to dance in their birthday suits. The playwright Marcella Evaristi even borrowed one of the costumes to wear in front of a studio audience for her BBC Scotland *Naked Radio* comedy sketch show.

When The Furbelows subsequently went on trial for their Liverpool outing and charged with 'insulting behaviour likely to cause a breach of the peace', it was not so funny. The participants were initially fined £25 each but when their legal adviser Art Law recommended they appeal, they foolishly did so. The aged judge, a Welsh Methodist Elder, decided to teach them a lesson. All four were jailed for two weeks which caused an uproar of protest throughout the print media. Tabloid and lifestyle magazines ran pages on the outrage.

Nowadays methinks it would be surprising if anyone gave them more than a passing glance. Well more than a glance maybe, and hopefully the world of art censorship is a more worldly and generous place nowadays.

Sights And Sounds In The Festival Sky

My first Edinburgh Military Tattoo was an auspicious occasion. It was 1965 and I was invited to the Royal Box by a daughter of the Secretary of State for Scotland. Both she and I were still at school. Her father was taking the Salute.

However, I had passed my driving test earlier that year and we followed the official limousine with its flapping flag and outriders through the crowds of the Royal Mile and onto the castle esplanade in my first car, a small and humble white Ford Capri.

On our arrival, a soldier jumped into the driver's seat and took my car away to park it. It felt terribly grown up and although this was three decades before the coloured spotlights, synchronised pyrotechnics and those astonishing projections onto the castle battlements, the show was awesome.

Marching pipe bands, the British Army with its kilted uniforms out in force, the Lone Piper playing *Sleep Dearie Sleep*, the hairs rose on the back of the neck.

The following year I was invited to a drinks party at the home of the feisty Brigadier Alistair Maclean, the Tattoo's director after Lt Colonel George Malcolm of Poltalloch and Captain Forbes Taylor. Brigadier Maclean was the man who laid down the military ground rules that the Tattoo must always go on regardless of the weather. Audiences were a hardy lot in those days. It always rains in Edinburgh in August and unless you are washed away, a wee bit of rain does you nae harm. Seriously, it makes the flowers grow, so I am told.

Little did I know then that 37 years later I would be approached by the Tattoo's Business Manager, the monumental Major Brian Leishman, to write the official history of the Edinburgh Tattoo, shortly afterwards elevated to Royal Edinburgh Tattoo.

And what a parallel it was to the Edinburgh Festival itself, beginning as a small parade in Princess Street Gardens organised by Philip Christison, General Officer Commanding Scotland, with the Queen of the Netherlands seated on a chair under an umbrella with the audience standing. It was that same August night of 1947 that Harry Lauder, Scotland's greatest music hall trooper died and the crowd stood in silence to remember him.

Such was the small parade's subsequent popularity that in 1950 it relocated onto the spacious Esplanade of Edinburgh Castle with Her Majesty Queen Elizabeth, with her daughters HRH Princess Elizabeth and HRH Princess Margaret in attendance, and Thomas Beecham conducting the Royal Philharmonic Orchestra.

When successive producers – Brigadier Jack Sanderson, Lt Colonel Lesley Dow, Major Michael Parker, Brigadier Melville Jameson, Major General Euan Loudon and Brigadier David Alfrey – theatrical drama was introduced, and the musicality was stepped up several notches. Ticket sales rocketed. With the appointment of Major General 'Buster' Howes as Chief Executive in 2022, I wish him well. The night fireworks over the castle and the distant sounds of the Tattoo on the wind have become as much a part of the Edinburgh International Festival as the great orchestras and theatricals of the official programme.

Perched on the castle rock high above the city, with the lights of the New Town and South Side twinkling below to form the centre of a great, all enveloping urban bowl under a big night sky, the Royal Edinburgh Tattoo reminds us all that Edinburgh is a truly great city in a truly great country in a great continent and in a great and challenging world.

I have now lost count of the number of times I have been to the Tattoo, either seated in the public stands or, more recently, in the VIP enclosure. The show has soared in popularity and surely remains one of the finest out-of-doors spectacles of all time.

With the close attachment of so many Scots families to Scottish Regiments coupled with an explosion of international tourism in the decades since that first small parade in Princes Street Gardens, the Royal Edinburgh Military Tattoo continues triumphant to this day.

From my home in Powderhall where the Water of Leith snakes lazily through housing developments, green spaces and industrial units towards its estuary in

Leith Docks, I feel privileged throughout the month of August to have my very own private firework display as seen from my sitting room window.

Before the Parade Passes By

It was also at the invitation of Major Brian Leishman, the retired Business Manager of the Edinburgh Military Tattoo, that in the late 1990s I became a judge at the Edinburgh Festival Cavalcade on Princess Street. This was then the Festival's opening out-of-doors extravaganza and it took place on the Saturday preceding the official Edinburgh International Festival's grand opening concert at the Usher Hall.

On the appointed day, the Lord and Lady Provost of Edinburgh (in my days Norman and Anne Irons, followed by Eric and Janice Milligan) accompanied by visiting VIPs, assembled on a dais, to start off with erected on the steps of The Royal Scottish Academy at the foot of the Mound but latterly in front of the Royal Overseas League on Princes Street. The judges, Brian Leishman, Wendy Jones, the irrepressible John Gibson from the *Edinburgh Evening News*, David Todd, PR supremo Martin Hunt, and I were given front row seats. On one occasion we were joined by Martin Hunt's friends, the actress Hayley Mills in town to support her son who was appearing on the Fringe, and the STV *Take the High Road* stars Eileen McCallum and Mary Riggans.

As with all such competitions, the conclusions of the judges were entirely good humoured and subjective, designed to give the greatest encouragement to all the remarkable community and youth groups given an opportunity to a create transitory statements of their being. Alas, when the crowds became too large for comfort, health and safety decreed the renamed Edinburgh Festival Carnival be relocated to Holyrood Park where, despite the roomy slopes of Arthur's Seat, the facilities were pronounced inadequate and untenable and it was decided to discontinue the event.

The Edinburgh Festival Cavalcade that I recall was certainly the most colourful and good natured of parades, featuring performers from the Tattoo, selected Fringe performers, and a pageant of gaudy floats manned by all sorts of local interests ranging from co-operative societies, the Lady Boys of Bangkok, to vibrant youth and ethnic groups from in an around the Edinburgh suburbs. It brought the citizens of Scotland's Capital face-to-face with what was about to envelope them in a blanket of fun, and the crowds that lined both sides of Princes Street were ecstatic.

I had previously only been a spectator but in 1996, the magician Fay

Presto, who was appearing in cabaret at The 369 Gallery, persuaded me to act as her chauffeur and drive her antique open-topped Triumph Herald, accompanied by my wingman Rory Knight Bruce, who was covering the Fringe for the *Londoner's Diary*. It was a warm and glorious summer's day and the backdrop of the old castle against an azure blue was incomparable. Camelot at its finest.

Now one of the problems of taking part in a great open-air public parade is that with the pipe bands, and marching soldiers and performers on foot and stage set lorries bursting with song and belching exhaust, the pace is, of necessity, critically controlled and not at all suited to an elderly vehicle prone to overheat.

Nevertheless, Fay Presto, blonde and sparkling in a cobalt blue dress, looked magnificent, waving like Royalty to the cheering masses. It was such a buzz, reminiscent of a crowd scene from the film *Evita*. Rory and I wore chauffeurs' caps and stared at the road in front of us while Fay and her mascot, Harvey, the white rabbit, lauded the adulation on the back seats.

To start off, the pace from Waverley was regular, less than 5mph, but having to stop and start every 20 yards soon took its toll on the car's radiator. Thankfully, we reached St John's Episcopal Cathedral at the West End before our trusty Triumph Herald came to a steaming and abrupt halt. Rory and I, even Fay and Harvey, were obliged to get out and push.

It was an undignified end to a highly exhilarating day, but happily none of the officials seemed in the slightest bit phased when we manhandled our exhausted steed into Lothian Road and Castle Terrace. No doubt they thought it was all part of the show.

Books Do Furnish a Room

With an increased demand from the literary world and general public at large for opportunities to interact with their favourite authors face-to-face (and buy their books, of course), the concept of book festivals was spawned throughout post-war UK in the wake of the Cheltenham Literary Festival launched in 1949. Oxford, Bath and Stratford-upon-Avon followed suit.

Edinburgh accordingly kicked off with its first 'meet the author' event held in the leafy surrounds of Charlotte Square Gardens in 1983. Initially conceived as a biennial occurrence, it became annual in 1997. The Edinburgh International Book Festival has since grown to over 900 events over two weeks. As a result of this, debatably, Edinburgh was nominated to become the first UNESCO City of Literature in 2004. Gloriously situated in the west end of Edinburgh's New Town, Charlotte Square surrounded by some of the finest Georgian architecture in the land, was annually transformed into a bustling village of tents and yurts, attracting famous fiction and non-fiction writers from far and wide.

The publishers of Margaret Atwood, Salman Rushdie, Gore Vidal, Alan Bennet, Harold Pinter and a raft of Edinburgh locals such as Alexander McCall Smith, Ian Rankin, and JK Rowling seized the opportunity. I even took part to promote four of my own non-fiction books, starting off with the graveyard slot of 9am on a Saturday morning.

But the atmosphere, intimacy and thrill of a live audience, even if it was not a full house, compensated for any early morning anxiety I might have had after a sleepless night. I did a lot better with the turnout on my subsequent appearances; there were great questions and answers. I actually sold a whole load of books.

In its way, the Edinburgh Book Festival also affords the opportunity for theatre. Probably my most vivid recall coincided with the publication of the edited *transcripts from the Trials of Oscar Wilde* in 2003 when Wilde's grandson Merlin Holland acted the part of his grandfather while Owen Dudley Edwards took on the role of his prosecutor Edward Carson, Dublin accent et al. Another highlight was the maverick politician Rory Stewart talking about his adventures on walking across Afghanistan and through the England/Scotland borderland.

The Edinburgh International Book Festival under its successive directors Jenny Brown, Catherine Lockerbie and Nick Barley also provided me with wonderful opportunities as a journalist to interview and interact with Germain Greer and Tina Brown, whom I had met in her *Tatler* magazine manifestation, controversially speaking in different decades about Diana, Princess of Wales. I was able to meet up with Diana Gabaldon from Arkansas, flushed with the success of her remarkable *Outlander* series. With the BBC Special Correspondent Allan Little as Chairman of the Board of Directors, its future in partnership with the University of Edinburgh in the purpose-built Edinburgh Futures Institute in 2024 looks assured but I am sure that all of us have happy memories of the tranquillity of Charlotte Square.

Over from his atelier in Paris, the late Jim Haynes was always a regular feature in the Press Yurt, and I remember so well becoming involved in a particularly animated conversation with his old pal Germain about censorship. The publisher Christopher MacLehose, a family friend, threw a splendid reception where I met some of his authors including Philip Ziegler who autographed my copy of his biography of Laurence Olivier.

Jim and I (I speak on his behalf as he is no longer with us) were particularly grateful to Frances Sutton, the calm, stylish former Edinburgh International Book Festival Press Officer, and her successors, for allowing us to make use of the Media yurts both at Charlotte Square, and since Lockdown situated at Edinburgh College of Art, as an escape from the Edinburgh Festival at large. Really good coffee.

If We Are Not Careful the Fringe Will Go Up in Smoke

As a columnist with the *Edinburgh Evening News* during the 1990s, I often found myself in the front line during petty feuds between Festivals and city, commerce, politics and culture. In August 1999, I was moved to pose the question, 'When is a festival not a festival?'

The answer was straightforward: When it is kept behind bars.

The very word 'festival' means a joyous celebration. In European countries, festivals spill out into the surrounding countryside and onto the city streets and street performance is a way of life.

Remember how wonderful it was during the heatwave of 1997, when Edinburgh could almost have been Paris or Berlin or Florence, with little pavement cafes and crowds everywhere celebrating the sunshine and blending together for a thrilling occasion of experimentation, music, dance, theatre, artworks, entertainment and love?

Nobody minded the leafleting. Nobody objected to the street theatre and the Fringe companies promoting their acts, with the centre of Edinburgh and the pedestrianised Royal Mile in particular becoming one great sunlit stage. It was fun and the visitors and the locals who chose to embrace it, loved it... Or at least most of them did... but then there is always some old misery guts determined to spoil the fun.

Promoted by yet another of those loud but invisible whingers so endemic in our poor northern capital, the Edinburgh Fringe suddenly announced that acts promoting themselves would henceforth be restricted by licence. To enforce this 'Red Shirts' were to be employed.

Red Shirts? Where did they come from?

And they wanted liability insurance too. Worse still, the beleaguered Paul Gudgin in his first year as Fringe Director, announced that he feared that if acts in the streets were not controlled, residents might start to complain.

I could not help but wonder who had got to him? So far as I was aware nobody to date had openly objected about street theatre and I would have thought the majority of residents of the Royal Mile, by virtue of living in such a historic thoroughfare, would be more accommodating than that.

But remember that 14 years earlier, just up the road, a young lady resident in Ramsay Garden had complained that the noise of building the spectator stands for the Tattoo was depriving her of beauty sleep! Given that this work took place during the day, one could not help but wonder how much time she spent in bed?

To my mind, if you choose to live in the heart of a bustling international city, you must accept, as they eventually did in Ramsay Garden, that for at least three to four weeks of the year, everyday life is going to involve somewhat more than cobbled streets populated by bickering councillors, bewigged lawyers, lovely views over the city north and south, and tartan souvenir shops. Such restrictions pose yet another problem for Fringe performers. How, with so many thousands of shows in town, are they to publicise themselves directly to a potential audience?

It is all very well and good if you are attached to The Gilded Balloon, Assembly or Pleasance with venues within walking distances of each other, but if you are stuck in a cupboard in Haymarket, or a church hall in Bruntsfield, you have to make a noise and work really hard to bring in the punters.

Alas, by the second millennium, the number of shows on the Fringe, deluged by the stand-up comedy circuit, have got out of control and at quite a lot of them, there are more people on stage than in the audience. In some cases, deservedly so.

When a group of the world's top clowns, Maski from the Ukraine, turned up having played to crowds of thousands in Poland, Germany and Denmark, and only six people turned out to see them in Edinburgh, there had to be something wrong. You could understand it if they were simply bad but they were not. They were brilliant. Only nobody knew they were there!

With the Fringe brochure resembling an oversize, old-fashioned telephone directory, it is for this very reason so many Fringe shows felt the need to take to the streets. Veteran performers who have been regulars for years, were beginning to feel they were being denied their self-respect.

I am not joking when I say that those of us who are privileged to live in this great northern city of Edinburgh, if we genuinely care about our national and international reputations, had best be careful. Edinburgh is already being seen by many of its citizens as a Mecca for partisan control freaks. So different from the sophisticated, enlightened and outward-looking citadel of three-quarters of a century ago.

Already in 1999, the message seemed to be going out, 'Don't come to Edinburgh – the natives are so unfriendly.'

That is so blatantly untrue.

CHAPTER EIGHT

By Waverley Station I Sat Down and Wept

IT MUST HAVE been early in 1979 that Andrew Brown embarked upon a biography of the Two Roberts, a project he mysteriously abandoned claiming he had left the manuscript on a train. Had we not heard that one before?

However, the catalyst was an introduction from John Craxton to the Canadian novelist Elizabeth Smart. During the 1940s, she had employed the painters Robert Colquhoun and Robert McBride as babysitters for her children.

Elizabeth's classic prose poem *By Grand Central Station I Sat Down and Wept*, was based on her pre-war love affair with the already married George Barker. The daughter of wealthy parents in Ottowa, she had fallen irredeemably in love with Barker's poetry which she had come across in a Charing Cross Road bookshop. On the spot, she decided to have children with him.

It took her some time to track him down to acquaint him with his destiny but she persevered and when World War II began, she raised enough money to rescue him from Tokyo University to bring him and his wife Jessica to the USA where they lived as a threesome. The rest is lyrically portrayed in Elizabeth's extraordinarily indulgent polemic.

In the autumn of 1980, the broadcaster Frank Delaney persuaded George and Elizabeth to appear on the same platform at an Edinburgh Festival writers' event held in the Assembly Rooms. Elizabeth gave readings from *By Grand Central Station I Sat Down and Wept* and George rendered his account of their affair. His version was called *Dead Seagull*, which probably says it all.

Whatever one's view of George Barker's morality in abandoning his wife to have children by Elizabeth, it was hard not to warm to his charm. When I first met him, he said to me, 'How extraordinary. One of my best friends is called Roddy Martine!'

And thus it was that I also met the fascinating and electrifying Elizabeth. She was adopted by all of us at The 369 Gallery, and Fionna Carlisle painted her portrait. Drinking at the Abbotsford with her and the younger, equally brilliant and beautiful Glasgow-Italian playwright Marcella Evaristi,

Elizabeth gripped my wrist and in her muffled Canadian burr announced, 'You know what? You would be the most wonderful painter. A truly great painter. But you're a bloody awful writer!' Marcella had an entirely different take on my talents. 'You're so f****ing *Daily Express*,' she would often repeat. I loved them both.

After the Krashny Dinner that year, Elizabeth wrote to me. 'Did I behave too badly?' she asked, continuing, 'Badly, yes, but too badly? I can see your face softly and kindly saying sssh! to me. I hate to be an ungrateful guest. But ten times for the same joke is a bit much when one is expecting to take off into glorious drunkeness!'

It was Andrew and Elizabeth who first took me to the Coach & Horses in Soho, where we encountered an inebriated Francis Bacon and the equally abusive publican Norman Balon. This was also where I first met Jeffrey Bernard, best known for his Low Life column in *The Spectator* and Keith Waterhouse's witty and insightful play *Jeffrey Bernard is Unwell*. Some years later, I was asked by *The Spectator* to look after Jeffrey when he visited Edinburgh. He was staying at the Roxburghe Hotel in Charlotte Square and when I arrived to collect him at 10am, the first thing he asked was where we could get a drink. His hands were visibly shaking. He was not the slightest bit interested in sightseeing.

It was early in the day so I took him to the Port of Leith. As soon as he had downed a half pint of vodka, the shaking stopped. Jeffrey was well again.

Elizabeth returned to Edinburgh the following January, a time of year when she felt she could best escape from her beloved Suffolk garden. She had become restless for a new adventure. She wondered if she might 'find succour in your stimulating city?'

In her poem 'The Bonus' (1977) she wrote:

> To be in a very unfeminine
> Very unloving state
> Is the desperate need
> Of anyone trying to write.

Having rented a small apartment in Stockbridge, she immersed herself in writing poetry, only occasionally sallying forth to socialise. She seemed perfectly happy. She even confessed to reading Walter Scott.

Her daughter Rose's premature death in the Spring of 1982 affected Elizabeth deeply and she returned to Canada to become writer-in-residence at the University of Alberta. In 1984, she published *In The Meantime* (Deneau, 1984), her last collection of poems.

Towards the end of 1986, Elizabeth called me to say that her photographer son Christopher was taking her to the Isle of Skye for a photo shoot. She suggested they might look in on Edinburgh on the way back. I was in London that weekend but loaned them my flat. Three months later, Christopher telephoned to say Elizabeth had died. He had stepped out from his Soho flat to buy a pint of milk.

On his return, he had found her slumped over the telephone which she had presumably answered. I regret that I did not attend her funeral in Suffolk but I was told that the wake had lasted several days. Elizabeth would have liked that.

Just before the 2004 Edinburgh International Festival began, a large poster on the front of the Gateway Theatre caught my eye. It read, *Each ... And Every Inch. The Life of Elizabeth Smart.*

It was a Theatre Cryptic production described as 'A walk through of sound installations, live music and 3D cinema – dedicated to the life of Elizabeth Smart and leading up to the novel that guaranteed her immortality.'

'How appropriate you should have the show here,' I told the young director Cat Boyd and I pointed across the road towards my front door. 'That was where Elizabeth was staying three months before she died. She loved Edinburgh.'

Sew On A Sequin

My spacious Georgian home at the top end of Leith Walk in Edinburgh's East End was ideal for entertaining. With high ceilings and east facing drawing room, there was a dining hall in which I could seat up to 20 at a 14ft-long trestle table I had rescued from a furniture warehouse in Causewayside.

Among those who came to stay with me for the Edinburgh Festival was the bouncy Mark Bunyan, styling himself 'The Gay Crusader.' In 1995, he was canonised by the California-based Sisters of Perpetual Indulgence as 'Saint Mark of the Musical Tendency.' Next there were Howard Rossen and Rick Seer, two theatre directors from New York. in charge of a troop of American drama students on the brink of off-Broadway fame.

On their return for a second year, their travel agent muddled up their booking dates and I ended up accommodating the cast overnight in sleeping bags on my sitting room floor. Another time, the All-Russia Theatre Company from Moscow, in town to enact Henry Miller's *The Crucible*, arrived for a party with their interpreter Ailsa Lamont and, with an absence of vodka, consumed several bottles of Scotch instead.

There were impromptu gatherings, singing around my Chapel Baby Grand. I have a vague recollection of the television presenter Simon Fanshaw duetting with either the polytetrafluoroethylene-wigged Australian comedian Bob Downe (aka Mark Trevorrow) or the actor David Benson, but this might just have been a bad dream. Alice Beberman brought the Canadian vocalist George Dvorsky and after supper, not knowing much about him, she and I sang songs by Cole Porter and Irving Berlin while he patiently listened. The following night, we cringed with embarrassment when he got up to sing like Enrico Caruso.

It appealed to me to mix up different worlds. The literary agent Giles Gordon argued with Timothy Clifford over whether or not Henry Raeburn was a great painter or just mediocre, and Giles became so animated that his, or rather my Chippendale chair collapsed under him.

A big Fringe success was *Instant Sunshine* headed up by Dr Allan Maryon-Davis and *The Times* columnist Miles Kington, a cousin of the voluminously bearded Laurence Blair Oliphant of Ardblair Castle and Blairgowrie Highland Games.

While the stages of the Festival Theatre, Playhouse Theatre, Royal Lyceum Theatre, and Usher Hall trembled beneath the weight of great orchestras and opera, I got into the habit of seeking out the cabaret haunts of the Fringe.

In 1996, I was in the audience to listen in exquisite pain to Clive James' protege, the magnificent and incomprehensible Cuban-American singer Margarita Pracatan. 'She never let the words or the melody get in her way,' observed James. 'Unlike us, she is without the fear of failure.' In 2001, I met the sparkling Joan Rivers at the Edinburgh Festival Theatre performing her Fringe show *Broke and Alone*. 'I love Edinburgh,' she announced. 'I've seen Hamlet in Polish and a Lesbian production of *Queen Leer*.'

More recently I have applauded Christine Bovill with her emotional recycling of the songs of Edith Piaf and Jacques Brel, the variety circus La Clique at the Underbelly and, only a couple of years ago, I was taken along to a venue up some dingy stairs on North Bridge to see the Australian drag artist Reuben Kaye. Nightlife at the Edinburgh Fringe is never mundane.

The magician Fay Presto first performed on the Edinburgh Fringe in 1996. She contacted me through a mutual friend whom she had met at the bar of Langan's Brasserie in London, where she table hopped. Sheena McDonald and I took her for lunch at the Shore Restaurant in Leith. Neither Sheena nor I knew what to expect but from the moment we arrived Fay took over the restaurant with her card tricks. She was back the following year for a late-night show with her own stand-up comedy troop, and a real chauffeur. She rented a flat in Moray Place from Elizabeth Fairbairn and threw a series of Sunday afternoon tea parties. It was at one of these I was introduced to the German theatre director Lutz Deisinger.

For over four decades my Edinburgh Fringe Festival notably centred upon two outstanding cabaret acts, Kit & The Widow (later morphed into Kit & McConnel) and Fascinating Aïda, who won a Perrier Award on the Fringe in 1984. I often, but fortunately not too regularly, sat stony-faced while being harangued with the banalities of stand-up comedy. Never sit in the front row! I am sorry Bill Burdett-Coutts and Karen Koren, and I am sure you must know, I rarely laugh for the sake of laughing. Only clever comedy, sophisticated, topical wit embedded in a musical score serves to crack me up.

I first came across Kit Hesketh-Harvey and Richard Sisson at McNally's, a venue run by Karen Koren in Haymarket in the early 1980s. It was the beginning of a 40-year stage door luvviedom and cemented enduring friendships. When the Widow, who always reminded me of a character from *Wind in the Willows*, finally divorced his stage partner, he was replaced by the equally talented James McConnel.

It was social commentary at its most outrageous and sublime, and not at all surprising that HM King Charles III should have sent a message to be read out at Kit's recent memorial service held in Convent Garden. Similarly, the effervescent Dillie Keane, founder of Fascinating Aïda, had made an unexpected entrance at one of my Festival parties during the 1970s. In those days I had no idea who turned up at my Festival parties. Everyone was welcome. I was such a groupie.

Since then the Edinburgh Festival has for me simply not been the same Edinburgh Festival without them. Now that Kit has passed on to that great cabaret platform in the sky, a lot of hilarity has gone out of our lives, and my life in particular.

No more will the bizarre plaid-kilted Mr Punch lookalike be seen parking his camper van outside his performance venue of Edinburgh Academy or emerging from his overnight yurt erected in the gardens of historic Hawthornden overlooking the River North Esk.

Although the trio of Fascinating Aïda (with latterly pianists Russell Churney and Michael Ralston) has gone through several manifestations with Lizzie Richardson, Marilyn Cutts, Charlotte Nytzen, Glenda Smith, Denise Wharmby, Issy van Randwyck and Sarah-Louise Young come to mind with Liza Pulman joining Dillie and the brave and enduring Adèle Anderson, the group's performances have attained new heights of hysterics, not least when Dillie, who is only marginally younger than myself, performs a cartwheel on stage.

It was while one of my Festival parties was in full swing in the 1990s that Lutz Deisinger appeared on my doorstep and was plainly offended that I failed to recognise him from Fay Presto's tea party three years earlier. He was again in town to search for cabaret acts for his two classic Berlin theatres, The Bar Jeder Vernunft and Tipi Am Kanzleramt. The Italian mime artist Ennio Marchetto, Fascinating Aïda and the Ukelele Orchestra are just three of the acts he coaxed to Schaperstrabe.

Endearingly shy but generous to a fault, and bearing a striking resemblance to Emilio Coia's not exactly flattering caricature of Anton Krashny, Lutz Deisinger had founded the Bar Jeder Vernunft with his partner Holga Klotzbach in 1992. The action takes place in a huge spiegeltent with table seating, and, since its beginning has launched the careers of such German super stars as Ute Lemper and Die Geschwister Pfister. Its larger, sister theatre, The Tipi Am Kanzleramt, occupies a gigantic Indian tent next to the Federal Chancellery.

Lutz's artistic genius remains instinctive; his enthusiasm is infectious. During his Festival visits, he often sees four shows in a day to feel the pulse of the new, more often than not discretely slipping out of the audience after 20 minutes when not impressed. Through him I was introduced to Melissa Madden Gray aka Meow Meow, the astonishingly gymnastic and melodic Australian singer/cabaret artist from Melbourne.

Her pianist on the Edinburgh Fringe was the rising American songwriter/ musician Lance Horne, a protege of my Upper East Side Manhattan friend Howard Rossen. The following year, I bought tickets for the Usher Hall to hear Meow Meow perform *Weimar Cabaret* on the official Festival programme with her countryman Barry Humphries, and the Australian Chamber Orchestra.

While foraging in a secondhand bookshop in Melbourne, the inimitable Barry Humphries (aka Dame Edna Everage) had come across a suitcase once owned by a Jewish refugee. It contained musical scores from the 1920s and 1930s. Recognising only too well what these represented, the now greatly lamented Humphries had set about scripting and unravelling that sardonic, sexually confused world of not so very, very long ago in the scheme of things; an age saturated with guilt, vanity and escapism, when nobody had a clue what was going on.

Sounds familiar, does it not?

With that same spirit that was adopted by Rudolf Bing and Bruno Walter over seven decades ago, I was proud that the Edinburgh International Festival should sponsor such a musical masterpiece of 20th-century Enlightenment for the 21st century. More please.

Voices from the Antipodes

Since my father was for three and a half years a prisoner of war in Singapore courtesy of the Japanese Emperor Hirohito, and I was born post-war on the island of Borneo in South East Asia, I was more than a little intrigued to discover that Jonathan Mills, who became Director and Chief Executive of the Edinburgh Festival in 2006, had written *Sandakan Threnody*, an oratorio for tenor, choir and orchestra.

I have since discovered that I have been to Sandakan, although I admit I was far too young to remember anything about it. Nevertheless, it is a name that has lingered long in my subconscious.

Let me explain. In 2005, I published *Scorpion on the Ceiling*, an account of my family's adventures in South East Asia. The story centres around the escape of my mother and middle sister when the Japanese army invaded Sarawak on Christmas Eve 1941. By walking 200 miles through a largely impenetrable Borneo Jungle, they eventually arrived off a Dutch boat in Australia via Pontianak and a seaplane to Batavia (Djakarta).

Meanwhile, my father was trapped in Singapore and among the 6,000 civilians interned in Changi Gaol which was built to hold 600 criminals. Had either parent been captured in Sarawak, they would have been interned in either the Batu Lintang camp or Sandakan in Sabah. Just possibly my father would have been among those sent off on those cruel and appalling death marches. The Japanese did not want any prisoners left to tell tales of the Hell they were forced to endure.

Having undertaken extensive research on the subject, I am painfully aware that several of my parents' friends died on those marches. I had read Agnes Newton Keith's moving *Three Came Home* (Michael Joseph 1950) and accidentally come across the plaintive message carved into timber by Cyril Le Gros Clark, Sarawak's Chief Secretary and Donald MacDonald, manager of the Sarawak Rubber Estates, shortly before they were unceremoniously shot and buried in some lonely woods near Keningau. In Jonathan's case, he was paying tribute to the 2,345 Australian and British prisoners who set off from Sandakan, only six of whom survived. Mercifully, both Jonathan's father Frank Mills at Sandakan and my father in Changi, Singapore, survived internment, otherwise neither of us would be here to write about them.

Knowing the universal vow of silence surrounding that brutal conflict on the other side of the world, I have never discussed this with him, but given that both of us have researched and written on the subject, I have always liked to think we have a certain amount in common. We were first introduced by Michael Shea at a performance of the Royal Edinburgh Military Tattoo in

2006, and I later attended one of those 'In conversation' lunchtime sessions between him and Richard Demarco at the Scottish National Portrait Gallery. In 2010, I photographed him on the roof of the EIF Society headquarters at The Hub on Castllehill for my *Scenes from a Life* exhibition at Henderson's Salad Table Restaurant. On all three occasions, I was reassured.

During Jonathan's reign Wagner's mighty *Ring Cycle* was performed by Scottish Opera at the Festival Theatre and in 2012, my old school friend Nick Oppenheim, having bought the tickets and taken us beforehand to the now closed Tower Restaurant on the top floor of the Museum of Scotland in Chamber Street, required his brother, sister-in-law and I to sprint around the corner during the interval and afterwards for our main and pudding courses. It brought an entirely new dimension to Tristan and Isolde.

Jonathan notably staged Berlioz's *Trojans* with the Mariinsky Opera and Valery Gergiev, Aldeburgh Music's production of Benjamin Britten's *Owen Wingrave*, both reflecting upon epic warfare and the trauma of personal conscience. Under his watch the Edinburgh International Culture Summit was introduced, a UNESCO-recognised biennial meeting held in conjuncture with Edinburgh's summer festivals took place and he became President of the EIFF International Jury. EFFE (Europe for Festivals, Festivals for Europe was initiated by the European Festivals Association).

The Edinburgh Festival was hopefully once again in safe hands for the second millennium. The powers that be must also have realised this as his term was twice extended before his successor, the Dublin-born Fergus Linehan, formerly Artistic Director of the Sydney Festival, was appointed to succeed him in 2014. Jonathan was another hard act to follow.

CHAPTER NINE

Freedom for Ukraine

IN 2022, IT seemed ironic that The Freedom Ballet Company of Ukraine should be appearing at the Edinburgh International Conference Centre on the Edinburgh Fringe as opposed to being part of the official Edinburgh International Festival. For it was exactly the calibre of performance for which the Edinburgh Festival had been created.

Described as a 'collaboration between dance, theatricality, emotion and technique' the presence of its cast, young Ukrainian men and women, less than six months after Vladimir Putin had launched his absurd Special Military Operation invasion of their homeland, added an immense poignancy to the show, not least in the knowledge that these young men and women would all soon be returning to fight for the survival of their country.

Most of the male performers had to be given special dispensation from Ukraine's Culture Minister to travel in the knowledge that only the arts could ram home the truth about what was taking place to a world otherwise preoccupied with its own turbulent domestic problems.

The brave slapstick, generic dance cabaret on a large stage with basic props might not have appealed to everybody who was there, notably the critic from the *Guardian* who gave it a bad review, but for the majority in the audience, it was deeply moving and reminiscent of an experimental, and mildly shocking, lost sophistication that would not have been at all out of place 75 years ago.

A Show That Must Dazzle to Stay on Stage

Forgive me, but I have no hesitation in unashamedly updating the sentiments of an article I wrote at the time of the 50th Edinburgh International Festival for *The Daily Mail*. This was prompted by a searing indictment from Frank Dunlop who has asserted that after his departure as Director, that the Edinburgh Festival had become tame, relying on a narrow band of established names from an almost exclusively Western artistic canon.

Frank Dunlop's comments followed on a controversial lecture delivered by Professor George Steiner, essayist and philosopher, who concluded that the Edinburgh International Festival had outlived its usefulness.

Both of these men knew what it was like to be on the receiving end of criticism, so their observations were not to be delivered lightly. They must have known that it is only too easy to savage the largest and most influential arts festival in the world for becoming stale. And at the same time it is hard to imagine how any festival can maintain the momentum indefinitely after half a century. Indeed, now after three-quarters of a century.

Originality, as Richard Demarco has always asserted and embodied throughout his life, demands revolutionary thought. Such thoughts are rarely understood or welcomed by the establishment.

But it was not always so. In the gloomy, post-war years of the last century, the Edinburgh Festival of Music and Drama shone like a beacon throughout the world, bringing nations together in the grey old capital of Scotland. It put Scotland on the global map as a homeland for artistic innovation and enlightenment.

In 1947, it would have been so easy to create a narrow, inward-looking Scottish ceilidh to boost national morale. Instead, huge international and aspirational ambitions prevailed. Only the very best on a world stage was called for, and only the very best responded – wonderful voices from Kathleen Ferrier, Joan Sutherland, Maria Callas and Plácido Domingo, Luciano Pavarotti and José Ferrero; orchestra conductors Malcolm Sargent and Claudio Abbado; the world's greatest musicians, from Yehudi Menuhin to Daniel Barenboim; dancers Dame Margot Fonteyn and Rudolf Nureyev.

Then there were the great orchestras and the legendary names of world theatre and entertainment – Marlene Dietrich, Ralph Richardson, Alec Guinness, Trevor Howard, Peter Ustinov and even Princess Grace of Monaco.

You might well ask why everybody wanted to come to the Edinburgh Festival in the first place? Over the years other festivals have sprung up, notably at Salzburg in Austria, Spoleto in Italy, Charleston in the USA, and there are countless other cultural platforms to choose from.

The answer as to Edinburgh's survival as an annual extravaganza over 76 years is that the performance and art world does not come here for reasons of prestige, although there is plenty of that involved. Performers flock here because, in addition to knowing it is the best place to be seen, there is an essential element of surprise. They all want to be part of it.

For performers and audiences alike, the three autumnal weeks of the Edinburgh International Festival, if you can climb over the bodies of the Fringe, enables you to be a part of the most exciting place on earth. Despite all the competing tourist traps, that still holds true.

Yes, times have changed drastically and attitudes and expectations are not at all what they were 76 years ago. Sadly it is the commonplace and mediocre that has been increasingly on offer. Where are those legendary *coups de théâtre*? Where are those great international art exhibitions pioneered by the legendary Richard Demarco?

To be fair, all of those in charge – Lord Harewood, Peter Diamand, John Drummond, Frank Dunlop and Jonathan Mills – have had to contend with the unwelcome ogre of political interference and an unashamed manipulation of purse strings, stifling originality. By the beginning of the 21st century, it was beginning to look as if the Fringe had taken over and won, if only by volume.

Mounting a great international festival is no mean challenge. Yet it should be no greater challenge than it was 76 years ago. Innovation and the shock of the new is required. With escalating costs on all sides, there more than ever needs to be a content that takes your breath away. In recent years it has been an overall inability to astonish that has made the Edinburgh International Festival vulnerable.

A truly international event cannot survive on the assumption that there will always be an audience because Edinburgh is pretty, with a nice castle and lots of historic distractions. It must thrill. It must tantalise. It must seductively dazzle. Otherwise it might just as well pack up while the going is good. Indeed, there are those who would probably like that.

However, that is not going to happen, at least not in the foreseeable future. Let me say that with the Budapest Festival Orchestra and London Symphony Orchestra in situ throughout, the Berliner Ensemble's interpretation of Brecht's *The Threepenny Opera*, flagged up under the direction of Barrie Kosky, Alvin Ailey's American Dance Theatre, and three challenging themes – 'Community over Chaos', 'Hope over Adversity', and 'A Perspective that's not one's own' – the Edinburgh International Festival of 2023 is off to a cracking good start.

In early May 2023, I was in the audience at the EIF Hub for an animated discussion between *The Scotsman* theatre critic Joyce McMillan and Nicola Benedetti, the very beautiful, highly intelligent incoming Director of the Edinburgh International Festival. The first Scots-born and first female EIF Director, Nicola was justifiably proud of the diversity of her first programme; also deeply conscious of the awesome commitment she has undertaken. As a classical solo violinist with the greatest orchestras in the world, performing in some of the grandest concert halls in the world, she still considers that the Edinburgh Festival is the finest crucible in the world for all of the arts.

On this she is 100 per cent focused and determined to listen. When I referenced my teenage journalism with *Lens*, she rather disconcertingly scribbled a memo in a small notepad. 'Such a great way to get schools involved,' she said. I was impressed.

'Where do we go from here?' Nicola asks in her introduction to the EIF Programme 2023, then continues. 'Above all, we go to you, and with you. This is your festival. It's you, our audiences, who will create its spirit of joy and discovery. I am excited to go on the journey with you in August.'

So if there is any further advice I might be bold enough to presume to give to her, it is that she should talk to her fellow Italo-Scot Richard Demarco. He has been there. He has seen it all.

APPENDIX I

The Demarco Archive

Richard Demarco

TWENTY-EIGHT YEARS AGO, in 1995, I was obliged to sell part of the Demarco Archive to the National Galleries of Scotland. This included 16 art works and a large section of the Demarco Library consisting of more than 14,000 items. Now, more than a quarter of century later, the Demarco Archive exists in two distinct parts. Part One is now owned by the National Galleries dating from the '40s decade to that of the '90s. This part of the archive is destined to be housed in a National Galleries multi-million-pound extension alongside the archives of the Scottish National Galleries, The Royal Scottish Academy and Historic Environment Scotland and which is to become a reality in 2026. I consider the second part of the archive, not only as an archive, but rather as a *Gesamtkunstwerk* – that is a collaborative large-scale art work. This consists of over 800 art works, including sculptures, paintings, drawings, prints and event photographs which are now defined as a new genre of contemporary art by Düsseldorf's Museum Kunst Palast.

The Demarco Archive contains examples of this new genre of art relating to artists such as Joseph Beuys, Ian Hamilton Finlay, Sandy Moffat, Li Yuan-chia, Jon Schueler, Günther Uecker, Paul Neagu, Tadeusz Kantor, Magdalena Abakanowicz, Marina Abramović, Patrick Heron, John David Mooney, Arthur Watson, Ainslie Yule, Margaret Tait, Helen Douglas, etc. This part of the archive is presently housed in Robert McDowell's Summerhall Arts Centre as well as in my studio in the garden of Terry Ann Newman's Milkhall Cottage at Howgate near to Penicuik in Midlothian, 11 miles from Edinburgh, as well as in my house in Lennox Street in the West End of Edinburgh.

At the very core of the part of the Demarco Archive that I am presently bringing up-to-date is my personal history of the Edinburgh Festival from the first Festival in 1947, over a long period of nine decades, to the Festival of 2023. This particular part of the archive also contains a number of significant publications and it therefore includes four Luath Press publications, including the one to be launched during this year's Festival. It is inspired by my personal experience of all 76 Edinburgh Festivals. It should be noted that the archive is fortunate to also exist as a sound archive now housed in the British

Library. It consists of 27 half-hour tapes, part of that National Library section entitled *Artists' Lives*. As a more recent and welcome addition to this archive with particular reference to the history of the Edinburgh Festival both official and fringe, there is the addition of countless hundreds of hours of film archive made by Marco Federici and Michael Lloyd.

They have collaborated on a number of occasions to focus on interviews I have made with those I regard as key figures in the history of the Edinburgh Festival such as Terry Lane, Frank Dunlop, Sheila Colvin, Jim Haynes, John Calder, Tamara Alferoff, Andrew Marr, Jimmy Boyle, Max Stafford-Clark, Angela Bartie, Brian Cox, Arthur Watson, Robert McDowell, Roddy Martine, Ian Crawford, George Bruce, Susan Mansfield, Charlie Ellis, Duncan Macmillan, Clare Henry, Cordelia Oliver, Mark Waugh, Richard Eyre and Edward Gage.

There are also films made by Ros Lambert, Samir Mehanović, Murray and Barbara Grigor, Gabriella Cardazzo, Mark Littlewood, Rory McEwen, Richard Ashrowan, Howard Walker, Norbert Attard, Andres Veiel, Robert Pöcksteiner, Andrea Miller, Steve Mardy, Noel Witts and Peter McGinn.

I have endeavoured to introduce the spirit of the Edinburgh Festival, in particular to Italy, Poland, Germany, France, Romania, Lithuania, Belarus, Ukraine, The Netherlands, Spain, to England, Ireland and Northern Ireland. I am therefore grateful to those who represented the following institutions who contributed more than their fair share to the spirit of internationalising the Edinburgh Festival. Among those institutions in Poland would be Wroclaw's Depot Museum, MOCAK (Museum of Contemporary Art in Krakow) and the Cricoteka, also in Krakow. In Romania, there is The Institute of the Present in collaboration with the National Museum of Art of Romania in Bucharest, The Brukenthal National Museum in Sibiu, The Brâncuși Foundation in Bucharest and the Foksal Gallery in Warsaw, as well as The Hugh Lane Gallery in Dublin, The Signet Library in Edinburgh, the Museum Kunst Palast in Düsseldorf and Dundee University.

There are also those who have studied the Demarco Archive and were awarded Doctorates: June Geddes from London University's Courtauld Art Institute, Aletia Badenhorst from Leeds Beckett University and Giles Sutherland from Dundee University.

It should be noted that the Demarco Archive at Summerhall is unique as it consists of an unbroken personal history of the Edinburgh Festival from 1947 until 2022. I find it difficult to believe that I am most probably the only person alive whose life has been blessed with the experience of the entirety of the Edinburgh Festival. I therefore ask myself the question: 'Should there exist in Edinburgh a museum dedicated to the Edinburgh Festival's history?'

Richard Demarco and Glenalmond College

Edward Schneider

RICHARD DEMARCO HAS had a long-established relationship with Glenalmond College, beginning in 1969 when he was invited by then art master Ronald Craig to come to Glenalmond to lecture to our pupils. This friendship and association with Ronald Craig propelled the Glenalmond art department to new heights, taking pupils on an exciting new journey, embracing the changes of the '60s and '70s and encouraging new and exciting ways of looking at and experiencing the arts in its broadest sense. This relationship blossomed and grew through the next decades as Richard became a regular fixture, lecturing pupils on various aspects of art, modern art, theatre, nature and the environment as well wider aspects of culture. This worked well as Richard is, by his own admission, and despite his varied careers as an artist, gallery and theatre director, art historian and social commentator, primarily a gifted and inspirational teacher. The culmination of his association with Glenalmond was his appointment as an Honorary OG.

As a teacher and lecturer, Richard brings a vast knowledge spanning a variety of subjects, as well as an unbridled passion to excite and inspire his pupils. His success as a teacher and lecturer is evident from the warmth and respect still expressed from pupils whom he met during his early days at Glenalmond, as well as those young people fortunate to hear his current lectures as he continues to inspire through his association with the College. Those former pupils include many who have gone on to work in the arts but, his ability to inspire went far beyond one genre and made a continuing and significant impact on pupils in all walks of life. Former pupils influenced by Richard include Hamish Pringle who was part of the Saatchi Brothers team and is now a full-time artist, Ian O'Riordan, former Keeper of Art at Edinburgh City Art Centre for three decades, Richard Ingleby, founder of the Ingleby Gallery in Edinburgh, who has been instrumental in promoting modern and contemporary art in the UK, David Weir who founded and directed the Dovecot Studios in its new home in Infirmary Street, Edinburgh, and the late Robbie Coltrane, who said to Richard that he was responsible for inspiring him to study at Glasgow

School of Art and from there to become an actor.

These are only a very few of the former Glenalmond pupils who have gone on to professions in the Arts. Glenalmond was also fortunate to be associated with Richard through various collaborations and exciting artistic projects. These ranged from participation in various art exhibitions such as the 2017 exhibition at Summerhall Arts Centre in the Demarco Wing which included contributions from both pupils and members of the Glenalmond Art Department with the publication foreword by Claudia Massie, to Glenalmond pupils being invited to stage a production of Cyrano De Bergerac at the 1998 Edinburgh Festival Fringe programme of the performing arts, sponsored by the Demarco European Art Foundation. These experiences opened new doors for Glenalmond pupils and allowed them exposure on an international stage which they would not have enjoyed without Richard's support and the support of the Demarco Foundation.

Much of Richard's own experience and views of the arts were shaped by his association with Joseph Beuys, one of the most important and influential artists of the second half of the 20th century. Working together, they moved the teaching of art out of the classroom and into nature, opening the world of nature and raising awareness of all things environmental years before the rest of the world realised how important this would prove to be. Richard's own teaching moved seamlessly between the classroom, the studio into the world of nature, teaching pupils to look more closely and to experience the world around them.

As we go forward together, there are plans for formal recognition for all that Richard has done, and continues to do, for Glenalmond. The College would like to establish The Demarco Scholarship for Glenalmond pupils to support study and travel connected with the arts. We are currently working to secure the necessary funding to endow this programme. Additionally, we are also exploring establishing ties with the Demarco Archive, which contains 75 years of information, photographs and art works connected with the Edinburgh Festival, to be used as a study centre for Glenalmond pupils and the wider community. We are also in the process, under Richard's guidance and through his connections, working to establish connections with the Signet Library and the Library at Traquair House. It is our intention to raise the profile of the arts at Glenalmond College as we celebrate the deep connection with Richard.

Richard's own inspiration and excitement continues to grow through his love of the natural world. His profound joy in nature is infectious. He brings his 93 years of experience to his teaching and indeed to every encounter as he journeys through life.

APPENDIX 3

Richard Demarco's Edinburgh Year by Year
(93 years… with a running commentary from the man himself)

1930

Richard Demarco was born 9 July in a private nursing home in Edinburgh's Grosvenor Street, now the Hilton Grosvenor Hotel; John Oswald Russell Martin born 11 June within the sound of Bow Bells; Tommy Connery born 25 August in Edinburgh's Fountainbridge; The Edinburgh Film Guild was founded. Donald Bradman scores 334 for Australia in a Test Match against England; Noel Coward's play *Private Lives* premiere; The Trocadero opens on Princes Street as a Thé Dansant'; R101 Airship crashes near Paris; Haile Selassie crowned Emperor of Ethiopia; Günther Uecker born in Wendorf, Germany.

RIP Sir Arthur Conan Doyle, 7 July.

1931

Royal Navy Mutiny at Invergordon; Britain enters into economic crisis by worldwide Depression; British politics thrown into disarray; Mahatma Gandhi visits Britain; Japan occupies Shanghai in the invasion of China. My parents inherited a world of silent films. The Versailles Peace Treaty was inconclusive. The stage was set for a Second World War.

1932

Richard Demarco's first memory of Pullman Train at Waverley Station involving a silver teapot, a teaspoon and a white-coated waiter. The Pullman was en route to Newcastle-on-Tyne where there were plans to establish a Demarco Thé Dansant in Gosforth; The atom was split by Cockcroft and Walton; BBC begins transmission from new BBC home; Brother Michael is born; Charles Laughton in Academy Award-winning film on *The Life of Henry VIII*.

My first memories were in a Pullman Carriage at Waverley Station whilst striking a silver teapot with a silver teaspoon. My first encounter with the natural world was as a two-year-old child running towards the seashore at Berwick-upon-Tweed through a field of tall grasses and wild flowers with a sea-breeze wafting the ozone-filled air in the morning sunshine.

1933

Second memory of running from the garden of house in Berwick-upon-Tweed through a field of long grass and wild flowers towards the North Sea in bright morning sunlight; Richard Demarco was living in the house of his mother's sister, Minnie. She was married to Alec Donnelly, the bugler of The King's Own Scottish Borderers stationed in their Berwick Barracks; Fred Astaire and Ginger Rogers star in film *Flying Down to Rio*.

Rudolf Bing, as an Austrian Jew, fled

Hitler's Germany to begin a new life in England.

1934

Premiere of Alexander Korda's film *The Scarlet Pimpernel* starring Leslie Howard; The first season of Glyndebourne opens; Richard Demarco's brother, Louis, was born on May 30; Cole Porter's musical *Anything Goes* premiere in New York; Charles Laughton stars as Mr. Barrett in the film *The Barretts of Wimpole Street*; Hawker Hurricane aircraft flew for the first time.

The Glyndebourne Opera Company came into being in Sussex and Rudolf Bing became its first director. The German people went to the polls on 19 August to vote Adolf Hitler into power as Fuhrer and Reich Chancellor.

RIP Sir Edward Elgar.

1935

Premiere of film *39 Steps*; Penguin Books launched; Mandatory driving test introduced; The Art Deco restaurant Rogano opened in Glasgow; Charles Laughton as Captain Bligh in the film *Mutiny on the Bounty*.

RIP TE Lawrence.

I was enrolled in St John's Roman Catholic Primary School in Portobello. I flew in a bi-plane from Portobello Beach, suitably dressed in a white fur suit.

1936

Jarrow March; The Atlantic Ocean liner *Queen Mary*'s maiden voyage from Southampton; Alexander Korda's film *The Shape of Things to Come* with film set as the interior of a space ship designed by Laszlo Moholy-Nagy as Richard Demarco's introduction to Bauhausian art; Premiere of the documentary film *Night Mail* by John Grierson; Richard Demarco begins primary school education at St John's Roman Catholic Primary School, Portobello; Awarded prize for Religious Knowledge at St John's Primary School; General Francisco Franco proclaimed Chief of the Spanish State; Germany and Italy recognise Franco's Fascist government; BBC's first television programme broadcast from the Art Deco building in Portland Place; King Edward VIII renounces his throne; The Crystal Palace is destroyed by fire.

I realised that the families of my mother and father, the Fuscos and Demarcos, had contrasting lifestyles on Portobello Promenade. The Fuscos' Marina Café was a wooden building, wedged between two wooden boathouses; Maison Demarco was Edinburgh's version of a Parisian café. I was driven by Marco Demarco, my aunt Cristina Demarco's chauffeur, in her Buick, the only American car in Edinburgh.

1937

UK forbids British citizens to fight in Spanish Civil War; Coronation of George VI; Premiere of *Gone with the Wind* and *Snow White and the Seven Dwarfs* at Art Deco County cinema in Bath Street, Portobello; Carmine Demarco wins The Powderhall Sprint in the Powderhall greyhound racing stadium; Tea at Jenners with parents; Carmine Demarco defeats Walter Donaldson to become East of Scotland Billiards Champion at the match played in The North British Hotel; Richard Demarco observes American troops arriving in charabancs at the main door of The North British Hotel; Airship *Hindenburg* explodes in New Jersey. Marshal Józef Piłsudski, liberator of Poland.

RIP JM Barrie.

1938

Neville Chamberlain and his Aide de Camp Frank Ashton-Gwatkin meet with Eduarde Daladier, the French Prime Minister, and St John Perse, Daladier's Aide de Camp, to persuade Adolf Hitler to help them declare peace with honour, in Munich; Frank Ashton-Gwatkin and St John Perse, as two poets, became friends at this fateful meeting; Len Hutton scores 334 in a Test Match against Australia; Jewish community in Germany endure 'Night of Terror'; Alfred Hitchcock's film *The Lady Vanishes* starring Basil Radford, Naunton Wayne, Margaret Lockwood, Michael Redgrave and Linden Travers; Nazi Germany annexes Austria.

The threat of World War Two began to loom large. Mussolini's Fascist government had invaded Abyssinia. My father, Carmino Demarco, knew that this did not bode well for the Italian community in Scotland.

1939

Nazi German invades Poland with a Blitzkreig; World War Two begins. 16 October first air raid over Forth; Nine-year-old Richard Demarco attends funeral of the two Luftwaffe airmen in Milton Road Cemetery; *Finnigan's Wake* by James Joyce is published; Richard Demarco evacuated with his mother and two younger brothers to Largs following Carmine Demarco's appointment as

manager of The Moorings; French surrender when German Army enters Paris; Mussolini invades Albania; Robert Donat wins Hollywood's Academy Oscar Award for his acting in the film *Goodbye Mr. Chips*. Thirty-five million gas masks are manufactured in Britain in anticipation of World War Two. In October this year, I narrowly escaped becoming the first child victim of the first Luftwaffe air raid in Britain. A Royal Air Force Spitfire's fusillade of machine gun bullets landed within inches of my bare feet, gleaming like jewels in the wet sand of Portobello Beach. They were aimed at the Luftwaffe *Junkel Bomber* in its death throes. I insisted that my mother took me to the funeral of the two young German pilots. A British Movietone News film provides proof that I stood by their graves as a child mourner.

1940

The Princesses Elizabeth and Margaret broadcast to the Nation; Tragedy hits the Italian community in Scotland with the sinking of the *SS Arandora Star* off the coast of Donegal; Largs, the world of Art Deco defined by the Castelvecchi family's The Moorings and the Nardini family's Café; Mussolini declares war in support of Hitler in June; The Demarco family of Elizabeth Demarco and her three young sons, bereft of their lodging accommodation in Largs, are seated on a park bench until kindly offered alternative lodging after an anxious four-hour wait; Dunkirk – Richard Demarco's uncle, Fr John Fusco, as a British Army Chaplain, is wounded on Dunkirk Beach during evacuation, his forehead wound is in the shape of a cross; Maternal uncles Noel and Francis join the Merchant Navy; Joseph Beuys plans to study medicine and is drafted into the Luftwaffe.

In this second year of World War Two, Oskar Fischinger was living and working in Los Angeles. As a German Jew, he had fled Hitler's Germany. He was the personification of the avant-garde artistic spirit of Germany in the 1930s. He laboriously worked on what must be regarded as hand-crafted colourful abstract images. He is commonly described as an animator and was the creator of a filmic masterpiece entitled *Fantasia*; it is one of the few Hollywood films to ascend to the condition of avant-garde art. I was, therefore, indebted to European artists who suffered the reality of Nazi Germany to give me my first experience of the language of the visual arts on the highest possible level.

RIP John Buchan.

1941

Nazi Germany invades Russia; From the windows of his tenement flat in Largs, Richard Demarco sees the night sky turn red from the air raid on Clydebank; German battleship *Bismark* sunk. Rudolf Hess lands in Scotland; Crete falls to Nazi Germany; Vera Lynn sings *The White Cliffs of Dover*; British troops embark from Largs beach in landing-craft taking them to a convoy of ships en route to North Africa; Italian submarine sinks HMS *Ark Royal* near Gibraltar; Joseph Beuys becomes Stuka navigator; Japan attacks Pearl Harbour.

Rudolf Hess flies to Scotland. A Clyde paddle-steamer voyage from Largs to Millport on the Island of Cumbrae.

RIP James Joyce.

1942

Fall of Singapore; Premiere of Powell and Pressburger's film *One of Our Aircraft is Missing*; Battle of El Alamein and the beginning of British victory in North Africa; Nazi German government begins sending Jewish population to Auschwitz; Italian Prisoner of War camp in Duddingston Village.

Landing-craft on Largs pebble beach involved the embarkation of British Army soldiers to awaiting convoys on the Forth of Clyde.

RIP Carole Lombard, wife of Clark Gable, dies in plane crash.

1943

Thirteen-year-old Richard Demarco leaves St John's Primary School and enters Holy Cross Academy in Class 1a; Italian Government surrenders; Carmine Demarco employed at Leadburn Farm; TS Eliot's *Four Quartets* published; Premiere of Powell and Pressburger's film *The Life and Death of Colonel Blimp*; Italian prisoners of war attend Mass at St John's Roman Catholic Church, together with uniformed Polish soldiers and British members of the Armed Forces forming half of the whole congregation to pray together in the Latin language; Roosevelt, Churchill and Stalin meet in Tehran; Joseph Beuys crashes in Crimea and life saved by Tartars.

Joseph Beuys survives life-threatening injuries from his Stuka bomber plane crash. His life is saved by Tartar tribesmen in the Crimea. Betty Maxton, an artist and schoolteacher, completed a portrait of myself and persuaded my parents and the Demarco family that I should become an art student and therefore benefit from a secondary school education. This led me to being enrolled at Holy Cross Academy. My father was obliged to find work as a labourer in the Midlothian landscape.

RIP Beatrix Potter.

1944

Richard Demarco experiences Laurence Olivier's film of Shakespeare's *Henry V*; Third assault on Monte Cassino; Polish soldiers take Monte Cassino; Paris liberated in August; Invasion of France on D Day; City of Aachen is liberated by US Army; Warsaw Uprising as Russian Army across the Vistula River is ordered not to provide support; Richard Demarco takes afternoon tea in the 18th-century house of Edward and Lucia Maher in the village of Duddingston, Edinburgh. Allied bombers destroy the Abbey of Monte Cassino. Joseph Beuys spends two years as a British prisoner of war.

1945

VE Day in May; VJ Day in August; The Yalta Conference lays the foundation of the Russian Communist empire governing Eastern Europe; Dresden blitzed; Germany surrenders in May; David Lean directs the film version of Noel Coward's play *Brief Encounters*; Labour Party landslide ousts Churchill's Conservative Party; Joseph Beuys is POW in Cuxhaven.

I was dismayed, as a 15-year-old schoolboy, to hear that two Atom bombs had been dropped on the Japanese cities of Hiroshima and Nagasaki. I was introduced to the literature of Charles Dickens by David Lean's film of *Great Expectations*.

1946

One-week vacation in Burntisland, providing 16-year-old Richard Demarco's first experience of River Forth from the Fife coast; Premiere of Terence Rattigan's play *The Winslow Boy*; First session of the United Nations held in London; British film premieres of *Great Expectations* and *Matter of Life and Death*; British National Health Service comes into being; Bread rationing imposed on Britain.

As a 16-year-old Holy Cross rugby player, I suffered a broken collarbone. I purchased my first copy of *Wisden, The Cricketers' Bible* and read it on a sunlit morning in the world of Portobello's Art Deco swimming pool where Tommy (Sean) Connery was employed as a life-guard.

1947

First Edinburgh International Festival comes into being with, after the coldest winter, three uninterrupted weeks of Festival sunshine; Richard Demarco's first experience of orchestral music from the Vienna Philharmonic with Bruno Walter conducting; Experienced Louis Jouvet's theatre company's French language production of Molière's *L'École des Femmes*.

Marriage of Princess Elizabeth to Prince Philip, Duke of Edinburgh; 'Hollywood Ten' blacklisted by American anti-communist committee; Joseph Beuys is art academy student under Ewald Mataré; From Portobello Public Library, Richard Demarco reads Gunby Hadath schoolboy novels illustrated by CM Brock, PG Wodehouse novel *Psmith* inspired by his Dulwich College schooldays, and Captain Marryat's novel *Mr Midshipman Easy*; Compton Mackenzie's novel published entitled *Whisky Galore*; Richard Demarco asks his father to demonstrate making a break of one hundred, as a champion billiard player, in the Bath Street Billiard Club, Portobello's Bath Street. Giles Gilbert Scott's Bankside Power Station was completed and I experienced the Angelic sound of Kathleen Ferrier's voice singing German Lieder. My life was blessed and transformed by the first ever Edinburgh Festival.

1948

Laurence Olivier and Jean Simmons as Hamlet and Ophelia in the film of Shakespeare's *Hamlet*; As a schoolboy, Richard Demarco appointed as manager of Edinburgh's Camera Obscura in Lawnmarket; Zionist state of Israel founded. World premiere in New York of Gian Carlo Menotti's opera *The Telephone*. I met the Scottish actor, Duncan Macrae, who invited me to the rehearsal and world premiere of Tyron Guthrie's historic production of *Ane Satyre of the Thrie Estaitis*. The Edinburgh Film Festival presented 100 films representing 25 nationalities in a programme devised by John Grierson.

1949

Last day at Holy Cross Academy; First day at Edinburgh College of Art; First meeting with John OR Martin and Douglas Soeder; Holy Cross Academy visit to Paris and Annecy via London and Calais; Ealing comedy *Passage to Pimlico* film premiere; St John's Catholic Parish Church cricket team was established. Richard Demarco played over 40 cricket matches, both for Holy Cross Academy as Vice-Captain and for St John's cricket team; China proclaimed a 'Peoples Republic' under

the leadership of Mao Tse Tung; George Orwell's novel *1984* is published; Richard Demarco is elected Captain of Holy Cross Academy's First Fifteen Rugby Team.

Holy Cross Academy introduced me to the reality of London and Paris and, what is most important, the avant-garde dance-theatre of Les Ballets des Champs Elysees. This production was my outstanding experience of the 1949 Edinburgh International Festival.

1950

Richard Demarco's Holy Year Pilgrimage to Rome with his father Carmine Demarco; At High Mass in St Peter's Basilica in Rome, Richard Demarco meets Peter Jansen who became Richard Demarco's German pen friend and introduced him to Thomas Mann's *The Magic Mountain*; Peter Jansen emigrated to USA to become Professor of International Literature at the University of Michigan; China enters Korean conflict; Richard Demarco is inspired by the art of fellow students George Mackay and Barbara Balmer and by the English war artists, Eric Ravillious and Edward Bawden.

The Edinburgh Festival, under the direction of Ian Hunter, presented two new Scottish plays – *The Queen's Comedy* by James Bridie and *The Atom Doctor* by Eric Linklater. The official programme was dominated by the genius of the Rembrandt exhibition. The Glyndebourne Opera presented two productions – *Ariadne auf Naxos*, an opera by Hugo von Hofmannsthal and *Le Bourgeois Gentilhomme*. The Edinburgh Film Festival presented 170 films.

1951

Premiere of the film *The Cruel Sea* written by Nicholas Monsarrat; Keith Douglas collected poems published; Richard Demarco visits Festival of Britain in London; The Stone of Scone stolen; Richard Demarco's 21st birthday party at 17 Bath Street, Portobello, the home of his cousins Norma and Christine Demarco; Richard Demarco awarded a small scholarship to travel to London, together with John Martin, staying in the Actors Club in Soho Square; Richard Demarco makes drawings of war-damaged buildings in London; Richard Demarco makes an oil painting of Tommy Connery as his life model.

This Festival was dominated, for me, by Ben Johnson's *Bartholomew Fair* at Church of Scotland's Assembly Hall. On the Edinburgh Festival Fringe, there was a production of Ewan MacColl's play *Uranium 235* performed by Theatre Workshop at Oddfellows Hall as part of the Edinburgh Peoples' Festival which was supported by the Scottish poet and folklorist Hamish Henderson. The Citizens' Theatre production of *The Thrie Estaitis* directed by Tyrone Guthrie. An exhibition of Spanish painting at The Royal Scottish Academy.

RIP Phillipe Pétain, aged 95, in prison.

1952

Princess Elizabeth becomes Queen Elizabeth II on the death of her father, King George V; Churchill returns to lead Conservative Party in Westminster; Agatha Christie's play *The Mousetrap* opens in London.

The New York City Ballet under the direction of George Balanchine. The Edgar Degas exhibition curated by Derek Hill; Premiere of Gian Carlo Menotti's *Amahl and the Night Visitors*. Claire Bloom and Alan Badel star in the Old Vic Theatre production of Shakespeare's *Romeo and Juliet*. Emlyn Williams' theatre production of Charles Dickens' *Bleak House*. I travelled to Paris by rail to begin work on my publication of what I entitled *My Paris Diary*, written and designed as my centrepiece for my diploma exhibition in 1953 as a design student at Edinburgh College of Art.

1953

Richard Demarco is elected Secretary and exhibition organiser of Edinburgh College of Art's Sketch Club; His etching attracts the attention of Sir William Gillies when judging the annual Diploma in Art influence of Samuel Palmer; Richard Demarco graduates from Edinburgh College of Art; Coronation of Queen Elizabeth II; *Waiting for Godot* premiered in Paris; Sean Connery as James Bond in *Casino Royale*; *The Quatermass* television play is broadcast; Film premiere of *The Wages of Fear* starring Yves Montand.

American National Theatre Ballet production of *The Square Dance*. The Marcel Marceau Mime Theatre Company. The Edinburgh Festival commissioned TS Eliot to write his play *The Confidential Clerk*.

The Old Vic Theatre production of Shakespeare's *Hamlet* with Richard Burton as Hamlet and Claire Bloom as Ophelia. As hotel receptionist, I welcomed them both to The Caledonian Hotel, as well as TS Eliot, Thornton Wilder and Alexander Fleming. Glyndebourne Opera presented the British premiere of their production of

Stravinsky's *The Rake's Progress* as well as Rossini's opera *Cenerentola*. There was an unforgettable Renoir exhibition at The Royal Scottish Academy. Orson Welles was invited by the Edinburgh Film Festival. He declared that the film industry was dying. RIP Dylan Thomas aged 53. RIP Eugene O'Neill.

RIP Hilaire Belloc.

1954

Richard Demarco graduates from Moray House Teachers' Training College; British Surrealist humour *The Goon Show* on BBC radio; End of rationing in Britain; Richard Demarco begins National Service in KOSB barracks in Berwick-upon-Tweed, and then to Royal Army Education Corps at Beaconsfield and becomes senior instructor, stationed at Royal Ordnance Army Corps Headquarters and Royal Electrical and Mechanical Engineers based at Bicester, 15 miles from Oxford; Roger Bannister's 4-minute mile; Forth Studios established in York Place by John Martin and Douglas Soeder; Joseph Beuys suffers nervous breakdown; Premiere of the film *The Maggie* directed by Alexander Mackendrick who had also directed the film *Whisky Galore*.

The Edinburgh Festival was dominated by Richard Buckle's historic exhibition celebrating the life of Diaghilev with over 1,000 exhibits, transforming the interior of Edinburgh College of Art. I was pleased to see that Richard Buckle relied on Leonard Rosoman as a muralist at Edinburgh College of Art. He was my inspiring mural teacher. The main Festival exhibition was an unforgettable manifestation of the genius of Cézanne as well as

an exceptional ballet production of Stravinsky's *The Soldier's Tale* with memorable performances by Moira Shearer and Robert Helpmann. This was the year when I began my National Service, training to be an infantry soldier fighting in North Korea at the historic King's Own Scottish Borderers barracks in Berwick-upon-Tweed. RIP Lionel Barrymore.

RIP Sir John Falconer.

1955

The Dam Buster's film premiere; Stirling Moss wins British Grand Prix; Ruth Ellis is hanged; ITV begins; Richard Demarco meets Dr John Thomson at Dominican Centre, Oxford University, who commissions him to make a suite of four watercolours to help illustrate his experimental work at the Radcliffe Hospital in Oxford.

Robert Ponsonby became the successor to Ian Hunter as the third Director of the Edinburgh International Festival. Thirty university rectors were invited to attend a conference entitled 'The Universities and the Arts'. Laurence Hardy and Madeleine Christie starred in Thornton Wilder's production of *A Life in the Sun*, directed by Tyrone Guthrie. Glydebourne Opera production of Giuseppe Verdi's opera of *The Barber of Seville* conducted by Carlo Mario Giulini. Douglas Cooper curated an unforgettable Gaugin exhibition. Vittorio de Sica attended his film *L'oro di Napoli*; he prophesied a revival of what he termed Neo-Realismo. David Baxandall, as Director-General of the National Galleries of Scotland, considered the Gaugin exhibition to be 'the greatest Festival exhibition of the series.'

1956

Premiere of Powell and Pressburger's
film *Battle of the River Plate*; Duke
of Edinburgh Award created; John
Osborne's play *Look Back in Anger*
premiere in London; Richard Demarco
attends performance in the Royal
Lyceum Theatre in Edinburgh with Lee
Klayme; Richard Demarco as Sergeant
in Royal Army Education Corps
teaching map-reading to REME soldiers,
Bicester and establishing friendship with
Boyd Tunnock, David Wheelock and
Major Henry T Morgan; Introduced to
Matthias Leber and Sebastian Littmann,
adopted sons of John Thomson; Richard
Demarco demob from National Service;
UK withdraws from Suez.

This was the tenth anniversary of the
Edinburgh Festival. The outstanding
theatre production *Under Milkwood*
was inspired by the poetry of Dylan
Thomas. Gene Kelly was invited to
celebrate the 10th Edinburgh Film
Festival and attend his film *Invitation to
the Dance*. It received Royal approval
by the presence of Queen Elizabeth,
the Duke of Edinburgh and Princess
Margaret. The Piccolo Theatre of
Milan presented their production of
Pirandello's play *Questa Sera Si Recita
A Soggetto*. The major exhibition
curated by Douglas Cooper was an
unforgettable manifestation of the
genius of George Braque. There are two
quotations which revealed his profound
and revolutionary vision of the world;
'Reality only reveals itself when it
is illuminated by a ray of poetry, all
around us is asleep' and 'Let us forget
things and consider only the relationship
between them'.

1957

Marriage to Anne Muckle at the
Church of St Ninian and St Triduana
in the parish of Restalrig in Edinburgh;
To London, Kings Cross Hotel; To El
Cuban, London's first coffee bar in
Kensington; Read Thomas Merton's
Elected Silence; First meeting with
Jim Haynes at an Oxford University
Dramatic Society's production of Ugo
Betti's play *Corruption in the Palace of
Justice*, followed by coffee in The Laigh
Coffee House; Britain refused entry into
European Union (EEC); Joseph Beuys
works on the van der Grinten brothers'
farm.

I was appointed Art Master at Scotus
Academy, Edinburgh.

RIP Oliver Hardy aged 65.
RIP Beniamino Gigli.

1958

Richard and Anne Demarco move to
the top flat in 18th-century building at
29 Frederick Street; Manchester United
plane crash in Munich; Film premiere
of *Saturday Night and Sunday Morning*
by Alan Sillitoe; Film of *Bridge over the
River Kwai* receives an Oscar; Painted
the Edinburgh mural at the Camera
Obscura with John OR Martin and
Peter McGinn; Dalai Lama flees Tibet;
Joseph Beuys marries Eva Wurmbach.

Tyrone Guthrie directed an Ulster
Theatre production at the Lyceum
Theatre of a play entitled *The Bonfire* by
Gerald McLarnon. Also at the Lyceum,
there was an unmissable late-night
entertainment performed by Dame
Peggy Ashcroft, and Osian Ellis. This
was entitled *Portrait of Women; From
Chaucer to Dylan Thomas*. This was
the year when Jacob Epstein completed

his masterpiece sculpture *Jacob and the Angel*. Alan Sillitoe published his novel *Saturday Night and Sunday Morning* and Harold Pinter's play *The Birthday Party* was premiered in London. However, the Edinburgh Festival programme was overshadowed by The Expo Exhibition in Brussels represented by the large-scale Atomium. This provided a glimpse into the future of culture and gave me nourishing food for thought regarding the Edinburgh Festival's future.

1959

Premiere in London of Harold Pinter's play *The Caretaker*; Richard and Anne Demarco, at the invitation of Gail Penners' parents, fly from Prestwick Airport on a KLM 4-engine flight to Idlewild (now JFK) Airport and then by road to Kennebunkport and thereafter to North Carolina, travelling by train, *Chattanooga Choo Choo, leaving Pennsylvania Station on Track* 29 and arriving in New Orleans Station where race relations make black population an underprivileged class.

This was the year when Jim Haynes completed his National Service and returned to the United States, riven by the horror of racial segregation. Edinburgh without the presence of Jim Haynes was unthinkable to me. I therefore felt it necessary to help him consider his future life to be in Europe and, in particular, Edinburgh then populated by those American Ivy League university students who were completing their 'Junior Year Abroad' and, of course, the cosmopolitan nature of the Edinburgh Festival. I cannot forget our meeting in New Orleans when I knew that I did, indeed, help

him make the decision which led him to live the remainder of his life in Europe and provide Edinburgh not only with the Paperback Bookshop but also with the Traverse Theatre Club. This was the year when the Edinburgh Festival Fringe Society was formed.

RIP Kay Kendall. RIP Stanley Spencer. RIP Mike Hawthorn; RIP Jacob Epstein.

1960

Independence Day for Cyprus; The Royal Shakespeare Company formed. Last 'call-up' for National Service; Jim Haynes opens the Paperback Bookshop; Alfred Hitchcock's film *Psycho*; Richard Demarco is commissioned to illustrate the BBC publications for Scottish schools, illustrating for example the Battle of Largs, Saint Columba's Missionary Travels throughout the Celtic Highlands and Islands, the pre-historic community centred on crannogs built offshore on Loch Tay, the Roman army building Hadrian's Wall between the Tyne and the Solway, and the steeples of the London churches, inspiring the children's folk songs. He was also commissioned by Forth Studios to illustrate Scottish National Trust brochures including those illustrating the historic architecture of Culross and Haddington. Richard Demarco was also commissioned by Arthur Oldham to design posters for programmes for Arthur Oldham's Scotus Academy productions of *The Pirates of Penzance* and *The Land of Green Ginger,* as well as record covers of the choral music composed by Arthur Oldham illustrating Christmas carols sung by the choristers of St Mary's Roman Catholic Metropolitan Cathedral, and for Cedric Thorpe Davie's *The Jolly Beggars.*

This was the year when, on a particular unforgettable evening, I experienced Ingmar Bergman's masterpiece film *The Virgin Spring*. It was the British premiere and, still quite stunned by the experience, I went unsuspectingly to what was an historic event in the Edinburgh Festival's history. I attended another world premiere but it was not of a film; it was at the Royal Lyceum Theatre which was only one-quarter full. It was *Beyond The Fringe*, proving beyond doubt that the programme of the official Edinburgh Festival is entwined with that of the Festival's Fringe.

The incomparable Beatrice Lillie also performed in a late-night entertainment at the Lyceum Theatre but her performance did not provide a theatrical experience which altered the Edinburgh Festival's future. This was the year that Boris Pasternak died, but it was also the year when the Edinburgh Festival visual arts programme, for the first time, presented an exhibition of living artists and, in particular, those who could be defined as defenders of the 20th century avant-garde. The exhibition was curated by Pierre Restany and it was entitled The New Realists. It included Yves Klein, Raymond Hains, Daniel Spoerri and his friend Arman, four of the most important 20th-century artists. RIP Aneurin Bevan.

RIP Clark Gable aged 59.

1961

'Beyond The Fringe' opens in London; University of Sussex founded; Muriel Spark's novel, *The Prime of Miss Jean Brodie*, published; Joseph Beuys appointed Professor of Sculpture at Kunstakademie Düsseldorf; Yuri Gagarin is the first man in space; Rudolf Nureyev defects to France.

This was the year when, again, a most important Edinburgh Festival visual arts experience in the form of the Jacob Epstein exhibition in, of all places, the expansive space of The Waverley Market, an extension of Edinburgh's Waverley railway station. This was the first year of George, Lord Harewood's directorship of the Edinburgh International Festival. Lord Harewood had chosen Alexander Schouvaloff to be his assistant director. Together, they were fully prepared to support my suggestion that the Festival should be presented in harmony with the Venice Biennale and the German city of Kassel's dOCUMENTA exhibition.

Lord Harewood wrote the illuminating foreword to the catalogue of the exhibition entitled *Masterpieces of French Painting from the Burrell Collection*. This was completely at home in The Royal Scottish Academy's galleries. The exhibition benefited from the tireless commitment of Joanna Drew who worked unremittingly for its success as the British Council's exhibitions curator.

RIP Sir Thomas Beecham. RIP Augustus John. RIP Grandma Moses aged 101.

1962

Richard Demarco appointed lecturer in Design for evening classes at Edinburgh College of Art.

The Edinburgh Festival benefited from what was known as The Writers' Conference. It came into being under the direction of John Calder and Jim Haynes. It brought the world's leading writers to Edinburgh University's McEwan Hall and, unlike the concept of the Edinburgh Book Festival later on, those attending were encouraged to exchange their thoughts as writers, sometimes leading to argument. I was introduced to JB Priestley and Lillian Hellman when I was asked by John Calder to drive them in my little Mini car from Musselburgh to Edinburgh city centre. I will never forget their conversation which was all about their appraisal of the writings of TE Lawrence.

I cannot forget this year because I was given the opportunity to present my first ever one-man exhibition in the newly opened Douglas and Fowlis Gallery. I sold 105 of my 115 watercolours and pen drawings but it was more important because it attracted Richard Buckle who became my first serious art patron and commissioned me to create an oil painting on a 16 x 9 ft canvas on the Spirit of Culture descending upon the City of Dundee for Dundee's Repertory Theatre. Another visitor was the world-famous American novelist William Burroughs, author of *The Air-Conditioned Nightmare* and also Abraham Rattner, the founder of New York's Stable Gallery.

This was also the year when I do believe the Traverse Theatre began its remarkable life. It resulted from a telephone conversation that I had with Patrick Prenter, then a Cambridge University undergraduate. He asked me if I could suggest an alternative Fringe venue to the Cambridge Footlights venue for two of his fellow undergraduates. Patrick Prenter's two friends were John Cleese and Tim Brooke-Taylor. I telephoned my good friend Tom Mitchell who had just bought a seven-storey 17th-century building in Edinburgh's Lawnmarket. This Cambridge University student theatre venue was entitled 'The Sphinx Club'. Five months later, it opened as the Traverse Theatre Club.

RIP Marilyn Monroe aged 36.

1963

Opening of the Traverse Theatre Club on 2 January; Drama Conference presented by the Traverse Theatre Club in the McEwan Hall which provides the ideal space for the Festival's first 'Happening' organised by Allan Kaprow, Mark Boyle, Ken Dewey and Carol Baker, includes a naked female wheeled across a balcony in the prestigious hall of Edinburgh University, causing a sensation; *Comedy, Satire and Deeper Meaning* at The Traverse written by Dieter Sebastian Grabbe, directed by Terry Lane; Installation of Mark Boyle's sculpture in the Traverse Theatre Club; Alec Douglas Home elected Prime Minister; Contraceptive pill made available.

Vice-Chairman of The Traverse Theatre Club until 1967.

The Edinburgh Festival was dominated, for me, by the successor to The Writers' Conference. This was The Drama Conference that brought the world's leading dramatists to the Edinburgh International Festival but it also introduced into the Festival the shock-tactics of those artists who would be known as performance artists.

They included the 'father of performance art', sometimes known as 'happenings'. He was the American-Polish artist Allan Kaprow, but he was aided and abetted by Mark Boyle, Ken Dewey and Carol Baker. The spirit of Dada had arrived to shock Edinburgh. The Traverse Theatre Club had opened its doors on a bitterly cold January night with two theatre productions directed by Terry Lane. They were Jean-Paul Sartre's *Huis Clos* and Fernando Arrabal's *Orison*. He, together with his wife, Rosamund Dickson, brought the open-stage spirit of the Stephen Joseph Theatre to The

Traverse. As Vice-Chairman of The Traverse Theatre Club's founding committee, I opened The Traverse Art Gallery with an exhibition of Polish posters in collaboration with the Polish Cultural Institute in London.

RIP John F Kennedy, assassinated in Dallas, Texas. RIP Jean Cocteau aged 74. RIP CS Lewis. RIP Aldous Huxley.

1964

To Wareham, Dorset, to meet Alastair Michie in his studio; BBC 2 television is born; The Forth Bridge is opened; Peter Brook directs *Marat Sade*; Richard Demarco drives Alexander Mackendrick and Larry Adler on a tour of the Highlands to the Pitlochry Theatre; Traverse Gallery exhibition in the Bank of Scotland building in George Street includes Mark Boyle, Xavier Corberó, Abraham Rattner; Pete McGinn introduces Richard Demarco to Susan MacDonald Lockhart who invigilates the Traverse Gallery exhibition in George Street. Sue later becomes the partner of Ian Hamilton Finlay and provides him with her family farm on a windswept hillside, 30 miles south of Edinburgh; Countess of Rosebery attends two performances at The Traverse Theatre Club of the British premiere of the Off-Off Broadway musical *The Fantastiks; An Evening with Sir Compton MacKenzie* at The Traverse; Richard Demarco commissioned by Richard Buckle to be one of the artists in the exhibition celebrating the 400th anniversary of Shakespeare's birth presented as part of the official Edinburgh Festival exhibition programme with artists such as Jean Hugo, Cecil Beaton, David Hockney, which also toured to

Stratford-upon-Avon, with Richard Demarco's three-dimensional painting of *As You Like It*.

Richard Demarco meets Robert Shure in Traverse Theatre restaurant, together with Susan Michie, whilst quoting Robert Shure's poetry; Harold Wilson elected Prime Minister; Richard Demarco is introduced to Patrick Heron in The King's Head in Chelsea by the Canadian artist, Bill Featherstone who was then living close to Patrick Heron's home at Eagles Nest at Zennor, near Land's End.

Tom Wright wrote the play *There was a Man*. It proved to be a tour de force because John Cairney brought Robert Burns fully to life. He performed this at a gala Traverse performance in which the guest was Lord Snowdon. He also performed this at John Calder's Opera Festival, also known as Ledlanet Nights. I regarded Ledlanet Nights as an extension of the Traverse Theatre Club world.

Of course, this year was dominated by the death of Sir Winston Churchill and Harold Wilson being elected as Prime Minister. I decided to present a major exhibition of seven international artists associated with the Traverse Gallery but not in the Gallery but in an office of the Bank of Scotland, on George Street. This exhibition was praised by Douglas Hall, Keeper of the Scottish National Gallery of Modern Art. It was providing proof that the Traverse Gallery was determined to present contemporary international artists. The artists were led by Abraham Rattner who was associated with New York's historic Stable Gallery and his wife, Esther Gentle, Allen Leepa who was a fellow New York-based artist, Xavier Corberó's sculpture received high praise from Robert Hughes, the author of

The Shock of the New, Olivier Herdies from Sweden, William Featherstone, a Canadian sculptor, as well as Mark Boyle, the London-based avant-gardist.

The major play of the official Edinburgh Festival programme was Michael Jeliot's production of Shakespeare's *Macbeth* presented by the Traverse Theatre on the open stage of The Church of Scotland's Assembly Hall.

1965

Alan Harrison Collection exhibition at the Traverse Gallery includes Louis le Brocquy, Karel Appel, Henry Moore, Graham Sutherland, Patrick Heron; The Beatles appointed MBE at Buckingham Palace; Joseph Beuys exhibition at the Schmela Gallery; Richard Demarco is invited by Sir Roland Penrose to a Friends of the Tate reception in the Tate Gallery at Millbank and introduces him to HRH Princess Margaret; Richard Demarco encourages HRH Princess Margaret to visit the Traverse Theatre and its New York equivalent, La Mama Theatre founded by Ellen Stewart; Richard Demarco meets Sir Roland Penrose in the Institute of Contemporary Art in Dover Street, London; Sir Roland Penrose, Norman Reid and David Baxandall as jury meet at London's Mall Galleries to select 100 paintings out of a submission of around 2,000 to be included in The Demarco Gallery's *Open Hundred* Edinburgh exhibition; John Martin invites Sir Roland Penrose and his wife, Lee Miller, and me, to dinner in Prestonfield House.

The year began with an extraordinary collection of art at the Traverse Gallery which questioned the inward-looking nature of the Scottish art world. It was an exhibition which brought together artists from the Alan Harrison Collection who was a Newcastle-upon-Tyne-based art collector. It represented the following leading English artists; Henry Moore, Graham Sutherland, Derek Hirst, Allen Jones, Henry Mundy and Patrick Heron as well as the doyenne of Irish artists, Louis le Brocquy, and William Johnstone who famously directed London's Camberwell School of Art.

The Traverse Gallery presented an exhibition of paintings by Patrick Heron and Bryan Wynter at Edinburgh University's Hume Tower in collaboration with the University, two of the leading artists of the School of St Ives. Unfortunately, this was the last year under the direction of Lord Harwood. His Directorship was cut short; he and his deputy, Alexander Schouvaloff, were totally supportive of my proposal that the official Edinburgh Festival should cease their programme of famous dead artists and focus on living artists, especially those who were living on the 'wrong' side of the Iron Curtain.

This was a bonus year at the Traverse Theatre Club. Memorable productions included *Green Julia* starring Jonathan Lynn who later co-wrote *Yes, Minister*, Edward Albee's *Zoo Story*, Robert Pinget's' *The Old Tune*, Robert Shure's world premiere of *Oh Gloria* directed by Max Stafford-Clark with Dinah Stabb, *The Wen* and *Orange Souffle* by Saul Bellow. The Scaffold established a cultural dialogue between Edinburgh and Liverpool, with Roger McGough, John Gorman and Mike McGear with *Lily the Pink*. Lady Rosebery attended the Fantasticks twice. *The Turquoise Pantomime* was devised and performed by Lindsay Kemp.

RIP Richard Dimbleby.

1966

During the Edinburgh Festival, The Richard Demarco Gallery opens at 8 Melville Crescent with 57 artists associated with London-based art galleries such as The Marlborough, Redfern, Hamilton, Axiom and Waddington; Exhibition at the Traverse Gallery of Iago Pericot and Polish Posters; Laker Airways is born; Joseph Beuys performs *Manresa* in Düsseldorf; Jorge Castillo exhibition at Melville Crescent; Also three exhibitions with Juuko Ikewada, Ian McKenzie Smith and William Rothgrave at Goldbergs Department Store. Director of The Richard Demarco Gallery to 1992.

The Richard Demarco Gallery's inaugural exhibition in 8 Melville Crescent in Edinburgh's New Town presented the art of Patrick Heron, Serge Poliakoff, Ben Nicholson, Victor Pasmore, John Houston and Robin Philipson.

RIP Walt Disney.

1967

Edinburgh Festival *Open 100* exhibition at Edinburgh University's Hume Tower; Demarco Gallery exhibition of Italian art from Italian National Gallery of Modern Art in Rome in collaboration with Giorgio di Marels; Italian avant-garde sculpture at Inverleith House; Richard Demarco appointed Director of Edinburgh International Festival's exhibition programme of international contemporary art; Dr Christian Barnard performs new heart surgery in Capetown; Retrospective exhibition of Patrick Heron; Julian Snelling, John Piper retrospective, tapestries by Aurèlia Muñoz and Sax Shaw; Exhibitions at The Demarco Gallery by Édgar Negret,

John Eaves, Nigerian artists from Osogbo, exhibitions by Martin Bradley, John Christoforou, Cecil King, Justin Knowles, Frank Phelan, retrospective of Patrick Heron, 15 UK artists participate in Warsaw exhibition including Rory McEwen, Patrick Heron and Robin Philipson.

Elected to the Society of Scottish Artists (SSA). I was appointed Director of the Edinburgh International Festival's programme of contemporary art. This began my 25-year directorship with the exhibition entitled 'The Edinburgh Open 100'. Over 2,000 artists competed for this exhibition with the three-man jury consisting of Sir Roland Penrose as Director of the London-based Institute of Contemporary Art, Sir Norman Reid, Director of the Tate Gallery, and David Baxandall who was the Director-General of the National Galleries of Scotland.

RIP Vivien Leigh. RIP Rita Hayworth.

1968

Richard Demarco is asked by The Canada Council to present the avant-garde art of Canada which results in the Edinburgh International Festival *Canada 101* exhibition at Edinburgh College of Art; Joseph Beuys at documenta; Richard Demarco with Édgar Negret as winner of the Venice Biennale's Sculpture Prize, resulting in a visit to Amsterdam; Richard Demarco's first visits to Poland and Romania; Students protest at Venice Biennale; Meetings with Paolo Patelli and Annely Juda, Gerald Furtz, Alan Bowness and Pierre Restany in Venice.

I was commissioned by The Canada Council to present the Edinburgh International Festival exhibition of Canadian contemporary art supported by the Art Gallery of Toronto, the Art Gallery of Vancouver and the Galerie National de Quebec in Montreal. RIP Robert Donat.

1969

Four Romanian artists exhibition at The Demarco Gallery, touring to Aberdeen Art Gallery – Bitzan, Neagu and the Jacobis; First flight of Concorde and sound barrier broken; Exhibition of Rory McEwen's *The Tweed Road* installation at Melville Crescent; Performance of *The Turquoise Pantomine* by Lindsay Kemp at Melville Crescent; Exhibition of concrete poetry and kinetic art at Melville Crescent; Duke of Edinburgh visits exhibition of Polish art at Melville Crescent; *Monty Python's Flying Circus* begins on BBC; Willy Brandt elected German Chancellor; USA astronauts land on the Moon 20 July; Richard Demarco watches the historic moment on Italian television in Rome. Elected Member of the Royal Society of Watercolour Painters (RSW). RIP Judy Garland.

The Demarco Gallery's exhibition of London-based artists at Edinburgh College of Art which included William Crozier, Mark Vaux and Tony Underhill, in collaboration with the Annely Juda Gallery. Also, at The Demarco Gallery in Melville Crescent, there was a major exhibition of the sculpture by Rory McEwen.

1970

Edinburgh International Festival exhibition Strategy: Get Arts. Richard Demarco guest of American government, touring from coast to coast, visiting many American universities such as Yale, Harvard, Chicago; Richard Demarco guest of West German Government; Joseph Beuys explores Rannoch Moor with Rory McEwen; Exhibition of Breakwell, Furnival Houldard, David Tremlett at Goldberg's Store; Richard Demarco makes film entitled *Walkabout Edinburgh*; Julian Glover and Timothy West, as James Boswell and Dr Johnson, visit Strategy; Get Arts exhibition at Edinburgh College of Art as members of the Prospect Theatre Company when the members of the Prospect Theatre Company used The Demarco Gallery as an addition to their Green Room during the Edinburgh Festival when Scottish Television were using the Gallery as an extension of their Festival office under the patronage of Tony Firth, Director of STV.

The Demarco Gallery's Festival exhibition was at Edinburgh College of Art with the palindromic title Strategy; Get Arts. This introduced the avant-garde artists of Düsseldorf to Britain; they included Joseph Beuys, Sigmar Polke, Blinky Palermo, Gerhard Richter, George Brecht and Günther Uecker.

1971

Edinburgh International Festival exhibition of 11 Romanian artists in Melville Crescent; Exhibition of Stefan Wewerka prints; Exhibitions of Eric Ritchie, Michael Craig-Martin, Li Yuan-chia, Phillipe Mora, Gordon Bryce, and five Belgium artists including Marcel Broodthaers at Melville Crescent; In November, exhibitions of Ed Rusche and Michael Peel at Melville Crescent; Richard Demarco lectures to Edinburgh University students Liberal Club and to students of the School of Divinity; to Brighton Polytechnic art school, and to the Law Society at The Roxburgh Hotel, Edinburgh; Taiwan expelled from United Nations to allow China to join.

The Demarco Gallery's official Festival exhibition was of Romanian artists at 8 Melville Crescent. They included Paul Neagu, Ion Bitzan, Horia Bernea, Ilie Pavel and Ovidiu Maitec. Bucharest's Bulandra Theatre was directed by Liviu Ciulei with their production of Bruckner's play *Leonce and Lena* at the Royal Lyceum Theatre. There was also a poetry reading was by Marin Sorescu; and Miriam Răducanu presented her contemporary dance performance art at The Demarco Gallery in Melville Crescent.

1972

First EDINBURGH ARTS experimental university of the arts; Robert Shure becomes Editor of The Demarco Gallery's publication *Parasol*; Richard Demarco attends filming of *The Wicker Man* in Dumfries and Galloway, invited to do so by Stuart Hopps; Sean Connery meets three film-makers from the Polish National Film School, Józef Robakowski, Ryszard Gajewski and Wojciech Bruszewski; Exhibitions of Gavin Scobie, Ion Bitzan, three South African artists including Kevin Atkinson at Hopetoun House; Uruguayan air crash in Andes of Catholic rugby team; Richard Nixon visits China. Became Director of Sean Connery's Scottish Education Trust 1972–73.

The Richard Demarco Gallery's official Festival exhibition *Atelier 72* was of the Polish avant-garde at Melville Crescent as well as at the Poorhouse in Forrest Hill in which Tadeusz Kantor's Cricot 2 Theatre performed their production of Stanisław Ignacy Witkiewicz's play *The*

Water Hen. Józef Szjana's production of *Replique* was performed at The Demarco Gallery. His installation on the façade of The Demarco Gallery was in homage to his fellow victims of Auschwitz. Magdalena Abakanowicz's sculptural installation linked St Mary's Episcopal Cathedral with The Demarco Gallery.

RIP William Boyd (Hopalong Cassidy).

1973

Second EDINBURGH ARTS summer school; Joseph Beuys' 12-hour Lecture at Melville College; At Saltire Society Gallery, Paul Neagu's Generative Art Group; Exhibitions at Melville Crescent of Kate Heron, Leon van Stadk; EDINBURGH ARTS participants included Tina Brown, Marina Abramović, Peter Selz and Margaret Tait; Tina Brown's play *Under the Bamboo Tree* is premiered at the Edinburgh Festival under the aegis of EDINBURGH ARTS '73; Sean Connery, together with Tina Brown and Auberon Waugh, attends Tadeusz Kantor's Cricot 2 Theatre's production of the Witkiewicz play *Lovelies and Dowdies*; Sydney Opera House opens.

Governor of Carlisle School of Art 1973–74. Scottish Sculpture exhibition at Fruitmarket Gallery, touring to Leeds and Glasgow; Exhibition and symposium at Bonito Oliva's *Incontri Internazionali d'Arte Roma*; to Motovun and symposium.

Another highlight of The Demarco Gallery's EDINBURGH ARTS Edinburgh Festival programme was a lecture by Frank Ashton-Gwatkin on the Arthurian legend delivered in the Abbey of Culross. There was also a film show and master class by Margaret Tait in The Demarco Gallery, and The 12-hour Lecture by Joseph Beuys in the

Melville College gymnasium, as well
as exhibitions of Austrian, French, and
Serbian artists from the Serbian student
art centre in Belgrade. Among them was
Marina Abramović who took part in a
programme of performance art.

RIP Noel Coward.

1974

Third EDINBURGH ARTS; Black
and White Oil Conference at Forrest
Hill Poorhouse; Exhibitions of French
artists including Christian Boltanski,
Serbian artists, Austrian artists, Anton
Christian, Richard Kriesche; Paul
Neagu performing *Going Tornado* at
Grampian Television; Exhibitions by
Ovidiu Maitec, Nigel Hall; Showing
of Ken McMullen's film of *Lovelies
and Dowdies;* Watergate trial begins in
Washington; Ulrike Meinhof jailed for 8
years. Appointed Kentucky Colonel USA.

The EDINBURGH ARTS '74
programme included five lectures by
Norbert Lynton, Sir Roland Penrose,
Colin Thompson, Douglas Hall,
David Baxandall. There were also
'actions' performed in the Forrest Hill
Poorhouse by Paul Neagu, Bill Beech,
Jane Whitaker, as well as lectures by
Magdalena Abakanowicz and Peter Selz.
The dance programme was directed by
Sally Potter and Jacky Lansley. Jud Fine
made a sculptural installation for one of
the pavilions at Hopetoun House. There
were also exhibitions by six Kansas City
Art Institute artists, from the Boston
Fine Arts Society and four Galleria del
Cavallino artists from Venice.

RIP Cole Porter aged 71. RIP Vittorio de
Sica.

1975

Fourth EDINBURGH ARTS; *From
Hagar Qim to Callanish*. Symposium
at Monteith House Gallery with Count
Panza and Karl Ruhrberg; Peggy Stuffi
and Paolo Patelli exhibition at Malta's
National Gallery. Recipient of Scottish
Arts Council Award £2,000.

The Italian artists Anselmo Anselmi and
Peggy Stuffi exhibited at the National
Gallery of Malta in Valletta as their
contribution to the exhibition entitled *To
Callanish from Hagar Qim*. In Malta, there
were plein air actions by Brian McDonald,
Paolo Patelli, Barbara Kozłowska and
Zbigniew Makarewicz. They were among
the artists who exhibited at the Fruitmarket
Gallery and at The Demarco Gallery
in Monteith House where there was an
international symposium on the subject of
The Artist as Explorer.

Among the participants were Count
Panza di Biumo, and Susan Brundage,
assistant to Leo Castelli in his New York
Gallery, as well as Richard England. Of
particular interest was David Jansheski's
dialogue with the inmates of The Special
Unit involving them in an exhibition
which he installed at the old Fruitmarket
Gallery in Market Street (now the City
Art Centre). The EDINBURGH ARTS
programme then established itself in
the primary school of Lochgilphead
and there a programme of avant-garde
actions took place inspired by the tidal
forces of Loch Gilp and the Celtic
history of Argyll and Bute. Devora
Cutler and her sister Wendy filmed the
Lochgilphead programme. There was
also the EDINBURGH ARTS expedition
to Berwickshire and Marchmont House.

RIP Arnold Toynbee (historian).
RIP General Franco. RIP Dmitri
Shostakovich.

1976

Fifth EDINBURGH ARTS. *From Hagar Qim to Ring of Brodgar*; Exhibition entitled 'Defence of the Innocent'; Jimmy Boyle and Joseph Beuys in collaboration at The Demarco Gallery in Monteith House; Also at Monteith House, exhibition of drawings by Dallas Brown, Il Lothvins lapscapes; Six artists selected by William Packer are Hall, Loker, Wayloe, Percy, Roberts and Stevens; 21–22 April, meetings planning EDINBURGH ARTS at RCA London and Burleighfield; Jimmy Carter becomes US President; The National Theatre opens on the South Bank, London; John Martin designs the 10th anniversary exhibition catalogue of The Demarco Gallery (1966–76). This contained essays by Richard Demarco, John Martin, Colin Thompson as Director-General of the Scottish National Galleries, Douglas Hall as Keeper of the Scottish National Gallery of Modern Art (SNGMA), Gabriella Cardazzo, Director of the Venetian Gallery, Galleria del Cavallino, Lady Jean Polwarth as Chairman of the Board of The Demarco Gallery, Cordelia Oliver, art critic of the *Guardian*, William Hardie, Director of Dundee City Art Gallery, William Buchanan, Art Director of the Scottish Arts Council, Edward Gage, art critic of *The Scotsman*, and Earl Haig as the Chairman of the Association of Friends of The Demarco Gallery.

Richard Demarco's essay, entitled *Beginnings in the Traverse* provides evidence that The Demarco Gallery has been born out of the Traverse Theatre Club Gallery and Jim Haynes' Paperback Bookshop and John Calder's Ledlanet Nights Opera Festival, and all of them were born out of the

miraculous reality of the founding of the Edinburgh International Festival in 1947 and, in particular the Edinburgh Festival under the direction of Lord (George) Harewood from 1961–65 who, together with his assistant, Alexander Schouvaloff, was responsible for Richard Demarco becoming Director of the Edinburgh Festival's programme of international contemporary visual art.

This publication contains invaluable archive material on The Demarco Gallery's 1968 Festival exhibition including open-air sculptures and paintings at Lord Linlithgow's Georgian palace of Hopetoun House, with a focus on the sculptural installations of three South African artists. The Demarco Gallery's 1969 Festival programme includes a Cambridge University late-night cabaret starring Clive James, Pete Atkin and Tony Buffery. Laurence Olivier and Frank Dunlop attended one memorable performance, sitting in the front row.

This was presented also with Lindsay Kemp's 'White Pantomime' and Geoff Moore's 'Moving Being' modern dance company, and Nancy Cole's one-woman show in homage to Gertrude Stein, as well as the Pakistan Raga music of Salamat and Nazakat Ali Khan introduced as friends of Rory McEwen and Ravi Shankar, and the late-night revue from Liverpool involving the poet John McGrath, Mike Gorman (the author of the popular song *Lilly The Pink)* and Mike McGear, the brother of The Beatles' Paul McCartney. This Festival programme provided proof positive that The Demarco Gallery was inspired by the spirit of the Traverse Theatre Club in which the visual and performing arts were intertwined. It should be noted that Sally Holman and

Elizabeth Lascelles set up The Demarco Gallery's Picture Rental Scheme in 1969. Exhibition entitled *Chinese Whispers* by Helen Douglas and Telfer Stokes.

Richard Demarco three-week lecture tour of USA, having been invited by the Government to tour for six weeks, (21 February to 12 March) Richard Demarco awarded Polish Gold Order of Merit.

The Demarco Gallery's EDINBURGH ARTS programme was entitled *From Hagar Qim to the Ring of Brodgar* indicating that it was about the physical expedition from the islands of Malta to those of Orkney. At the Edinburgh College of Art, there was Tadeusz Kantor's Cricot 2 production of *The Dead Class*. At The Demarco Gallery in Monteith House, there was a presentation of Diane Cilento's film entitled *Turning* inspired by the ritual of the Whirling Dervishes. Eliza Ward of The Royal Shakespeare Company presented a programme of 20th-century music by Kurt Weill and Bertolt Brecht at the Episcopal Cathedral of St Mary's.

1977

Sixth EDINBURGH ARTS; Exhibition at Fruitmarket; artists involved included Sillani, Osborne, Neagu, Nash; Choral recital at St Magnus Cathedral, Kirkwall; EDINBURGH ARTS expedition to Sardinia, Malta and France; Exhibitions of Anna Constantinou and Diohande, two Greek artists at Monteith House, and also Alistair Park and Angelo Bozzola, Matussek and Pletsch; Joseph Beuys' *Honeypump* at documenta 6 for 100 days.

There was an exhibition at the Fruitmarket Gallery curated by Paul

Overy of six Scottish artists, Ian Hamilton Finlay, Will Maclean, Fred Stiven, Glen Onwin, Eileen Lawrence and Ainslie Yule. I also curated two EDINBURGH ARTS exhibitions at the Fruitmarket.

RIP Charlie Chaplin aged 88.

1978

Seventh EDINBURGH ARTS via Sardinia, Malta, France; Exhibition at Monteith House of *Art of the Invisible and Visible*; Exhibition of three Romanian artists – Bernea, Dragomiresco, Stoica; Exhibition by Elise Taylor and George Levantas, also at Monteith House; *That Sinking Feeling* film by Bill Forsyth also starred Richard Demarco; EDINBURGH ARTS '78 exhibitions were presented at the Fruitmarket Gallery. I was invited to lecture at the Kunsthalle in Düsseldorf. This lecture was attended by Joseph Beuys, Jurgen Harten and Georg Jappe. This year was marked by the exhibition in Monteith House with an accompanying publication entitled *The Artist as Explorer*, which I wrote, illustrated and designed.

1979

Eighth EDINBURGH ARTS; Voyage on *The Marques* from Devon to Kinsale to the Scilly Isles, to Brittany and the Channel Islands, and then overland to Greece; Exhibitions Galeria Foksal and also at Third Eye Centre; American Embassy in Tehran is seized by Iranian students; 18 soldiers die in Warren Point ambush, Northern Ireland.

The Demarco Gallery Festival exhibition was focused on Jimmy Boyle as a sculptor and his work in The Special

Unit of HMP Barlinnie. The Demarco programme was defined by a voyage on board the sailing ship in the form of the barque *The Marques*. This was a replica of Charles Darwin's HMS *Beagle*. It sailed from the coastline of Devon to those of Cornwall, Somerset and Wales to Dublin, then to the Isles of Scilly and to St Ives where Patrick Heron delivered a lecture on the history of the School of St Ives.

Another feature of this Edinburgh Festival programme was an exhibition of artists from the Muzeum Sztuki in Łódź and the Foksal Gallery in Warsaw in the architects' studios of Nicholas and Limma Groves-Raines and Michael Spens in the Canongate, as well two exhibitions at the Fruitmarket Gallery of the paintings of Stanisław Ignacy Witkiewicz and Edward Krasiński. There was also an overland EDINBURGH ARTS expedition that I led from Carnac to Paris to Le Centre Pompidou and the studio of Brâncuşi, through France and Italy to the studio in Puglia of the Belgian artist, Norman Mommens and, from there, to Greece and the world of John Zervos in Athens.

RIP Merle Oberon.

1980

Ninth EDINBURGH ARTS. 78-day circumnavigation of The British Isles; *Edinburgh in the Thirties* exhibition at Monteith House in collaboration with Cranley School; Scottish Arts Council withdraws annual grant as a direct result of Joseph Beuys taking legal action against the Secretary of State in protest of Jimmy Boyle having to move from the Special Unit to Saughton Prison in Edinburgh; publication of the book by Anthony Howell of his performance

work *Homage to Morandi*; it was related to his *Theatre of Mistakes*.

The 34th anniversary of the Edinburgh Festival was celebrated by the Edinburgh International Festival Committee under the Chairmanship of The Lord Provost, Tom Morgan. He was fortunate to have the wise advice of such veterans of the Festival Committee as Lady Rosebery and Lord Cameron with Ronald Mavor as Deputy Chairman.

The official Edinburgh International Festival programme contained a memorable Scottish Ballet production of *The Tales of Hoffmann* directed by Peter Darrell, Artistic Director of Scottish Ballet. This was complemented, for me, by the National Theatre's production of the morality play *The Passion*, directed unforgettably by Bill Brydon. There was also Mike Ockrent's production of Lillian Hellman's play *Watch on the Rhine*, with magnificent performance by Peggy Ashcroft. John Drummond invited Tadeusz Kantor to present his Cricot 2 Theatre production of *Wielopole Wielopole* at Moray House gymnasium.

The Demarco Gallery was provided with a temporary ideal Festival venue on the Royal Mile in the architects' office that Nicholas and Kristin Groves-Raines shared with Michael Spens. This was indeed an ideal venue for Joseph Beuys to conduct a three-day master class for the 1980 EDINBURGH ARTS.

Joseph Beuys created a diptych entitled *The Jimmy Boyle Days* on two blackboards. I had invited Joseph Beuys to meet Jimmy Boyle in The Special Unit of HMP Barlinnie in Glasgow. Jimmy Boyle was being removed from The Special Unit after years of exemplary behaviour as a sculptor and writer.

Joseph Beuys protested by going on a hunger strike and wrote to Scotland's Secretary of State in support of Jimmy Boyle as an artist and not as a convicted criminal. I had invited Joseph Beuys to celebrate the 10th anniversary of the exhibition Strategy; Get Arts.

Unfortunately, the year 1980 revealed the inevitability of an ever-widening gap between my concept of art as 'a gift', and therefore unencumbered by a price tag, and the Scottish Arts Council's concept of art as within an art industry. The Scottish Arts Council removed its annual grant to The Demarco Gallery. The Chairman of the Visual Arts Committee addressed me with these words – 'You have brought dishonour to the meaning of art; you have brought dishonour to the meaning of art in Scotland; you have brought dishonour to the meaning of The Demarco Gallery!!'

Of course, I did not manage by myself to achieve the enormous task of bringing dishonour to the meaning of art. As a result, ever since 1980, the Scottish Arts Council (now renamed Creative Scotland) has declined to offer my annual programme annual grant to help to pay the basic running cost to develop the Demarco Archive as a *Gesamtkunstwerk*. RIP Steve McQueen.

RIP Peter Sellers aged 55.

1981

Tenth EDINBURGH ARTS; Ainslie Yule exhibition in The Demarco Gallery, Jeffrey Street. An outstanding contribution to the 1981 Edinburgh Festival was The San Francisco Ballet production of Shakespeare's *Romeo and Juliet* at The Playhouse Theatre. Johannes Cladders curated the collection

of the Mönchengladbach Museum in The Scottish National Gallery of Modern Art in the Royal Botanic Garden Edinburgh. This included Joseph Beuys' *Forrest Hill Poorhouse Doors*. This masterpiece was physically installed by Scottish artists George Wyllie and Dawson Murray. Their signatures can be found on the rear.

This exhibition was planned for The Demarco Gallery but, without a Scottish Arts Council annual funding grant, the exhibition was under the aegis of the Scottish National Gallery of Modern Art. It should be noted that Johannes Cladders purchased *The Poorhouse Doors* to be exhibited along with the blackboard diptych that Beuys created in honour of his friendship with Jimmy Boyle. It was entitled *The Jimmy Boyle Days*.

Joseph Beuys was accompanied by his family. They stayed in the East Lothian village of Humbie because I wished Joseph Beuys to explore the world of Sir Walter Scott. This meant that Joseph Beuys wished to visit the grave of Sir Walter Scott in the precincts of Dryburgh Abbey. This grave is beside that of Field Marshall, The Earl Haig. I arranged for Joseph Beuys to visit the studio of his son, Lord (Dawyck) Haig. They had fought against each other at The Battle of the Bulge in France. Joseph Beuys and his family, together with Johannes Cladders, were welcomed to Bemersyde Castle to see Lord Haig's studio and art collection.

Joseph Beuys removed *The Poorhouse Doors* from Forrest Hill to Edinburgh College of Art, and then to the Scottish National Gallery of Modern Art in The Royal Botanic Garden Edinburgh, in collaboration with the

Mönchengladbach Museum of Art, to become an addition to the exhibition curated by Johannes Cladders of the collection he established at the Mönchengladbach Museum. This exhibition expressed the long-standing friendship and collaboration between myself and Johannes Cladders.

RIP Hoagy Carmichael.

1982

Eleventh EDINBURGH ARTS; During the period of Martial Law, Polish Tapestry exhibition in Fruitmarket Gallery; Studio International re-launched in Venice during Biennale; Fabrizio Plessi exhibition in Jeffrey Street, also Ainslie Yule; Richard Demarco invited to attend conference in Varese by Count Panza di Biumo.

The Demarco Gallery exhibition at Edinburgh College of Art was in homage to the life and work of Rolf Jährling as a patron of Joseph Beuys and the avant-garde artists of Düsseldorf. This exhibition was supported by the Goethe Institut and was presented in the exhibition rooms of Edinburgh College of Art in which the Strategy; Get Art exhibition was made manifest. The Demarco Gallery, in collaboration with Edinburgh City Arts Centre, presented an exhibition of Piranesi etchings. John Drummond was appointed Edinburgh International Festival Director. Peter Ustinov directed and performed in his production of *The Marriage*, and English translation of Nikolai Gogol's text at the Royal Lyceum Theatre. (NB. Peter Ustinov joined the Association of Friends of The Demarco Gallery and was pleased to play the role of the Laird of Inversneky. Dresden State Opera presented a production of *Ariadne auf*

Naxos at the King's Theatre).

There was an Edinburgh Festival exhibition of Man Ray photographs at The Royal Scottish Academy. The Medici Quartet led by Paul Robertson performed in the Freemason's Hall. A discussion on the future of the Edinburgh Festival took place at St Cecilia's Hall led by Frank Dunlop and chaired by Michael Billington.

The Demarco Gallery presented an exhibition in collaboration with the Gray Art centre of Piranese Drawings and Prints at the City Arts Centre from the Piranese Collection in the Avery Library in New York's Columbia University.

RIP Leonid Brezhnev aged 75.

1983

Twelfth EDINBURGH ARTS. *Varese Engagement* exhibition; *Art of the Andes* exhibition at Edinburgh City Arts Centre; Lecture at Southampton College of Art, meeting with Terry Ann Newman as art student, part of Richard Demarco's lecture tour of English art schools devised by Richard Noyce.

The Edinburgh Festival exhibitions for The Demarco Gallery were 'The Varese Engagement with Modern Art' from the Collection of Count Panza di Biumo in Jeffrey Street, and Art from the Andes at the City Arts Centre. This included an international conference entitled *Housing the Arts in the 21st Century* at Edinburgh University's Hume Tower. John Drummond, the Director of the Edinburgh International Festival, was inspired by The Vienna Secession. However, this year was marked by the book launch and exhibition at The Demarco Gallery in Jeffrey Street of Jim

Ede's book and collection in his house in Cambridge which became a unique art gallery known as Kettle's Yard. The book launch took place in the presence of Jim Ede and his friend, David Baxandall, as well as Lord MacLeod of Fiunary and Professor Barry Wilson, a board member of The Demarco Gallery.

Among the highlights of the 1983 Edinburgh International Festival was the sculptural installation by Denise Marika at Mellerstain House in Berwickshire in the landscape of Lord Binning's estate. This exhibition was focused on the increasing numbers of refugees fleeing from world conflicts. The Demarco Gallery exhibition in Monteith House on the Royal Mile celebrated the 20th anniversary of the Traverse Theatre Gallery in collaboration with Angela Wrapson, Chair of the Traverse Theatre Committee.

I contributed to the first issue of *Studio International*, edited by Michael Spens with an essay on the exhibition in the Zurich Museum of Art curated and conceived by Harald Szeemann. This was entitled *Towards a Total Art Work*. I suggested to Michael Spens that, as the Contributing Editors of *Studio International*, they should be Mario Amaya in New York, Wiesław Borowski in Warsaw, Nobua Nakamura in Tokyo, Pierre Rastany in Paris, Karl Ruhrberg in Düsseldorf, Dorothy Walker in Dublin and Nick Waterlow in Sydney, Australia.

There was The Demarco Foundation Gallery at Edinburgh College of Art in collaboration with Rolf Jährling, Director of Galerie Parnass in Wuppertal. Artists included Bazon Brock, Charlotte Moorman, Nam June Paik, Tomas Schmit, Wolf Vostell,

Hans-Peter Alvermann and Joseph Beuys. The exhibition catalogue contained texts by Annely Juda, Karl Ruhrberg and Rolf Jährling.

The exhibition in The Demarco Gallery in Jeffrey Street was inspired by Count Giuseppe Panza's collection in the Villa Litta in Varese. It was entitled The Varese Engagement with Modern Artists and included Bruce Nauman, Donald Judd, Richard Serra, Dan Flavin, James Turrell, Robert Morris, George Segal, Jan Dibbets and Joseph Kosuth. The Demarco Conference took place on the theme of Housing the Arts in the 21st Century. Speakers included Johannes Cladders, Giuliano Gori, Count Giuseppe Panza, Arthur Watson, Frank Dunlop and John Drummond and was held at the David Hume Building of Edinburgh University.

RIP Joan Miró.

1984

Thirteenth EDINBURGH ARTS; *Demarcation* as a 12-day conference at Edinburgh College of Art; Anzart exhibition with Australian and New Zealand artists; Oakham School master class directed by Martin Minshall at Edinburgh College of Art; Robert Fraser Gallery artists exhibition; French sculpture exhibition in collaboration with Michael and Sandra Le Marchant of The Bruton Gallery of work by Bourdelle and Rodin; *From Scratch* New Zealand music performance in Edinburgh College of Arts Sculpture Court; Joseph Beuys visits Japan; Four Polish policemen on trial for murder of Fr Jerzy Popieluszko; Richard Demarco observes parishioners of Fr Popieluszko's church in Warsaw on 24-hour guard against armed police. Appointed Officer of the British Empire (OBE).

Anzart exhibition at Edinburgh College of Art – Australian and New Zealand artists. *Demarcation '84*, a 12-day conference and exhibition at Edinburgh College of Art. Exhibition from The Smithsonian Institution at The Royal Museum of Scotland. *Art and the Human Environment*, Dublin, was a case study at the National Gallery of Ireland as an extension of *Demarcation '84*; David Rintoul played the role of The King of Scotland in the Scottish Theatre Company's production of *The Thrie Estaitis* directed by Tom Fleming in the Church of Scotland Assembly Hall.

As a key contributor to the 1984 Edinburgh Festival's Theatre Programme, Tom Fleming asked me to help fund the travel costs of transferring the production to participate in the Warsaw International Theatre Festival. This I did by contacting Polish Airlines (LOT) who provided two of their jet planes to transport the cast and set of this production from Edinburgh Airport to Warsaw Airport. The Tom Fleming production was awarded the First Prize of the Warsaw Theatre Festival.

On 14 August, there was a whole day symposium, part of the 12-day conference at Edinburgh College of Art on the impact of Information Technology on Art and Art Education. The morning session was chaired by Wilton S Dillon of the Smithsonian Institute. Session One: Ken Gray on Parallalism in Art & Technology; Sculpture. Session Two: Wilton Dillon on High technology and Human Freedom. Afternoon Session: Lectures by Gavin Ross and David Hebditch.

Frank Dunlop began his

eight-year directorship of the Edinburgh International Festival. I was interviewed for the directorship but my interview was unsuccessful. If I had succeeded, I would have been the first Edinburgh citizen to have been given the opportunity to promote the contemporary avant-garde artists to bring the Edinburgh Festival to become in fruitful dialogue with the Venice Biennale.

RIP Richard Burton aged 59.

1985

Fourteenth EDINBURGH ARTS. Four Foksal artists exhibition at The Demarco Gallery in Jeffrey Street and Arthur Sackler buys the complete exhibition and then donates it to the collection of Tufts University in Chicago; Diohande and Anna Constantinou exhibition; David Mach exhibition at Foksal Gallery Warsaw; Edinburgh Festival Fringe Babel Theatre production; EDINBURGH ARTS expedition to Dorset to Jonathan Phipps' Portland Sculpture Park via London and Winchester; participants included the sculptor Magdalena Jetelová recently escaped from Czechoslovakia. (Janet Treloar, Terry Ann Newman, Connie Byam Shaw, Lorna Green); Joseph Beuys installation at Museo di Capodimonte, Naples.

In The Demarco Festival Gallery in Jeffrey Street, there was an exhibition of four Foksal Gallery artists, Leon Tarasewicz, Tomasz Tatarczyk, Andrzej Szewczyk, Tomasz Ciecierski. This exhibition was donated to the University Art Gallery in Chicago. A programme of alternative Polish Theatre was presented by The Demarco Gallery as part of the official Edinburgh Festival.

Two outstanding contributions were Zofia Kalińska's production of *The*

Maids by Jean Genet, and a production by Poland's leading performance arts company Akademia Ruchu with their version of *The English Lesson*. The Demarco Gallery emphasised the importance of the cultural dialogue between European countries divided by the Iron Curtain.

RIP Orson Welles aged 70. RIP Phil Silvers. RIP Rock Hudson aged 59.

1986

Fifteenth EDINBURGH ARTS; Edward Dwurnik exhibited at Bath and London art fairs; The Demarco Gallery's exhibition and theatre programme during the Edinburgh Festival at Heriot's School and performance of The Scipion Nasice Sisters Theatre from Slovenia; Polish exhibition at Blackfriars Church as inaugural Festival exhibition; Exhibition of Austrian artist Ludwig Redl in Blackfriars Church; Joanna Przybyła's sculptural exhibition at Traquair House; Two EDINBURGH ARTS expeditions to Poland, 4 January (participants included Mark Boyle, Alastair McLennan) and, post Chernobyl disaster, in June; In July, The Demarco Gallery presented 'The Windows of Marlborough' exhibition for Marlborough Festival, Wiltshire (Ainslie Yule 1st prize, Terry Ann Newman 2nd prize, awarded by Mel Gooding); First publication of *The Independent* newspaper; Space shuttle *Challenger* explodes.

The Demarco Gallery presented the Scipion Nasice Sisters Theatre production by the Slovenian Group Irwin at George Heriot's School. The exhibition of Group Irwin was at The Demarco Gallery in Blackfriars Church, together with the paintings of Polish

artists. John David Mooney's sculptural installation was also at Blackfriars Street and at George Heriot's School.

During the 1986 Edinburgh Festival, The Demarco Gallery made good use of the large-scale venue provided by George Heriot's School. I put together a Festival programme of 22 theatre programmes and five exhibitions in celebration of the 40th anniversary of the Edinburgh Festival and the 20th anniversary of The Richard Demarco Gallery. I can never forget what I now consider as the main event in my programme. It involved, for the first time in Western Europe, the Scipion Nasice Sisters Theatre production of *Marija Nablocka*.

This was described as a retro-gradistic event by the organisers of this historic theatrical experience from Ljubljana, the capital of Slovenia. It was 'a fusion of impulses, executed through a fusion of disciplines, using Bertolt Brecht's play *Baal*. The performers grapple with the collusion between appetites and indivisible desires. On one hand, a political necessity and on the other authoritarianism. The production wraps the audience into a situation where they are united or perhaps compelled not to contemplate a theorem but to experience a process.' The audience was reduced to no more than one dozen. They were blindfolded and led to the stage by two of the performers and placed with their heads through holes on the wooden stage. Beside each of their heads was a flaming torch. As expected, the police closed this production after four performances as a fire risk. This extraordinary example of performance art was linked to an exhibition of the artists of Group Irwin at The Demarco Gallery in Blackfriars Street. The artists of Group Irwin expressed the political ambitions of the people of Slovenia who did not wish to be identified with Field Marshal Tito's concept of a united Yugoslavia.

These artists undoubtedly helped to develop a political situation which led to the Balkan War and the collapse of Marshal Tito's regime. During this year, there were two EDINBURGH ARTS expeditions to Poland, first in January. The Chernobyl disaster delayed the second EDINBURGH ARTS expedition from April until June. Among the participants were artists Terry Ann Newman, Larry Wakefield, Mary McIver, Don McGovern, Rudi Calonder and Angela Weyersberg. All of them contributed to the 1986 Edinburgh Festival exhibition. RIP Joseph Beuys 26 January.

RIP Harold Macmillan (Earl of Stockton) aged 92. RIP Cary Grant. RIP Elizabeth Smart. RIP Andy Warhol.

1987

Sixteenth EDINBURGH ARTS; Mladen Materić with Tattoo Theatre and Group Irwin at Blackfriars Church; The Demarco Gallery exhibited in art fairs in London and Bath; Lunch meeting with Suzanne Pagé. External Examiner at Stourbridge School of Art 1987–90.

Sir Peter Maxwell Davies and Sir Yehudi Menuhin directed the Scottish Chamber Orchestra with a performance of Beethoven's Symphony No.3. A performance of the Edinburgh Festival Chorus was conducted by Arthur Oldham of *The Damnation of Faust* by Berlioz. Mladen Materić directed *Tattoo Theatre* at The Demarco Gallery's Blackfriars Church.

A highlight of the official Edinburgh Festival Theatre programme was *The History of the Horse*, a production by The Theatre Gorky of Leningrad starring Evgeny Lebedev.

The Demarco European Art Foundation's contribution to the 1987 Edinburgh Festival programme was undoubtedly the exhibition *Bits and Pieces* which celebrated the genius of Joseph Beuys and commemorated his untimely death from his war wounds at the age of 64 in January of last year.

I was grateful to the Paul Van Vlissingen Foundation for the generous support which made this exhibition possible. An historic addition to the visual arts dimension in the history of the Edinburgh Festival. I was also indebted to Arthur Watson, the founder and director of Aberdeen's Peacock Printmakers and Bristol's Arnolfini Gallery. Their respect for the genius of Joseph Beuys made it possible for the exhibition entitled *Bits and Pieces* to be toured to Aberdeen and Bristol. It was given this title by Caroline Tisdall who was gifted *Bits and Pieces* as an art collection celebrating their shared experience of the Celtic Central Heritage of Europe.

Bits and Pieces was presented in The Richard Demarco Gallery in Blackfriars Street together with an exhibition catalogue, fully illustrated. Also presented was a contemporary exhibition celebrating the unique landscape of Loch Maree with photographs and text by Paul Van Vlissingen and Caroline Tisdall. The two exhibitions were in every sense complementary because they celebrated the fact that Joseph Beuys, together with Heinrich Böll, had founded the Green Party in Germany.

RIP Fred Astaire. RIP Claire Boothe
Luce. RIP Jean Anouilh (French
dramatist).

1988

Seventeenth EDINBURGH ARTS;
Tavola exhibition by Mario Merz at
Blackfriars Church in collaboration
with the Scottish Sculpture Trust;
Edinburgh Festival symposium on 100th
anniversary of Hugh MacDiarmid;
Art in a Cold Climate Channel 4
film directed by Murray and Barbara
Grigor; Exhibition in collaboration
with Peacock Printmakers in Collegium
Artisticum, Sarajevo Festival; Yasser
Arafat refused visa to USA to address
United Nations; Lockerbie air disaster.

Appointed Cavaliere della Repubblica
d'Italia. Recipient of *Scotland on Sunday*
Critics Award for contribution to the
visual arts programmes of the Edinburgh
Festival. There was the celebration
of the 10th anniversary of the death
of Hugh MacDiarmid in the form of
a conference at Blackfriars Church
which included David Gascoigne, Mary
McIver, Sorley Maclean and Norman
MacCaig.

In collaboration with the Scottish
Sculpture Trust, there was an exhibition
of the thought-provoking sculpture
by Mario Merz at Blackfriars Church.
Mladen Materić directed *Moonplay*
at The Demarco Theatre in the
Grassmarket in collaboration with
Dione Patullo. EDINBURGH ARTS
expedition to Sarajevo and exhibition in
collaboration with Peacock Printmakers
and the Galerija Grada Zagreb and
Marijan Susovski.

A noteworthy official Edinburgh
International Festival production was La
Zattera Di Babele Theatre Company's

Towards Macbeth; A Prologue. This was
presented in association with Regioni
Siciliana Assessorato Turismo e Beni
Culturali at The Demarco Gallery in
Blackfriars Church, travelling in three
buses from Edinburgh en route to South
Queensferry and then by ferry across the
Firth of Forth to Inchcolm Island. This
production was directed and performed
by Carlo Quartucci and Carla Tato. The
company included Juliet Cadzow and
Johnny Bett who had key roles as Scottish
actors working with Italian actors.

The Edinburgh Fringe Director Michael
Dale published *Sore Throats and
Overdrafts*, his account of the history
of the Edinburgh Festival Fringe. It was
first published by Precedent Publications
Ltd. The introduction was written by
Miles Kington and contained essays
by Andrew Dallmeyer, Edith Simon,
Charles Maclaren, Bernard Levin,
John Milligan, Alistair Moffat, Jim
Haynes, Carol Main, Clive Wolfe,
Patrick Brookes, and Jeremy Taylor.
Their essays comprised a multi-faceted
account of the Edinburgh Fringe from
1947 to 1988.

Michael Dale also included his
insightful interview with Allen Wright,
The Scotsman's most respected arts
journalist, as well as with Dr Jonathan
Miller who had become Chairman of the
Fringe Society in 1984. Rowan Atkinson
was also interviewed and revealed
how in 1979, he first performed on the
Fringe as a schoolboy. This publication
provided an invaluable history of the
Fringe. It followed that, together, Alistair
Moffat and Michael Dale transformed
the Fringe programme and, indeed, gave
the Fringe the professional structure it
needed to cope with the ever-increasing
number of performing arts companies
attracted to Edinburgh.

1989

Eighteenth EDINBURGH ARTS. *Roma Punto Uno* exhibition at Blackfriars Church of 50 Rome-based artists; Three Portuguese artists, Helena Almeida, Paula Rego and Ruth Rosengarten; The Demarco Gallery's Edinburgh Festival exhibition programme included Dutch artists on Inchcolm Island; Polish artists exhibition at Blackfriars Church, including an installation by Magdalena Abakanowicz, in collaboration with MOMA Oxford; John Betts directs *Macbeth* on Inchcolm Island; EDINBURGH ARTS expedition to Poland; Richard Demarco, Jane MacAllister, John and Terry Newman visit Moscow and Leningrad; Berlin Wall breached; Massacre in Timisoara; Nicolae Ceaușescu overthrown; Václav Havel elected President of Czechoslovakia; Pope John Paul II meets Mikhail Gorbachev in Rome.

Edinburgh Festival in Dundee was a programme in collaboration with Dundee Rep. This included Oskaras Koršunovas opera production of 'Hello Sonya New Year', The Belarus State Theatre production of 'Dodge' by the Belarusian Shakespeare F Alekhnovitch Theatre, the Yvette Bozsik Company production in collaboration with the Katona József Theatre of Budapest of two productions entitled *Two Portraits* and *The Miraculous Manadarin*. Also, The Demarco Inchcolm Theatre production of John Bett's adaptation of Shakespeare's *Macbeth* starring John Cairney as Macbeth and Gerda Stevenson as Lady Macbeth. There was the exhibition of postal art in collaboration with the Scottish Postal Board at Blackfriars Street, contemporary art from The Netherlands in association with The Netherlands

Contemporary Art Foundation, Amsterdam at Blackfriars Street, and on Inchcolm, and the television *Portrait of Richard Demarco* as a film for BBC2 as an 'Edinburgh Nights Special' directed by Andrea Miller and produced by Douglas Mackinnon.

At the Edinburgh College of Art, there was an impressive exhibition celebrating the distinguished career of Sir Robin Philipson as a painter. This added a much-needed visual arts manifestation to the programme of the Edinburgh Festival Fringe. The most memorable work of art was that expressed in the sculptural installation in a medieval room within the walls Inchcolm Abbey. Using light and what appeared to be a formless paper sculpture, there was revealed in all its glory Michelangelo's statue of David. This was the contribution by Diet Wiegman to the exhibition *Contemporary Art from The Netherlands*.

RIP Laurence Olivier. RIP Salvador Dalí. RIP Dione Patullo.

1990

28 November, Margaret Thatcher resigns; *French Spring* exhibition on Inchcolm Island, at Blackfriars Church and at SNGMA; Opening of The Burrell Collection in Glasgow; Official Venice Biennale Scottish Pavilion in Giardini with three artists, David Mach, Arthur Watson and Kate Whiteford; *Burns, Beuys and Beyond* exhibition for Glasgow European City of Culture; Oakham School Festival production of *Nero My Hero*; Soviet Government changes Russian Constitution. External Examiner for Wolverhampton School of Art.

The Demarco Gallery's 'Road to Meikle Seggie' exhibition was presented in collaboration with Fonds régional d'art contemporain Nord Pas-de-Calais and L'Institut français d'Écosse as an Edinburgh Festival exhibition at Blackfriars Street. Mimmo Rotella conducted a master class at Blackfriars Street resulting in two master works, one of which was sold at Sotheby's in aid of The Demarco Gallery and the other gifted to the Scottish National Gallery of Modern Art. *Pictlandgarden* was an exhibition at Blackfriars Street by Günther Uecker in celebration of the 20th anniversary of Strategy; Get Arts. RIP Paulette Goddard.

RIP Tadeusz Kantor.

1991

Twenty-first anniversary Edinburgh Festival exhibition at Blackfriars Church of PENTAGONALE PLUS together with a conference at Kingston University, Napier University and The Demarco Gallery; Cricot 2 Theatre returns to Edinburgh Festival, without Kantor, with the production *Today is my Birthday* at The Edinburgh Festival Theatre; Marina Abramović exhibition in collaboration with MOMA Oxford; Exhibition of Hungarian and Romanian artists; BBC film; Matthew Macfadyen in the Oakham School production of *Touched* at Blackfriars Church; EDINBURGH ARTS voyage across the English Channel on ss *Maria Assunta* from Chatham to Calais; Richard Demarco commissioned to make The Tall Ships suite of prints at Peacock Printmakers; Two-man exhibition, Will Maclean and Richard Demarco, at Artspace Gallery, Aberdeen, entitled *The Artist as Voyager*.

EDINBURGH ARTS expedition to Budapest to create works in situ for

exhibition at the Academy; works by Ainslie Yule, Terry Ann Newman and Helen Brough acquired for National Gallery of Hungary by László Beke; International Science Festival; *Margaret Gardner and Thomas Merton: A Correspondence*; Interview with Paul Neagu in Timisoara for BBC filmed expedition from Budapest by Andrea Miller; Terry Waite released from prison in Iran; Serbian army bombards Dubrovnik. Appointed Chevalier de l'Order des Artes et des Lettres (France). Appointed Honorary Fellow of the Royal Incorporation of Architects of Scotland (FRIAS).

PENTAGONALE PLUS symposium with keynote address by Rt Hon Gianni di Michelis, Italian Minister for Foreign Affairs was presented at Napier University and Edinburgh City Council, together with an exhibition in The Demarco Gallery in Blackfriars Church in celebration of 21st anniversary of the Edinburgh Festival in collaboration with Kingston University, and Oakham School contributed a theatre production for the Festival of Stephen Lowe's play *Touched*. This introduced Matthew Macfadyen and Tiffany-Alice Pershke to The Demarco Gallery's Edinburgh Festival programme. The television *Portrait of Richard Demarco* as a film for BBC2 was an 'Edinburgh Nights Special' directed by Andrea Miller and produced by Douglas Mackinnon of the Edinburgh Arts journey to Budapest and Timisoara.

RIP Dame Margot Fonteyn. RIP Robert Maxwell.

1992

Barbara Balmer's portrait of Richard Demarco is exhibited at the Scottish National Portrait Gallery; John Major wins election; Anglican Church approves women priests; Annus Horribilis for HM Queen with Windsor Castle fire; *Electo Imprimata* portfolio of prints – Printmaking at art schools in Ghent and Strasbourg, directed by Arthur Watson and Mary Modeen; Demarco East European Art Foundation established; *Burns, Beuys and Beyond* group exhibition at Blackfriars Church; Bulgarian Choir tour of UK from Edinburgh Festival to Eton College and Downside Abbey; Richard Johnson and Sophie Thomson directed by Nicholas Fogg as a homage to Weisz.British International Institute of Theatre Award. Polish International Institute of Theatre Award. Director of the Demarco East European Art Foundation.

Rachel Weisz and Sasha Hails performed *Talking Tongues,* a play at the Demarco Foundation in Blackfriars Church under the direction of David Farr which was a Cambridge Footlights production by Rose Garnet. There was a performance by David Mach, setting alight his sculptural matchstick portrait of myself. The Kingston University Quartet performed with the Royal Shakespeare Company and Dorothy Tutin at the Demarco Festival in St Mary's Cathedral in collaboration with Kingston University. Rick Cluchey conducted the San Quentin Drama Workshop.

RIP Marlene Dietrich.

1993

Rachel Whiteread wins Turner Prize; Cheltenham Festival exhibitions by Terry Ann Newman and Jane Bywater; Symposium at Villa Foscarini Rossi in Italy, in collaboration with Kingston University; Exhibitions of Hungarian and Austrian artists, Ainslie Yule

sculpture installation entitled *Seven Score Years and Ten*; Budapest Art Fair; *Witnesses of Existence* exhibition at Kingston University and The Tabernacle Gallery London. Director of The Demarco European Art Foundation-Appointed Professor of European Cultural Studies, Kingston University 1993–2000. Honorary Doctorate from Atlanta College of Art. Trustee Kingston Demarco European Cultural Foundation. Awarded Picker Fellow, Kingston University 1993–94.

Six Bosnian artists from besieged Sarajevo at the Demarco Foundation's Edinburgh Festival venue at St Mary's Primary School in collaboration with Kingston University as well as a British Council supported play from Serbia in a programme involving Bosnia and Serbia in the beginning of a necessary peaceful cultural dialogue.

RIP John Osborne. RIP Anthony Burgess. RIP Rudolf Nureyev.

1994

Tony Blair replaces John Smith as Labour leader; *Captain Corelli's Mandolin* published; *Bridging the Gap* for the Edinburgh Festival programme at St Mary's School; Damien Hirst exhibition and action for *Agongo* at St Mary's School; Channel Tunnel opens; Danny Boyle's film *Shallow Grave* premiere; *The Bridge of Mostar* and *Homage to Beuys* exhibitions; To Morocco on lecture tour; Ceasefire in Yugoslavia.

Damien Hirst installation for the opera *Agongo* written by artist Daniel Moynihan for The Demarco Gallery in St Mary's School. The Estonian Youth Theatre produced Shakespeare's *Romeo and Juliet* in the courtyard of St Mary's School, and the symposium in collaboration with Colin Sanderson, Director of Artiscience entitled *Bridging The Gap* between Art and Science and between East and West Europe.

RIP General Stanisław Maczek. RIP Lindsay Anderson.

1995

Damien Hirst wins Turner Prize; 25th anniversary of Strategy; Get Arts with Henning Christiansen and Ursula Reuter performing an 'action' entitled *100 Hammer Blows Against Warmongers* at Edinburgh College of Art and on Rannoch Moor with George Wyllie; Graham Smallbone opens the 'Old School' at Oakham School on 2 March with production of Shakespeare's *Pericles;* Graham Smallbone, as Oakham School's Headmaster, gifts Oxford English Dictionary to Richard Demarco; Artists Deryck Healey, Alastair Niven, and Kevin Dagg install sculpture at Traquair House, inspired by the history of Traquair; *The Garden Route* expedition from Hampton Court via the Isle of Wight and via Terry Ann Newman's studio in Dorset with John Latham, Barbara Steveni, Robert Lamb and Portland Sculpture Park students, Downside Abbey via Garsington Hall, Yorkshire Sculpture Park and Little Sparta to Udny Castle Gardens in Aberdeenshire. Awarded Glasgow Royal Philosophical Society Arts Medal. Delivers Adam Smith Lecture, Fife College.

The Hungarian dance company of Yvette Bozsik who performed *The Miraculous Mandarin* and *Yellow Wallpaper* at Dundee Rep for the 'Edinburgh Festival in Dundee'. This programme included the Lithuanian Oskaras Koršunovas Theatre Company and the former President of Lithuania, Vytautas Landsbergis playing the music of Čiurlionis, and the Latvian Stella Polaris Theatre company.

EDINBURGH ARTS took *The Garden Route to the Edinburgh Festival*, from Kingston University, Hampton Court, The Royal Palace Garden in Brussels, Stonerwood Park, Quarr Abbey, Portland Sculpture Park and Clavell House in the south of England, Yorkshire Sculpture Park, Bemersyde, Traquair House in the Scottish Borders, and ending at Udny Castle in Aberdeenshire.

1996

Dolly the Sheep created by Edinburgh University; Dunblane massacre; Carnegie Mellon University artists exhibition at St Mary's School; Charles and Diana divorce; Edinburgh Festival exhibitions at St Mary's include Judith Lamb, Jimmy Boyle, Rene Nisbett and George Wyllie; Belarusian language *Macbeth* at Ravenscraig Castle, Fife; Richard Demarco invited by Rear Admiral John Lippiett to lecture at the Royal Navy School of Navigation at HMS *Dryad*, Portsmouth; Appointed Commander of the Order of St Lazarus. Honorary Doctorate of Law, Dundee University. Elected Honorary Member of the Scottish Arts Club.

The Belarusian State Theatre performed Shakespeare's *Macbeth* at Ravenscraig Castle, Kirkcaldy, in collaboration with Fife College.

RIP Ella Fitzgerald 15 June aged 79. RIP Peter Diamand.

1997

New Labour sweeps to power. 1,400th anniversary of St Columba's death – Colmcille Irish-Scottish exhibition in Donegal, Ireland and Edinburgh; Manresa Symposium at St Mary's School with Fr Friedhelm Mennekes SJ and Jimmy Boyle, Alastair MacLennan, Dom Aidan Bellenger OSB, John Haldane; JK Rowling's *Philosopher's Stone* is published; YBA *Sensation* exhibition in London.

This year marked the 30th anniversary of the inaugural exhibition of ROSC in Dublin in 1967 and the expedition organised by the Association of Friends of The Demarco Gallery to Dublin to experience what proved to be the beginning of a fruitful dialogue between Scotland and the Republic of Ireland.

During this Festival, the Demarco Foundation presented an exhibition celebrating the 1,400th anniversary of the birth of Saint Columba (St Colmcille). This exhibition was presented in the Demarco Foundation's gallery in St Mary's Roman Catholic Primary School after it had been exhibited in the Art Centre in Letterkenny in County Donegal. There were six Irish artists and six Scottish artists represented, plus Joseph Beuys who defined himself as a Germano-Celt. George Wyllie created a sculptural installation on the roof of St Mary's School.

EDINBURGH ARTS expedition in the form of a pilgrimage from the grave of Edward Elgar in Little Malvern and to that of Shakespeare's grave in Stratford-upon-Avon. A symposium was held in collaboration with Artiscience and the University of Dundee with Prof George Steiner speaking on the interface between Art and Science. Ian Crawford published his personal history of the Edinburgh Festival. He entitled this Goblinshead publication *Banquo on*

Thursdays, subtitled 'The Inside Story of Fifty Years of the Edinburgh Festival'.

Commodore John Lippiett, Director of The Royal Navy's School of Navigation in Hampshire, invited me to lecture on The Demarco Gallery's circumnavigation of the British Isles on board the Sailing Ship *The Marques*, a replica of Darwin's *HMS Beagle*. This 1980 EDINBURGH ARTS voyage explored the interface between the worlds of Nature and Culture on the coastlines linking the British Isles with the Republic of Ireland and with Brittany.

RIP Diana, Princess of Wales. RIP Mother Teresa. RIP Rudolf Bing.

1998

EDINBURGH ARTS expedition to Dubrovnik Festival with Demarco artists in Otok Gallery exhibition with artists including Edwin Owre, John David Mooney, Terry Ann Newman, Robert McDowell, Arthur Watson, Ian Howard; European Youth Parliament, led by its founder, Bettina Carr-Allinson, welcomed by Mary James as Headmistress at St Leonard's School resulting in the opera premiere of *Europa*, directed by Professor Nigel Osborne in collaboration with Timothy Neat, with masterclasses by Arthur Watson, Nicholas Fogg, Zofia Kalińska and Ariel Dorfman; Good Friday Treaty; Omagh bomb, Co. Tyrone; Honorary Peers to be abolished in House of Lords; Croatian Folk Choir from Pakrac at Birkhill, Fife, and Edinburgh Festival as well as the McManus Gallery, Dundee; Exhibition of Demarco artists from Dubrovnik Festival at New Parliament House for Edinburgh Festival.

Appointed Green Cross Trustee. Elected Fellow of The Royal Society of Arts.

EDINBURGH ARTS expedition to Dubrovnik in collaboration with Peacock Printmakers of Aberdeen and the Galerija Grada in Zagreb in preparation for the Demarco Foundation's EDINBURGH ARTS Croatian dimension in the Dubrovnik Festival involving Edwin Owre in a sculptural installation entitled *Aura – A Beacon* for Dubrovnik Harbour, an EDINBURGH ARTS exhibition linking Croatia with Scotland. Artists then created new work for the Edinburgh Festival. The European Youth Parliament created and performed the world premiere of the opera *Europa* under the direction of Nigel Osborne.

RIP Ted Hughes.

1999

Jill Dando's murder; Ros Lambert's film entitled *The Road to Meikle Seggie*, with Richard Demarco in conversation with Guido de Marco as the Maltese President, Richard England and Norbert Attard; *Art and the Sea* exhibition at the National Maritime Museum, Malta; *Labrynth* exhibition at the Matthew Gallery, Edinburgh University, including George Wyllie's tribute to Joseph Beuys; Malta Pavilion at Venice Biennale with four Maltese artists, including Norbert Francis Attard. The Malta–Scotland cultural dialogue *From Hagar Qim to Little Sparta* with an exhibition resulting from the collaboration between Ian Hamilton Finlay, Richard England and John Borg Manduca, as well as sculptural installations by John David Mooney and Norbert Francis Attard for the St James Cavaliere in Valletta as an art museum. The visit of the Maltese Minister of Culture, Louis Galea, was hosted by the Demarco Foundation. The Minister attended the Festival Tattoo as the guest of the Lord Provost Eric Milligan.

RIP Lord (Yehudi) Menuhin.

2000

To Malta for Maltese Millennium celebration in Valletta JD Mooney's sculptural installation at St James Cavalier and also Norbert Attard sculpture installation; Concorde crash.

Appointed Professor Emeritus of European Cultural Studies, Kingston University. Elected Honorary Vice-President of The Rose Theatre, Kingston-upon-Thames.

The exhibition entitled *70/2000 on The Road to Meikle Seggie*, a Kingston University's Picker Gallery exhibition was presented at the Edinburgh City Art Centre in collaboration with Ian O'Riordan, Keeper of Fine Art, in celebration of my 70th birthday. The Demarco Foundation's, in collaboration with Xela Batchelder's Rocket Productions, presentation of *Chagal, Chagal* by the Belarusian Theatre Yakub Kolas of Vitebsk won a Festival Fringe First.

RIP Tim Stead aged 70. RIP Sir Alec Guinness aged 86.

2001

John OR Martin and Richard Demarco exhibition at Peter Potter Gallery, Haddington; Foot and Mouth closes rural Britain; 2nd term for Tony Blair; Demarco exhibition moves from Kingston University to Oxford Brookes University, John Ruskin's home at Brantwood, Coniston Water, and to the National Gallery of Lithuania in Kaunas, in collaboration with British Council in Lithuania; Exhibition of Lithuanian Art at Edinburgh Festival in Edinburgh College of Art; *Windows of Marlborough* exhibitions in shop windows in the High Street in collaboration with the Marlborough Festival. Elected Honorary Royal Scottish Academician.

There was an exhibition celebrating the 200th anniversary of the birth of Robert Burns and 200th anniversary of the birth of Charles Darwin and also, an exhibition of Belarusian art from the academy of Minsk. The Demarco EDINBURGH ARTS Festival was in Alloa, in collaboration with Clackmannanshire County Council, and Zofia Kalińska's production of *Dybuck* in Edinburgh. EDINBURGH ARTS made an expedition to Cumbria with Elliot Rudie, Colin Sanderson and Eric Wishart in collaboration with the University of Lancaster and John Ruskin's Brantwood House in collaboration with the director, Howard Hull.

2002

Beyond Conflict exhibition for Mercy Corps at Commonwealth Games, Manchester, opened by the Countess of Wessex, moving to the Apex Hotel for the Edinburgh Festival in collaboration with BlinkRed, The Royal Museum of Scotland and The Royal Scottish Academy with financial support from The Russell Trust; artists included Arthur Watson, Bill Scott, Doug Cocker, Gareth Fisher, Joy Alstead, Elaine Shemilt, Merylin Smith, Marian Leven, Will Maclean, Lys Hansen, Barbara Balmer, Joyce Cairns, Alan Robb and Ian Howard, with congratulations from Nelson Mandela and HM Queen Elizabeth II, with statements by MEPS

including Hans-Gert Pöttering, leader of the European Union's Christian Democrats, and Struan Stevenson; it then moved to Brussels to the European Parliament; Demarco Foundation's *Festival of the Sea* for Forth Ports, Leith, and *Edinburgh's Shoreline*; Richard Demarco (with Terry Ann Newman) exhibition of watercolours, Rockcliffe Gallery.

Polygon's *Morning Star* publication defined as an archaeology of Scotland's culture (1960–200) with the apt title 'Justified Sinners'. It is entitled by the artists Ross Birrell and Eck Finlay. The contributing editor was Steve Robb, the then archivist of the Demarco Archive and is part of a series of pocketbooks. Richard Demarco contributes a text which he wrote on New Year's Day in 1972 entitled 'From Twenty Reflections and Resolutions of a Gallery Director on Facing the Art World in 1972'.

There is also a page devoted to Richard Demarco's drawing of Marina Abramović in performance at The Fruitmarket Gallery during the 1974 Demarco Gallery's EDINBURGH ARTS programme. There are also Richard Demarco's *Event Photographs* inspired by key events at Edinburgh College of Art by artists involved in the exhibition Strategy; Get Arts; and performance art events by Paul Neagu on the shoreline of Inchcolm Island, and Tadeusz Kantor's *Demarcation Line* and his Cricot 2 Theatre production of Witkiewicz's play *Lovelies and Dowdies*. This Event Photograph shows Kantor in relation to two participants of EDINBURGH ARTS '73, Sean Connery and Tina Brown.

There is also an Event Photograph of the Scottish Arts Council football match versus The Demarco Gallery as part of the 1973 EDINBURGH ARTS programme as well as Event Photographs of Joseph Beuys and Buckminster Fuller contributing to this programme of *The Black and White Oil Conference* in The Demarco Gallery's Forrest Hill Poorhouse.

Beyond Conflict exhibition and conference presented by the Demarco Foundation in collaboration with The Royal National Museum of Scotland and Mercy Corps Scotland at the Apex Hotel Grassmarket. This was also presented at the European Parliament in Brussels.

RIP Michael Demarco. RIP HM Queen Mother aged 101.

2003

Demarco Archive exhibition at 8 Melville Crescent courtesy of Scottish Arts Council; David Silcox in Edinburgh; England win rugby world cup; SNGMA Demarco Archive exhibition curated by Ann Simpson of the 1960s, in Keiller Library; Sonia Rolak, Wanda Casaril, Bill Scott, Arthur Watson exhibition at Demarco Roxy; Demarco Archive 40th anniversary at Edinburgh City Arts Centre; Norbert Attard exhibition at Apex Hotel; Mother Teresa beatified.

Richard Demarco delivers the Discovery Lecture; Dundee University Belarusian Yakub Kolas State Theatre of Vitebsk production of Gogol's *Diary of a Madman* was presented in collaboration with Xela Batchelder's Rocket Productions, as well as *Birds of Sarajevo*, a Haris Burina play from Bosnia which was awarded a Fringe First.

2004

New Scottish Parliament building completed, designed by Enric Miralles;

Demarco Archive RSA artists at RSA curated by Arthur Watson; Demarco Archive in Keiller Library, Scottish National Gallery of Modern Art; Exhibition at Edinburgh Quay for Scottish Canals entitled *Scottish Canalscapes* includes artists Ian Hamilton Finlay, Arthur Watson, Archie Sutter Watt, Janet Treloar, John Hale, Terry Ann Newman, John David Mooney, Bill Scott, Elizabeth Blackadder, Margot Sandeman, Valerie Sadler, and curated by Charles Ryder, 11–27 August; and Demarco Archive exhibition at Ocean Terminal, Edinburgh; Simon Sharp and David Lowe masterclass in Stockbridge Theatre Workshop inspired by Goethe's Italian Journey; *A Day down a Goldmine* with a performance by Bill Paterson and George Wyllie; A warehouse fire destroys part of the Saatchi art collection; First NHS hospitals become Foundation Trusts; The European Union admits ten new member states.

George Wyllie's *A Day Down a Goldmine* was performed at Edinburgh Theatre Workshop, as well as *Conversations with Richard Demarco* at The Royal College of Surgeons, in collaboration with Rocket Productions.

RIP Jeremy Rees. Obituary in *Artwork*.

2005

Demarco Archive moved to Skateraw Barn Gallery from New Parliament House and from the Gallery at Ocean Terminal in Leith Docks; Harold Pinter wins Noble Prize; *Strategy; Get Arts Revisited* exhibition; EDINBURGH ARTS 1972–80 in Keiller Library; Symposium on Blinky Palermo sculpture re-painting at Edinburgh College of Art; Demarco Festival programme at

Demarco Roxy Art House, including Mexican Theatre, and Munich theatre with Shakespeare's *Midsummer Night's Dream* promenade in Prestonfield House grounds; Tsunami disaster in Indian Ocean. Demarco Archive exhibition at Johnny Watson's Skateraw Barn Gallery was opened by Patricia Ferguson MSP, Minister of Culture, at Skateraw near Dunbar, East Lothian.

2006

Charles Kennedy resigns as Liberal leader; Menzies Campbell succeeds him; Demarco Archive exhibition at Skateraw Farm Barn near Dunbar, East Lothian, opened by Patricia Ferguson MSP as Scotland's Minister of Culture; Demarco exhibition at Glasgow Art Fair.

Elected Honorary Member of the Royal Watercolour Society (RWS). Awarded Honorary Doctorate from Wrocław Art Academy of Fine Art. RIP Ian Hamilton Finlay. RIP Muriel Spark. RIP John Profumo. RIP Fred Truman. RIP. Alexander Lukashenko, poisoned by Russian agents in London.

Demarco Archive exhibition at Skateraw Barn Gallery, opened by Sir John Leighton, Director-General of the Scottish National Galleries.

RIP Moira Shearer. RIP Sir John Drummond.

2007

Gordon Brown becomes Prime Minister; *A Highland Decade* exhibition at RSA. Demarco Archive exhibition at Lambs Gallery, Dundee University; Focus on Demarco Archive at Keiller Library SNGMA; MIMA, Middlesbrough Institute of Art, opens in January.

Appointed to the Office of Commander of the British Empire. Appointed Honorary Visiting Professor of Fine Art, Dundee University. Awarded the Silver 'Gloria Artis' Medal by Minister of Culture of Poland in Warsaw. Awarded Honorary Doctorate from Stirling University.

I was featured in Alexander McCall Smith's serial novel *44 Scotland Street* published by *The Scotsman* and Polygon. *Demarco's Festival,* as an Edinburgh International Festival exhibition at The Scottish National Portrait Gallery, was at the invitation of Sir Jonathan Mills as the Festival Director. It also included a 21-day conference on the history of the Edinburgh International Festival.

2008

Razem exhibition of Polish artists living and working in Scotland at Demarco Roxy Art House; Boris Johnson elected Mayor of London; End of Woolworths stores. Elected Honorary Fellow of Edinburgh College of Art. Awarded Honorary Citizenship of the City of Łódź, Poland. Awarded The Pillar of Leith Silver Medal. Two contributions to the Demarco Foundation's Festival programme were from Downside School. They were Roland Reynolds' play *Stalemate* and Downside School's homage to George Melly directed by Kevin Byrne.

2009

Demarco Archive moves from Skateraw Barn to Craigcrook Castle, Edinburgh; Carol Ann Duffy appointed Poet Laureate; Demarco Archive exhibition at Telford College; Exhibition of Demarco Archive entitled *Then and Now* at Polish

National Film School, Łódź, and at Telford College; Marcin Brzozowski, Polish National Film School, directs *Zoriuska*, at the Demarco Edinburgh Festival Theatre in collaboration with Sweet Theatre Productions.

Strictly Cam Laughing by Cambridge University, a Demarco Edinburgh Festival programme linked the world of Cambridge University Footlights.

RIP Cordelia Oliver aged 86.

2010

Ten Dialogues exhibition at Royal Scottish Academy; David Cameron and Nicholas Clegg form coalition government; Exhibition at Southampton City Art Gallery celebrating the history of The Demarco Gallery marking Richard Demarco's 80th birthday with works from the City Collection including those by Wilhelmina Barns-Graham, Ian Hamilton Finlay, Patrick Heron, Roger Hilton, William Scott and Bryan Wynter, curated by Alice Workman, private view in October. Awarded Glenfiddich Award. Delivers Sir William Gillies Annual Lecture, National Gallery of Scotland. Awarded Honorary Fellowship from The Rose Bruford College of Theatre and Performance. Awarded the Grand Cross Order of Merit of the Federal Republic of Germany. Awarded the Polish 'Bene Merito' medal.

Opera and Jazz was a production at the Demarco Festival Theatre at Craigcrook Castle of a musical programme which ranged from opera to popular music. The editor of *Art Mag*, Ian Sclater, published an essay entitled *Man on a Mission*, outlining the nature of the Demarco Archive as exhibited in Craigcrook Castle.

2011

Master Class by Richard Demarco and Arthur Watson at Hill of Tarvit, Fife, during the Cupar Arts Festival; Exhibition of Richard Demarco's drawings of Cupar's historic alleyways in relation to exhibition and installation by Kate Downie RSA; 'Pitman Painters' at Glasgow's Theatre Royal and meeting with Trevor Fox.

Awarded Honorary Doctorate from Southampton Solent University. Received the 'Celebrating Heroes' Award from USA. Selected artist from Scotland for the Biennale di Venezia del Mondo. *Traumatikon* was a production directed by Teresa and Andrzej Welminski in collaboration with Rose Bruford College at Robert McDowell's newly acquired Summerhall. An exhibition at Craigcrook Castle was entitled *Biennale de Venezia nel Mondo*, linking the Venice Biennale with Edinburgh.

2012

A Multi-Media Thing theatre at Tom Fleming Centre, Stewart's Melville College, a celebration of the art and life of Bogusław Schaeffer, the Polish artist and avant-garde composer. Awarded the Gold 'Gloria Artis' Medal of Poland. Awarded The Great Scot for the Arts. For The Festival of Culture and Politics at the Scottish Parliament, I was invited to consider the relationship between the John Murray Archive and the Demarco Archive. This also involved George Wyllie as an artist and Struan Stevenson as a Member of the European Parliament.

2013

Demarco Archive moves from Craigcrook Castle to Robert

McDowell's Summerhall Arts Centre; Masterclass to Royal College of Art students at Redoubt Art Centre and afterwards at Towner Art Gallery Eastbourne; Highland Shakespeare Theatre Company's production at Beauly, Inverness-shire; Exhibition of Richard Demarco's Edinburgh prints at The Scotsman Hotel; Forth Studio exhibition at Southampton Solent University curated by John OR Martin in collaboration with Trevor Thorne; Demarco Foundation exhibition at Sonia Rolak Gallery during Venice Biennale; Exhibition of Richard Demarco's paintings celebrating the 200th anniversary of the birth of Mikhail Lermontov in the Art Gallery of The National Library for Foreign Literature in Moscow; Voted a 'European Parliament Citizen of the Year'. Awarded The Edinburgh Prize by The Lord Provost of Edinburgh in the City Chambers.

The Demarco Archive is moved into its current home of Summerhall Arts Centre, thanks to the patronage of Robert McDowell, where a portion of the archive is able to be displayed. Dr Angela Bartie, the historian, published her history entitled *Edinburgh Festivals' Culture and Society in Post-war Britain*. It focused on the history, both social and cultural, of the Edinburgh Festival and the impact of the Traverse Theatre Club and Art Gallery on the Edinburgh Festivals in the 1960s.

RIP Ronald Craig. RIP Lord Fraser of Carmyllie. RIP Sir David Frost.

2014
Elizabeth Oxborrow-Cowan produced a comprehensive report on the Demarco Archive for the Scottish Government

with comments from such experts as archivist Louisa Riley-Smith, and conservator Christopher Wood of Tate Galleries; Hauser and Wirth Gallery, Bruton, Somerset, opened with a private view; Professor Pedriali's Edinburgh University event inspired by Emilio Gadda with a conference at Cassino University, The Abbey of St Benedict at Monte Cassino with a violin recital by Nicola Benedetti followed by dinner in Casa Lawrence in Picinisco, and then in the British Embassy in Rome; Posthumous award to Lord Fraser of Carmyllie at the Polish Embassy in London; *Anamnesis* exhibition and conference in Wrocław inspired by the life and work of Richard Demarco and Poland; Gwen Hardie and Masha Fingaiu; Exhibition of paintings by Janet Treloar in Norwich Cathedral.

Discussion with Andrew Neil in the Hawthornden Lecture Theatre; Richard Demarco celebrated birthday at Fingask Castle, Perthshire; Christmas event as Loretto School teacher Archibald Buchanan-Dunlop organises famous Christmas Peace between British and German soldiers to celebrate Christmas in No-Man's Land on the Western Front; 450th anniversary of Shakespeare's birth.

Marc Glöde was the curator of the exhibition at the Summerhall Arts Centre in Edinburgh inspired by the life and art of Tadeusz Kantor. This exhibition was later transferred to the Polish Cultural Institute in Berlin. I was pleased to be invited to lecture on how I introduced Tadeusz Kantor to Joseph Beuys during the 1973 Edinburgh Festival. Stephen McKenna exhibited his European paintings at Middlesborough Institute of Modern Art (MIMA).

RIP Bill Wright. RIP Michael McLaughlin

(Australia). RIP Hugh Dodd.

RIP Roy Oxlade. RIP David Jansheski. RIP. Andy MacMillan.

2015

Jim Haynes awarded Honorary Doctorate at Napier University having donated his archive to the University; Richard Demarco's 85th birthday party at Stonerwood Park; Centre Pompidou archivists research Demarco Archive at Summerhall Arts Centre, Edinburgh; Richard Demarco lectures at Le Centre Pompidou; Graham Fagan represents Scotland at Venice Biennale; Richard Demarco lectures at Royal College of Physicians; 'Kantor, Beuys, Demarco' exhibition at The Museum of Contemporary Art Krakow.

This was the UNESCO Year of Tadeusz Kantor in celebration of the 100th anniversary of his birth. The main exhibition was the one inspired by The Black Madonna of Czestochowa and Scotland's national flag, a white Saltire cross on a blue background symbolising the martyrdom of Saint Andrew. This exhibition took place as a Demarco Foundation exhibition in the St John's Scottish Episcopal Church in the West End of Princes Street. It was part of a programme linking the world of culture with that of religion. I gave a lecture at the Venice Biennale inspired by the screening of three films produced by Gabriella Cardazzo and directed by Duncan Ward. These films were inspired by the Cricot 2 Theatre of Tadeusz Kantor. This lecture and film screening took place under the aegis of the Academia of Venice. There was also an exhibition inspired by the Luath Press publication The Road to Meikle Seggie of my original illustrations to the

bi-lingual Anglo-Italo publication in the gallery of The Scottish Storytelling Centre. The exhibition and publication were co-presented by the Italian Cultural Institute in Scotland. Stefania del Bravo, the Institute's Director, contributed an essay, as did Donald Smith, the founder of the Scottish Storytelling Centre. There was also a performance at Summerhall Arts Centre by Aletia Badenhorst. This included a conversation between Miriam Margolyes and Aletia Badenhorst.

In the summer of this year, there was a lavish programme entitled Edinburgh Festivals. In its 178 pages, there was one page devoted to the official Edinburgh Festival programme in the Usher Hall of Mozart's Requiem performed by the Budapest Festival Orchestra conducted by Ivan Fisher. There was also a reference to a new musical drama performed by the Chicago Chamber Orchestra.

2016

Exhibition at Scottish National Gallery of Modern Art entitled Richard Demarco and Joseph Beuys; A Unique Partnership related to the exhibition entitled A language of drawings; 6th Sokolowsko Performing Arts Festival and in Wrocław in collaboration with Marek Mutor's Depot History Centre; Józef Chrobak and Martyna Sobczyk from MOCAK, Krakow, research Demarco Archive. Awarded Honorary Doctorate from Leeds Beckett University.

Emballage was the title of an outstanding example of performance art by Leeds Beckett PhD student Aletia Badenhorst. It was written, directed and performed by Aletia Badenhorst at Summerhall Arts Centre. It was inspired by The Demarco Gallery and Foundation's long-standing commitment to performance art and, in particular, Tadeusz Kantor, Paul Neagu and Joseph Beuys as exponents of performance art. It also celebrated long-established dialogue I have had with Professor Noel Witts, linking the academic world of Leeds Beckett University with the Demarco Archive.

2017

Anne Marie Gilmour exhibition at Summerhall; Eric Ritchie exhibition at Doubtfire Gallery, Edinburgh; Exhibition at The Fruitmarket Gallery of William Kentridge and Vivenne Koorland; Richard Demarco attended Anthony Howell's recreation of *The Theatre of Mistakes* at Alex Sainsbury's Raven Row in London.

At Summerhall, I presented an exhibition in celebration of the life of Ronald Craig as artist and Art Master at Glenalmond College, Perthshire. This exhibition provided proof positive that art teaching at a secondary level of education must be identified with art education on a tertiary level. It also supported the Beuysian concept that everyone is an artist and that Joseph Beuys' definition of the quintessential nature of his art was simply that he was, first and foremost, an art teacher.

RIP Stephanie Wolfe Murray, funeral at Peebles. RIP Stephen McKenna.

2018

Wrocklaw Breaks the Iron Curtain exhibition and symposium at Polish Arts Centre, London; Glenalmond College exhibition at Summerhall; Downside Abbey Centenary; *Six Degrees West* Demarco Festival exhibition; James O'Brien poetry book launch; Demarco

posters exhibition at Creative Scotland's Gallery.

Art, Truth and Time was published by Luath Press. It contained eight essays by Sister Anselma Scollard OSB. This year was marked also by an exhibition of the art of Gunnie Moberg and Margaret Tait and the inspiration they derived from the Orcadian world.

RIP John Calder. RIP John Oswald Russell Martin.

2019

Exhibition of Romanian artists who were introduced to the Edinburgh Festival at The Demarco Gallery in Melville Crescent. It was entitled 24 *Arguments* in National Museum of Art, Bucharest, presented by The Institute of the Present; Exhibition of the Demarco Archive at Burgh Hall Art Centre, Dunoon, with a focus on the art of Andrew Marr, Terry Ann Newman, Sarah Waters and Fernanda Zei and symposia and lectures in Summerhall and Venice. To Venice Biennale – exhibition and conference in La Scuola Grande di San Marco; Exhibition of the Demarco Archive in the Italian National Museum in the Castello Pandone, Venafro, with symposium directed by Deirdre MacKenna; Stephen McKenna memorial exhibition in Dublin. Richard Demarco interviewed Caroline Wiseman for Michael Lloyd's film entitled *Art or Artifice*.

Appointed Honorary Member of the Mihai Eminescu International Academy, Bucharest. The Demarco European Art Foundation presented an EDINBURGH ARTS expedition linking the waters and coastlines of the Firth of Clyde with the waters and coastline of the Venice Lagoon and the history of the Edinburgh

Festival with that of the Venice Biennale. It linked the world of The Dunoon Burgh Hall in Argyllshire with La Scuola Grande di San Marco, the civic hospital of Venice. Terry Ann Newman and Sarah Waters paid homage to Joseph Beuys' use of felt in the exhibition in Dunoon and among the artists who participated in the exhibition in La Scuola Grande were Andrew Marr with oil paintings, John Hale-White with bronze sculptures and Sonia Rolak with pencil drawings.

Giuliano Gori's Fattoria di Celle made a photographic celebration of Ian Hamilton Finlay's sculptural installation in The Gori Collection which was inspired by the olive groves of Tuscany. This exhibition was an expression of art as a healing balm. There was a programme of 11 days during which a programme of lectures, discussions and performances including those by Stephen Partridge and Elaine Shemilt, and conversations with Andrew Marr and his good friend Francesco da Mosto. Marco Federici was there to film the 11 days during the first week of the Venice Biennale, as well as the exhibition in Dunoon and both were featured in his documentary *Rico*.

The Second Decade of the Third Millennium in the Christian Era ended in the Italian Renaissance world of Venice in the interior of La Scuola Grande di San Marco. The long history of this working civic hospital of Venice in which the history of medical science is interlocked with that of the history of the visual arts suggests that there should be a fruitful dialogue between medical science and the visual arts. They underline the obvious fact that they are both concerned with the process of healing physical and mental illnesses.

Through my two very good friends, Krzysztof Noworyta and Marek Mutor, my two books, *The Road to Meikle Seggie* and *The Artist as Explorer* were published in Polish by the Centrum Historii Zajezdnia of Wrocław. RIP Janet Treloar. RIP Elizabeth Roberts, RIP Bogusław Schaeffer. RIP Catherine Carnie.

RIP Alan Smith. RIP Merilyn Smith.

2020

To Aldeburgh, to Andrew Marr exhibition, and *Alive in the Universe* symposia directed by Caroline Wiseman; Meeting with Humphrey Burton, former head of BBC arts programmes; Visits to the studios of Miche Fabre Lewin and Flora Gathorne-Hardy; Meeting with Sir John Leighton at Summerhall.

Bill Williams, as the Editor of *Artwork*, invited me to contribute an essay on the future of the Edinburgh Festival. The result was an essay entitled 'Edinburgh without a Festival' in which I questioned the future of the Edinburgh Festival because of the widening gap between the reality of the official Festival and that of the Fringe. This was also the year in which the Covid-19 pandemic forced the Edinburgh Festival to be dramatically reduced. However, the work on that part of the Demarco Archive undergoing the process of being developed and enlarged continued without serious interruption.

I was indebted to Jamie Macfarlane and Arthur Watson for their preparedness to help install a studio in the back garden of Terry Ann Newman's cottage at Howgate in Midlothian. It must be defined as a 'Studio' containing a vitally important library and workspace for a chronological collection of publications and correspondence, plus innumerable photographic images to make an archive installed as an extension of the Demarco Archive which exists in Robert McDowell's Summerhall Arts Centre in Edinburgh and in my house in Edinburgh. RIP Maria Stangret. RIP Roma Tomelty. RIP James Sherwood.

This was the year of my 90th birthday. Unfortunately, it coincided with the full impact of Covid-19 as a global pandemic, making the Edinburgh Festival an impossibility.

Roddy Martine and Tamara Alferoff were introduced in a filmed interview made by Michael Lloyd at Summerhall Arts Centre. Their memories of the Edinburgh Festival in the Sixties provide invaluable information on the early years of the Traverse Theatre Club, as well as Jim Haynes' bookshop. Tamara was an Edinburgh University undergraduate; Roddy Martine was a 16-year-old Edinburgh Academy schoolboy.

Meeting with Lord (Jamie) Crathorne and Victoria (Tor) Callander Agnew at Milkhall; Jamie was a good friend of Michael Spens and was a fellow member of The Demarco Gallery board of trustees in the late 1970s.

Correspondence with Alexander and Susan Maris with regard to Joseph Beuys having dinner of Danish smorgasbord at The Howgate Inn, on the evening of his first day introduction to the United Kingdom. It should be noted that this was the first of his eight visits to Scotland.

Telephone conversation with Tino Trova in St Louis (USA) regarding his father, the Italo-American sculptor Ernest Trova, who achieved fame with his series of *Falling Man* bronze sculptures.

RIP Sir Sean Connery.

2021

Festival by the Sea was the title of a festival which extended the concept of the Edinburgh Festival to include the sea-girt reality of North Berwick and the world of the Firth of Forth. This took place in The Marine Hotel in the form of a conversation between me and Brian Taylor, former BBC political editor dealing with the affairs of the Scottish Parliament. The main contribution to the Edinburgh Festival by the Demarco Archive at Summerhall Arts Centre took the form of a Festival exhibition celebrating the 100th anniversary of the birth of Joseph Beuys.

For me, the highlight of this Edinburgh Festival was the exhibition dedicated to the art of Los Angeles-based, Italo-American artist Tom Marioni by Brian and Lesley Robertson at their Zembla Gallery located in the Scottish Border town of Hawick and one of my favourite galleries on The Road to Meikle Seggie.

Tom Marioni introduced me, in 1970, to his fellow Californian artists when I was the guest of the American government on a three-week tour of the cultural life of the United States. He personified the spirit of the American artist as an avant-gardist with a particular focus on the interface between music and the visual arts. Tom Marioni made an important contribution to The Demarco Gallery's 1973 Edinburgh Festival programme. It was inspired by the main gallery space at The Demarco Gallery in Melville Crescent and intrigued David Baxandall, the Director-General of Scotland's National Galleries.

I enjoyed my meeting with Ros Lambert at Milkhall, bringing back memories of her career as a film maker inspired by the concept of The Road to Meikle Seggie, linking the cultural life of Scotland to that of Malta and the road from Meikle Seggie that leads via the war-torn city of Mostar in Bosnia. Ros Lambert now lives in Spain. Her film footage includes historic images of my meetings with Guido de Marco, the President of Malta, Richard England, Malta's leading architect, and Norbert Francis Attard who represented Malta during the Venice Biennale. Richard England met Joseph Beuys in Edinburgh in 1970, prior to the Edinburgh Festival together with Maltese artists Gabriel Caruana, Mary di Piro and John Borg Manduca.

Arthur Watson produced his large-scale publication *Demarco; 2020* as a celebration of my 90th birthday at Fingask Castle in Perthshire. It contains 31 contributions by such friends as Marina Abramović, Jimmy Boyle, June Geddes, Murray Grigor, Fiona Hyslop MSP, Sir John Leighton, Laura Leuzzi, Adam Lockhart, Jane MacAllister, John McAslan, Terry Ann Newman, Glen Onwin, Radu Varia, Johnny Watson, Charles Ryder, Kirstie Meehan, Noel Witts and Arthur Watson. This was, for me, an all-time precursor to the programme of the Edinburgh Festival. It coincided with a performance of The Highland Shakespeare Company, under the inspirational direction of Sunny Moodie and was linked to the planting of an oak tree as a memorial to Joseph Beuys.

This was also the year when I planted an oak tree, together with a Basaltic stone, at Edinburgh College of Art in celebration of the 50th anniversary of the 1970 exhibition of artists from Düsseldorf and the publication *Strategy; Get Arts; 35 Artists who broke the*

Rules. This must be regarded as a unique academic resource into the history of the Edinburgh Festival. It is published by Alexander Hamilton and *Studies in Photography*, edited by Professor Christian Weikop of Edinburgh University and I must congratulate them both on the excellence of the publication.

RIP Jim Haynes.

2022

BBC Television Scotland screened Marco Federici's 85-minute documentary film entitled *Rico* as the story of my life and which was narrated by Brian Cox. The Demarco Archive was made manifest in an exhibition celebrating the 75th anniversary of the Edinburgh Festival coinciding with the 200th anniversary of The Signet Library in Parliament Square. This exhibition related to the Demarco Archive exhibition at the Summerhall Arts Centre in relation to an exhibition at Dom Polska in Edinburgh curated by Krzysztof Noworyta and Marek Mutor.

These three exhibitions were presented within the civic boundaries of Edinburgh. However, my concept of The Road to Meikle Seggie extends the reality of the Edinburgh Festival beyond Edinburgh into the world of nature existing in the landscape and history of Scotland. The Road to Meikle Seggie is the road to the farmscape of Scotland. It suggests that the world of agriculture should be identified with the world of culture. Therefore, the Demarco Archive programme is found also found at Traquair House in Peeblesshire, as well as in Arthur Watson's Window Gallery in Perth, and in The Dunoon Burgh Hall, in the sea-girt world of the Cowal Peninsula.

The Demarco European Art Foundation's exhibition in The Signet Library was perhaps the most significant manifestation of the Demarco Archive. It provided proof positive that the history of the Demarco Archive is deeply embedded in that of the history of Scotland and, in particular, the period of The Scottish Enlightenment, when Sir Walter Scott arranged for it to be housed in what must surely be regarded as an architectural masterpiece; a perfect celebration of the spirit of the Enlightenment all over Europe since it heralded the 20th-century as one hundred years of global conflict and, therefore, sorely in need of the language of all the arts as a healing balm.

The Signet Library provided the ideal exhibition space in Edinburgh. It was one of three which were in Edinburgh and the others were on what I defined as The Road to Meikle Seggie, the road which leads into the world of nature in Scotland; the world of farmscape because Meikle Seggie is the name of a working farm.

Lord Kames, one of the luminaries of the Scottish Enlightenment, declared that 'agriculture was the most important of all the arts.' Of course, I am most grateful to Anna Bennett and her colleagues at The Signet Library for having invited me to curate this exhibition.

I am hoping that I can provide a satisfactory answer to the question asked by Nicola Benedetti as the newly elected Director of the Edinburgh International Festival. Her question was timely and thought-provoking; 'Where do we go from here?' She was wisely quoting Martin Luther King as he fought against the injustice of racial segregation. Under her directorship, the Edinburgh Festival must surely have a future.

The main contribution to the Demarco Foundation's Edinburgh Festival 2022 exhibition programme was entitled *The History of Seventy-Five Edinburgh Festivals* exhibited, at the invitation of Anna Bennett as The Signet Library's Deputy Chief Executive, in the library in Parliament Square. The exhibition was related to an interview on the nature of the Demarco Archive as a total art work, a veritable *Gesamtkunstwerk*, in which I was involved in conversation with Amanda Catto, the Director of Visual Arts at Creative Scotland. The exhibition was related to others such as that of the large-scale photographs by Alexander Lindsay in the Bowhouse Gallery in the East Neuk of Fife, the Window Gallery of artist Arthur Watson in Perth, the exhibition celebrating the genius of Hamish Henderson as a poet, folklorist and academic. Among the artists involved in this celebration were Terry Ann Newman, Sandy Moffat, Arthur Watson, Hugh Buchanan, Charles Nasmyth, Helen Douglas and Jonathan Freemantle.

The University of Dundee was awarded a £200,000 Arts and Humanities Research Council grant for research and a publication entitled *Richard Demarco; The Italian Connection*, edited by Dr Laura Leuzzi, Professor Elaine Shemilt and Professor Stephen Partridge, with additional support from the Instituto Italiano di Cultura in Scotland and the engineering company of Antonio Buono.

The Edinburgh International Festival Mass at St Mary's Roman Catholic Cathedral, with *The Sixteen* providing inspirational singing. There was the private view at Dom Polski, the Polish House in Edinburgh, and the installation of a mural painting by the homeless women of New Delhi installed by Charty Dugdale. I had a Luath Press 'in conversation' with David Pollock on his history of the Edinburgh Festival, at the Quaker Meeting House. Beyond Borders Festival opened at Traquair House on 27 August directed by Mark Muller Stuart and his wife Catherine Maxwell Stuart.

RIP Angela Lansbury.

2023

This year has been focused on the need to find ways in which I collaborate with Marco Federici and Michael Lloyd to make films inspired by The German, Romanian, Polish, Traverse Rooms that I have installed at Summerhall Arts Centre in relation to the 360Art Foundation's four workshops.

These four installations need to be related to the rooms dedicated to the art of Joseph Beuys, John Martin, Trevor Thorne, Terry Ann Newman, Christ Wainwright, Margaret Tait, Ainslie Yule, Arthur Watson, Li Yuan-chia, John Hale, Ronald Craig, Diane Howse, Janet Treloar, Jerzy Nowosielski, Sonia Rolak, Ian Hunter, Robert McDowell, Piccolo Silani, Giancarlo Venuto, John David Mooney, Sandy Moffat, Jonathan Freemantle, Rose Strang and Walter Dalkeith. All in relation to The Road to Meikle Seggie and to the Signet Library exhibition 2022 entitled *The History of the Edinburgh Festival*, together with the concept of 'Event Photography' in collaboration with the Museum Kunst Palast in Düsseldorf.

This year, at Summerhall Arts Centre, there is the book launch of Dundee University's publication *Richard*

Demarco; The Italian Connection edited by Dr Laura Leuzzi, Professor Elaine Shemilt and Professor Stephen Partridge, published by Libbey Publishing Ltd of East Barnet, Herts and distributed worldwide by Indiana University Press, Bloomington, Indiana USA with a preface by Amanda Catto, Director of Contemporary Art at Creative Scotland.

The showing of Marco Federici films, plus Sunny Moodie's *Homage to Victor MacDougall*, the spirit of Fingask Follies 'Having a Good Time', is expressing the spirit of the Demarco Festival programmes of cabaret which included *The Scaffold* with Roger McGough, John Gorman, Mike McGear, and the Cambridge Footlights with Clive James and Tony Buffery.

RIP Barry Humphries. RIP Kit Hesketh-Harvey. RIP Sir James Dunbar-Nasmith. RIP Hugo Burge.

Bibliography

Arcari, Virginia, *Picinisco – Uncovering 1,000 years of History*, Virginia Arcari, 2017

Astaire, Lesley and Martine, Roddy, *Living in Scotland*, with photographs by Fritz von der Schulenberg, Thames & Hudson, 1997

Bellman, David (ed), *A Journey from Hagar Qim to the Ring of Brodgar* with an introduction by Lucy Lippard; *Notes for a Descriptive Phenomenology* with an introductory essay from David Bellman.

Beuys Kantor Demarco , MOCAK (The Museum of Contemporary Art), Krakow, 2015 (In English and in Polish with a foreword by Maria Anna Potocka)

Birrell, Ross and Finlay, Alec (eds), *Justified Sinners – An Archaeology of Scottish Counter-Culture 1960–2000*, Pocket Books (Polygon Press), 2002

Boyle, Jimmy, *A Sense of Freedom*, Pan Books, 1985

Boyle, Jimmy, *The Pain of Confinement*, Pan Books, 1985

Bruce, George, *Festival in the North: The Story of the Edinburgh Festival*, Robert Hale, 1975

Carlin, Norah (ed), *Holy Cross Academy: The Life and Times of a Catholic School 1907–1969*, illustrated with drawings by Richard Demarco, New Cut Press, 2009

Collins, Hugh, *Autobiography of a Murderer*, Macmillan, 1997

Collins, Hugh, *Walking Away*, Rebel Inc., 2001

Crawford, Iain, *Banquo on Thursdays: The Inside Story of 50 Years of the Edinburgh Festival*, Goblinshead, 1997

Dally, Jenny and Jacob, Mary Jane (eds), *Magdalena Abakanowicz: Writings and Conversations*, Abakanowicz Arts and Cultural Foundation, Skira Editore, 2022

Demarco, Richard, *Artysta Jako Odktywca* with a foreword by Krzysztof Noworyta. Published in Wroclaw in Polish Language by the Depot Gallery.

Demarco, Richard, *A Life in Picture*, Northern Books, 1978

Demarco, Richard, *Droga Do Meikle Seggie* with a foreword by Thomas Wilson. Published by Wroclaw in Polish language by the Depot Gallery.

Demarco, Richard, *The Road to Meikle Seggie,* with a foreword by Stefania Del Bravo and an essay by Donald Smith – 'The Road Goes On', Luath Press, 2015.

Demarco, Richard, *The Italian Connection* edited by Laura Leuzzi, Elaine Shemilt and Stephen Partridge, John Libbey Press

Dudley Edwards, Owen, *City of a Thousand Worlds: Edinburgh in Festival*, Mainstream, 1991

Exhibition Catalogue: Demarco European Art Foundation Exhibition of Maritime Art 'A Festival of Sea' at Leith Docks. Demarco European Art Foundation in collaboration with Forth Ports PLC, Aberdeen Assets Management and Giclee UK and the archive of James and Pamela Currie.

Exhibition Catalogue of *Bougé*. Presented by The Richard Demarco Gallery as part of the Official Exhibition Programme of the Edinburgh Festival 1984 in collaboration with the Ministry of Culture in Paris, Institut Français d'Écosse in Edinburgh, Musée des Beaux Arts, Beune Centre D'Action Culturelle, Monbeliaro with an introduction by Andre Laude 'Tu Boiges, Tu Vis, Je Vois.' Curated by Georges Daldachino.

Gordon Bowe, Nicola and Cumming, Elizabeth (eds), *The Arts and Crafts Movements in Dublin & Edinburgh 1885–1925*, Irish Academy Press, 1998

Henderson Scott, Paul (ed), *Spirits of the Age: Scottish Self Portraits*, Saltire Society, 2005

Hogg, Brian, *Cosmopolitan Scum! Edinburgh, The Arts and the Counter Culture*, Nove Mob (Ink) Publishing, 2019

MacArthur, Euan and Watson, Arthur (eds), *Ten Dialogues: Richard Demarco, Scotland and the European Avant Garde*, Royal Scottish Academy, 2010

Martell JF, *Reclaiming Art in the Age of Artifice*: A treatise, critique, and a call to action, Evolver Editions, North Atlantic Books, 2015

Martin, Marilyn (ed), *Kevin Atkinson: Art and Life,* The Kevin Patricia Atkinson Trust and Print Matters Heritage, 2022

Martin, John OR (ed), *The Demarco Collection and Archive: An Introduction,* Demarco Archive Trust

Martine, Roddy, *Edinburgh Military Tattoo,* Robert Hale, 2001

Martine, Roddy, *Scorpion on the Ceiling: A Scottish Colonial Family in South East Asia,* Librario, 2004

Martine, Roddy, *This Too Shall Pass: Reminiscences of East Lothian*, Birlinn, 2009

Montgomery, Bryan, *Pictures for an exhibition*: Works Collected by Bryan Montgomery during the past 30 years, The Richard Demarco Gallery in collaboration with SITE (Scottish International Trade Exhibitions Limited) and Andy Montgomery Ltd, 2021

Mooney, David John, *Vatican Observatory and the Arts: The Sculpture of John David Mooney at Castel Gandolfo,* University of Notre Dame Press, 1999

Murawska-Muthesius, Katarzyna and Zarzecka, Natalia (eds), *Kantor was Here: Tadeusz Kantor in Great Britain,* Black Dog Publishing, 2011

Nasmyth, Charles (ed), *Hamish Henderson A Conversation Piece: A Portrait in Six Conversations,* Fife Global Press, 2022

Pollock, David, *Edinburgh's Festivals: A Biography*, Luath Press, 2023

Royle, Trevor, *A Diary of Edinburgh*, with pen drawing illustrations by Richard Demarco, Polygon Books, 1981

Scollard OSB, Sister Anselma, *Art, Truth and Time: Essays on Art,* with a foreword by Richard Demarco, Luath Press, 2019

Sheeler, Jessie, *Little Sparta: The Garden of Ian Hamilton Finlay,* with photographs by Andrew Lawson, Francis Lincoln, 2003

Spens, Michael and Janet Mackenzie (eds), *Studio International* Special issue, Vol. 207, No. 1,030

Stanley, Tim, *Whatever Happened to Tradition? History, Belonging and the Future of the West*, Bloomsbury Continuum, 2021

Swan, Douglas, *Ein Moderner Klassiker (A Modern Classic),* ed. by Axel Wendelburger, Museum August Macke Haus, Encounters Hans-Bonn Exhibition, 2020

Tisdall, Caroline, *Joseph Beuys: Bits and Pieces,* with an introduction by Caroline Tisdall and Richard Demarco, Richard Demarco Gallery in association with the Arnolfini Gallery, Bristol and Red Lion House, 1987

Watson, Arthur (ed), *Richard Demarco 2020,* Demarco Archive Trust and Duncan of Jordanstone College of Art, 2021

Weikop, Christian, 'Anselm Kiefer's Occupations through a Glass Darkly', *Studies in Photography: Understanding the Past,* ed. by Alexander Hamilton, Scottish Society for the display of Photography, 2021

Weikop, Christian, *Strategy: Get Arts: 35* 'Artists Who Broke the Rules', *Studies in Photography,* 2021.

Watson, Arthur (ed), *Richard Demarco 2020,* Demarco Archive Trust and Duncan of Jordanstone College of Art

A Survey of History, an essay by Frank Ashton-Gwatkin Inspired by EDINBURGH ARTS. Edited by David Bellman. Research and Art Work by Jeanne Sanschargrin and Carol Swift. Caledonian Press. Published by Richard Demarco Gallery 1976.

Endnotes: Taking the Long View (pp17–33)

1   Unreferenced quotations from Demarco come from talks, public and private conversions, and media interventions between 2020 & 2023. These include videos directed by Marco Federici and Michael Lloyd.

The most recent comments quoted come from discussions between Richard Demarco, Roddy Martine, and Edward Schneider, and the author in April 2023.

2   M Modeen, 'Drawing as Place-Making', in Demarco 2020, Demarco Archive 2020; R Demarco, *A Life in Pictures (Edinburgh)*: Northern Books, 1995).

3   M Davis, 'The Richard Demarco Archive: Accessing a 40-year Dialogue between Richard Demarco and the European Avant-Garde', *Journal of the Scottish Society for Art History*, Vol. 11, 2006.

4   *Richard Demarco; Joseph Beuys: A Unique Partnership* (Edinburgh: Luath Press, 2016).

5   J Jones, 'The man who fell to earth', *Guardian*, 19 July 1999.

6   F *Fukuyama*. 'The populist surge'. American Interest, Vol. 13, No. 4, 2018.

7   W Gordon Smith, 'A Godfather who plays to the gallery', *The Observer*, 6 August 1989.

8   A Camus, *Create Dangerously* (London: Penguin, 2018), p. 29.

9   A Applebaum, *Twilight of Democracy* (London: Penguin, 2020); T Snyder, *The Road to Unfreedom: Russia, Europe, America* (London: Penguin, 2018).

10 R Demarco, *The Challenge of the New Europe*, Stanley Picker Lecture 1992.

11 P Long, *The Architect and the Artists*, in P Long & J Thomas (eds) Basil Spence: Architect (Edinburgh: National Galleries of Scotland, 2007).

12 B Spence, *Phoenix at Coventry*: The Building of a Cathedral (London: Fontana, 1964).

13 D McLean, 'Violent anti-Italian riots in Edinburgh recalled 80 years on', *Evening News*, 10 June 2020.

14 Edinburgh Festivals at 75: Richard Demarco; David Pollock in Conversation, 26 August 2022.

15 C Ellis, 'Relativism and Reaction: Richard Hoggart and contemporary conservatism', in: S. Owen (ed)*Richard Hoggart and Cultural Studies* (London: Palgrave, 2008).

16 R Samuel, *Theatres of Memory*: *Volume II*-Unravelling Britain (London: Verso, 1998) p. 356.

17 O Bennett, *Cultural Pessimism* (Edinburgh: Edinburgh University Press, 2001).

18 D Pollock, *Edinburgh's Festivals: A Biography* (Edinburgh: Luarth Press, 2022, 2023).

19 R Keat, Cultural Goods and the Limits of the Market (London: Macmillan, 2000).

20 R Keat, 'Scepticism, authority and the market', in R Keat, N Whiteley & N Abercrombie (eds) *The Authority of the Consumer* (London: Routledge, 2004), p. 30

21 R Hoggart, *Desert Island Discs*, BBC Radio 4, 15 October 1995.

22 R Hoggart, *Only Connect* (London: Chatto & Windus, 1972), p. 83.

23 A Sinfield, *Literature, Politics and Culture in Postwar Britain*, new edition, (London: Continuum, 2004), p. 276. 24 R Hoggart, *Between Two Worlds* (London: Aurum, 2001).

25 D Harding, 'Cultural Democracy -Craigmillar Style', https://www.davidharding. net/?page_id=33

26 'Demarco and Boyle in conversation', https://www.youtube.com/ watch?v=FkImrmSIAdE

27 J Boyle, *The Special Unit*, in Demarco 2020, Demarco Archive 2020.

28 J McGuigan, *Cultural Populism* (London: Routledge, 1992).

29 A Peacock, *Paying the Piper* (Edinburgh: Edinburgh University Press, 1993); R Towse, 'Alan Peacock and cultural economics', *Economic Journal*, 115 (2005), pp. 262–76,

30 J Berger, *Ways of Seeing* (Harmondsworth: Penguin, 1972), p. 88.

31 P Buckley Hill, *Freeing the Edinburgh Fringe* (Desert Hearts Books, 2018).

32 B Venables, 'How Comedy Captured the Edinburgh Fringe', *The Skinny*, Issue 143, August 2017.

33 J Haynes, *Thanks for Coming* (London: Faber & Faber, 1984).

34 A Marwick, *Culture in Britain since 1945* (Oxford: Blackwell, 1991).

35 R Shaw, & G Shaw, 'The Cultural and Social Setting', in B Ford (ed) *The Cambridge Cultural History of Modern Britain:* Vol. 9 (Cambridge: Cambridge University Press, 1992).

36 G Mulgan, 'Culture', in D Marquand & A Seldon (eds) *The Ideas That Shaped Post-War Britain* (London: Fontana, 1996), pp. 197–198.

37 M Tracey, *The Decline and Fall of Public Service Broadcasting* (Oxford: Oxford University Press, 1998); C. Dunkley, 'Courageous programming (deceased)', *Financial Times*, 22 March 2000.

38 J. Arlidge & P Bazalgette, 'Why this is now the golden age of TV', *The Observer*, 9 September 2001.

39 HU Obrist, *Ways of Curating* (London: Penguin, 2015) p. 46

40 'Richard Demarco threatens to burn his arts archive', *The Herald*, 20 September 2021.

41 J Campbell, 'Edinburgh's Granton Waterfront: National Galleries of Scotland announces plans for major art facility', *Edinburgh Evening News*, 31 March 2023.

42 HU Obrist, *Ways of Curating* (London: Penguin, 2015) pp. 30–33.

43 K Meehan, 'The Demarco Archive at the National Galleries of Scotland', in Demarco 2020, Demarco Archive 2020. M Davis, 'The Richard Demarco Archive: Accessing a 40-year Dialogue between Richard Demarco and the European Avant-Garde', *Journal of the Scottish Society for Art History*, Vol. 11, 2006.

44 D Daiches, P Jones, & J. Jones (eds) *A Hotbed of Genius* (Edinburgh: Edinburgh University Press, 1986)

45 T Royle, *A Diary of Edinburgh* (Edinburgh: Polygon, 1981), p. 5.

46 R Scruton, *Culture Counts* (New York: Encounter Books, 2007).

47 D Murray, 'Roger Scruton: A man who seemed bigger than the age', *Spectator*, 12 January 2020.

48 R Scruton, *Beauty: A Very Short Introduction* (Oxford: Oxford University Press, 2011).

49 R Scruton, 'Kitsch and the Modern Predicament', *City Journal*, Winter 1999.

50 C Weikop, *Strategy: Get Arts -35 Artists Who Broke the Rules* (Edinburgh: Edinburgh University Press, 2021).

51 R Birrell & A Finlay, *Justified Sinners: An Archaeology of Scottish counter-culture (1960–2000)* (Edinburgh: Canongate, 2001).

52 M Abramović, *Walk Through Walls* (London: Penguin, 2016), p. 58.

53 A Camus, *Create Dangerously* (London: Penguin, 2018).

54 M Abramović, *Walk Through Walls* (London: Penguin, 2016), pp. 56-61.

55 R Demarco, 'Edinburgh without its Festival', *Artwork*, May/June 2020.

56 B Logan, 'The Edinburgh Fringe is too long, too expensive and too gruelling. It must change or die', *The Guardian*, 29 August 2022.

57 E Lawson, 'Edinburgh Festival Fringe faces 'existential threat', warns chief executive', *Independent*, 11 April 2023.

58 W Quinn, 'Festival is too busy, says Fringe pioneer', *The Observer*, 29 June 2008.

59 C Wilhelm, 'The Brexit Tree', http://clemenswilhelm.com/portfolio/thebrexittree/

60 P Wohlleben, *The Power of Trees: How Ancient Forests Can Save Us if We Let Them*, translated by J Billinghurst (Vancouver: Greystone, 2023).

Index

Note: this index comprises people referred to in Parts 1 and 2

Luath Press Limited

committed to publishing well written books worth reading

LUATH PRESS takes its name from Robert Burns, whose little collie Luath (*Gael.*, swift or nimble) tripped up Jean Armour at a wedding and gave him the chance to speak to the woman who was to be his wife and the abiding love of his life. Burns called one of the 'Twa Dogs' Luath after Cuchullin's hunting dog in Ossian's *Fingal*. Luath Press was established in 1981 in the heart of Burns country, and is now based a few steps up the road from Burns' first lodgings on Edinburgh's Royal Mile. Luath offers you distinctive writing with a hint of unexpected pleasures.

Most bookshops in the UK, the US, Canada, Australia, New Zealand and parts of Europe, either carry our books in stock or can order them for you. To order direct from us, please send a £sterling cheque, postal order, international money order or your credit card details (number, address of cardholder and expiry date) to us at the address below. Please add post and packing as follows: UK – £1.00 per delivery address; overseas surface mail – £2.50 per delivery address; overseas airmail – £3.50 for the first book to each delivery address, plus £1.00 for each additional book by airmail to the same address. If your order is a gift, we will happily enclose your card or message at no extra charge.

Luath Press Limited
543/2 Castlehill
The Royal Mile
Edinburgh EH1 2ND
Scotland
Telephone: 0131 225 4326 (24 hours)
Email: sales@luath.co.uk
Website: www.luath.co.uk